Luftwaffe Fighter-Bombers over Britain

Other Chris Goss titles available from Crécy Publishing

Luftwaffe Seaplanes
A pictorial history of Luftwaffe sea and float planes between 1939 and 1945
0 947554 93 9

The Luftwaffe Fighters' Battle of Britain
The inside story: July-October 1940
0 947554 81 5

The Luftwaffe Bombers' Battle of Britain
The inside story: July-October 1940
0 947554 82 3

Bloody Biscay
The story of the Luftwaffe's only long range maritime fighter unit,
V *Gruppe/Kampfgeschwader* 40, and its adversaries 1942-1944
0 947554 87 4

It's Suicide but it's Fun
The story of 102 Squadron
0 947554 59 9

Brothers in Arms
An account of August-September 1940 through the deeds of two opposing fighter units,
609 Squadron of the RAF and 1/*JG*53, a Luftwaffe *Staffel* based in northern France
0 947554 37 8

Luftwaffe Fighter-Bombers over Britain

The Tip and Run Campaign, 1942-43

Chris Goss
with Peter Cornwell and Bernd Rauchbach

Crécy Publishing Limited

First published in 2003 by Crécy Publishing Limited
All rights reserved

A CIP record for this book is available from the British Library

ISBN 0 947554 97 1

Printed and bound by
The Cromwell Press Ltd.

Crécy Publishing Limited
1a Ringway Trading Estate, Shadowmoss Road, Manchester M22 5LH
www.crecy.co.uk

Contents

Acknowledgements

I always find this one of the hardest things to do. Having researched this book for so many years, trying to remember each and every person who has helped gets harder the older I get! However, first and foremost thanks must go to Bernd Rauchbach and Peter Cornwell. Bernd has been my co-researcher for nearly 15 years and without him, his diligence, patience, help and advice, I would not be able to undertake at least half of my researching and writing. As to Peter, I have known him for much longer. His help with my research, even when I was still at school, was always freely given and he has been more than generous with this help over the years. Knowing his interest in the early 'tip and run' attacks and his encyclopaedic knowledge of things Battle of Britain made him eminently suitable to be the main contributor to Chapters 1 and 2. Next comes Mark Postlethwaite who yet again proof read and constructively criticised/advised the manuscript – all corrections and comments have been taken on board. Finally, one must not forget the late *Oberst* Erhard Nippa for his kind foreword, written even though he was not in the best of health.

Understandably, with a book of this size, contributors were many. I have elected not to thank here those whose vivid and vital accounts are in the main text, preferring to thank them *en masse* and by including their accounts. However, the following people or organisations have also been a great help:

Frank Arnold, Bezner Family, Gill Bolam (PMA, RAF Innsworth), *Bundesarchiv/Militärarchiv*, Freiburg, *Bundesarchiv/ Zentralnachweisstelle*, Aachen, Pat Burgess, Don Caldwell, Clarke Family, Graham Day (AHB), Heinz Ebeling, Helmut Eberspächer, Peter Feiger, *Frau* I Geburtig, Franek Grabowski, Grahl Family, Manfred Griehl, Steve Hall, Mrs Jennie Hickman, Otto Hintze, Phil Irwin, Heinz Jahner, Dr Ingrid Jensen, Terry Knight (Cornwall Studies Library), Sqn Ldr Tony Liskutin, W Matusiak, Victor Mölders, Christian Möller, Morzinek Family, Nash Family, Barry Needham, Z Nentwich, Jaroslav Popelka, Dieter Prym, Otto Putz, Winston Ramsey ('After the Battle'), Geoff Rayner, Fred Richards, Dr Fritz Sauer, Andy Saunders, *Frau* R Schammert, Bruno Stolle, *Frau* L Storsberg, Andy Thomas, Chris Thomas, *Herr* W Wenger, *Frau* E Weyl, Richard Wittmann, *Herr* Wöllmann (WASt, Berlin), Ken Watkins.

Finally, I do this every time but thanks to my wife Sally who has put up, yet again, with me being locked in the study, posting tonnes of letters and answering all sorts of phone calls at all times of the day and night. Also to my 3 daughters, Kat, Megan and Alexandra – thanks for letting me get to the PC!

Chris Goss

Glossary and Abbreviations

AA	Anti-aircraft
Ac	Aircraft
AC	Aircraftman
AFC	Airforce Cross
Angriff	Attack
ARP	Air Raid Precautions
ASI	Air Speed Indicator
ASR	Air Sea Rescue
ATS	Auxiliary Territorial Service
Aufklärungsgruppe	Reconnaissance Wing.
Bf	*Bayerische Flugzeugwerke*
BRT	British Registered Tonnage
CO	Commanding Officer
Cpl	Corporal
Deutsches Kreuz in Gold	German Cross in Gold (award for bravery)
DFC	Distinguished Flying Cross
DFM	Distinguished Flying Medal
DSO	Distinguished Service Order
E/a	Enemy aircraft
Ehrenpokal	Honour Goblet
Einzelmeldung	Detailed report such as detailing the activities of *Luftflotte 3*
Eiserne Kreuz (EK)	Iron Cross
Ergänzung (Erg)	Training
Erprobungsgruppe (ErprGr)	Experimental Wing
Experten	Ace
Flugbuch	Logbook
Flugzeugführer(F)	Pilot
Feindflug	Operational flight
Feldwebel (Fw)	Flight Sergeant
Fg Off	Flying Officer
Flak	Anti-aircraft fire
Flieger (Flg)	Aircraftman
Fliegerkorps	Air Corps
Flt Lt	Flight Lieutenant
Flt Sgt	Flight Sergeant
Flugmeister	Air force Non-Commissioned Officer
Frontflugspange	Mission clasp-awarded for operational flights

Führer	Leader
FW	Focke-Wulf
Gefreiter (Gefr)	Leading Aircraftman
Generalmajor	Air Commodore
Generalmajor oberst	Air Chief Marshal
Geschwader (Gesch)	Group (three Gruppen) commanded by a *Geschwader Kommodore (Gesch Komm)*
Gp	Group
Gp Capt	Group Captain
Gruppe (Gr)	Wing (three *Staffeln*) commanded by a *Gruppen Kommandeur (Gr Kdr)*
GRT	Gross Registered Tonnage
Hauptmann (Hptm)	Flight Lieutenant/Captain
HE	High explosive
Hrs	Hours
Ia	Operations Officer
IAS	Indicated Air Speed
ITW	Initial Training Wg
Jabo	*Jagdbomber*-fighter bomber
Jaboeinsatz	Fighter-bomber operational flight
Jafü	Fighter Leader or operational level of command
Jagdgeschwader (JG)	Fighter Group
Kagohl	See *Kampfgeschwader*
Kampfgeschwader (KG)	Bomber Group
Katchmarek	Nickname for wingman
Kg	Kilogram
LAC/LACW	Leading Aircraftman/Aircraftwoman
Lehrgeschwader (LG)	Operational Training Group
Leutnant (Lt)	Pilot Officer/2nd Lieutenant
Lt der Matrosen Artillerie	Naval Coastal Artillery Lieutenant
Luftflotte	Air Fleet
Luftgaukommando	Air Administrative District HQ
M	Missing
Major (Maj)	Squadron Leader/Lieutenant Commander
Me	Messerschmitt
MG	Machine gun
ML	Motor Launch
NCO	Non-commissioned officer
NO	*Nachtrichen Offizier*-responsible for communications
Oberfeldwebel (Ofw)	Warrant Officer/Master Sergeant
Obergefreiter (Ogefr)	Senior Aircraftman

Oberkommando der Luftwaffe (OKL)	*Luftwaffe* High Command
Oberleutnant (Oblt)	Flying Officer/1st Lieutenant
Oberst	Group Captain/Colonel
Oberstleutnant (Obstlt)	Wing Commander/Lieutenant Colonel
OKL	*Oberkommando der Luftwaffe*
	Luftwaffe High Command
Panzer	Tank
Plt Off	Pilot Officer
POW	Prisoner of war
Revi	Reflector gun sight
RFA	Royal Fleet Auxiliary
RFC	Royal Flying Corps
Ritterkreuz (RK)	Knights Cross
Ritterkreuz mit Eichenlaub	Knights Cross with Oakleaves
RN	Royal Navy
RNAS	Royal Navy Air Service
Rotte	Two aircraft tactical formation
Rottenflieger	Wingman
Rottenführer	*Rotte* Leader
Schlachtgeschwader (SG)	Ground Attack Group
Schnellkampfgeschwader (SKG)	Fast Bomber Group
Schwarm	Four aircraft tactical formation led by a *Schwarm Führer*
Seenotdienst	Air-sea rescue
Sgt	Sergeant
Sqn	Squadron
Sqn Ldr	Squadron Leader
Stab	Staff or Headquarters
Staffel	Squadron, commanded by a *Staffel Kapitän (St Kap)*
Stabsfeldwebel (Stfw)	Senior Warrant Officer
Störangriff	Nuisance attack
Stuka	Junkers 87
Sturzkampfgeschwader (StG)	Dive Bomber Group
Tiefangriff	Low-flying attack
TO	*Technischer Offizier* (Technical Officer)
Unteroffizier (Uffz)	Sergeant
USAAF	United States Army Air Force
WAAF	Women's Auxiliary Air Force
Werk Nummer (Wk Nr)	Serial number
Wg Cdr	Wing Commander
Zerstörergeschwader (ZG)	Heavy Fighter Group
zS	*zur See*-German naval rank suffix
+	Killed

Foreword

by

OBERST (Ret'd) ERHARD NIPPA

This very impressive, objective, fair and enlightening publication will show the reader the origin, idea, planning and preparations of German fighter-bomber 'tip and run' missions over southern England from spring 1942 until early summer 1943. I experienced these missions as a pilot with 10(*Jabo*)/*JG* 2 and, from early 1943 on, as *Staffel Kapitän* with 15/*SKG 10* flying Messerschmitt Bf 109s and then Focke-Wulf 190s. As one of those *Jabo* pilots who had been in service the longest, I think I am able to express my opinions about this publication.

In March 1941, I commenced training as a fighter-pilot and eventually joined the *Ergänzungsgruppe/JG* 2 at Cazaux/France in July 1941. It was here that I realized that I had a limited ability as a fighter pilot but then coincidence or fate solved my problems. The *Geschwader* was looking for volunteers to build up a special *Jabo-Staffel*. I volunteered and in September/October 1941 was transferred to 13/*JG* 2 based at Beaumont-le-Roger. Together with the *Staffel Kapitän Oblt* Frank Liesendahl and *Oblt* Fritz Schröter, *Ofw* Gerhard Limberg (who later became Chief of Staff of the Federal German Air Force from 1974-1978) and two or three NCOs, I was one of the first pilots to begin this special training. Some time later, *Lts* Wenger and Fröschl and several NCOs joined our *Staffel*. At the end of our training, our strength was about 10-12 combat ready pilots and with some difficulty, the *Staffel* was able to maintain the same level of strength nearly all the time.

One saw oneself as a member of a special unit faced with extreme demands, strain, danger and high risk. If you were aware of it or not, this resulted in a feeling of being a member of an élite unit. The *Staffel Kapitän*, pilots, mechanics and the administrative staff – nearly everyone felt an accepted member. The result was a decisive contribution to the motivation and willingness which created the preconditions for the *Jabo* missions and the resultant successes.

Special training included flying at low-level over land and sea, even in bad weather, very close formation flying and bomb dropping using the *Liesendahl-Verfahren*. Frank Liesendahl was the initiator – a tough, skilful, and if necessary, uncompromising advocate of his ideas, thoughts, conclusions and demands. He was an experienced fighter pilot who had gained experience of bombing sorties with the Bf 109. He realized that fighter aircraft were not, and could not, be successful in fulfilling these two roles but that special *Jabo*-attack tactics and techniques, together with special training of pilots and total change in role, could be an effective and promising method of attack. Against a lot of opposition and even criticism, especially from the other fighter units, Liesendahl succeeded in convincing higher authorities of his ideas and plans.

Jabo tactics involved taking off in *Staffel* formation and approaching the target flying at the lowest level and in strict radio silence. Formation flying, especially at low-level, placed additional demands on the pilots – it was very difficult when the seas were rough and even more demanding in foggy or hazy weather with a calm sea when you could not make out the horizon. This was the most strenuous and nerve-wracking part of the mission and some pilots had to be replaced because they were not able to cope with these demands and the strain.

In this publication, the Liesendahl Process' attacks are extensively described. One should add that it was necessary, especially for survival, to introduce some changes and variations in the way of attacking ships and specific targets. For example, gunners on board ships and on the coast were prepared and knew the direction of our approach so we flew our attacks from different directions, sometimes attacking after passing over the target and turning back.

Oblt *Erhard Nippa, Russia, 1944* (Nippa)

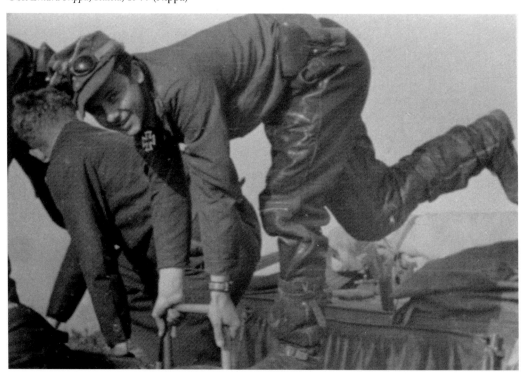

It is not necessary for me to add comments on the attacks and missions because the author has researched the facts with great care. One must emphasize his constant effort for objectivity and fairness in assessing and reviewing these events, showing the consequences of mistakes which often resulted in unnecessary damage and the loss of people and material. However, it is surprising to learn how successful and effective our two small units were – these facts were not known by us at the time. This book frankly and honestly shows the effects and successes in attacking the primary targets like ships, harbours, military installations and public utilities. It also shows the large number of successful attacks on secondary targets. The psychological effect on the population in large parts of southern England was considerable and was admitted by British military and political leaders. Particularly important was that because these 'tip and run' raids could not be detected early enough, it meant that defensive measures could only come into action when the attacks had been carried out; they also ensured that considerable British defence assets were tied down by these attacks.

In the final analysis, it can be said that 'tip and run' missions were successful. However, without reservation, one can agree with the question asked by the British: why did the *Luftwaffe* abandon such a successful offensive method which did not require much technical effort? Of course, these are questions that will remain unanswered.

I thank the author for this successful, objective and fair description of the events of that time, the sequence of attacks and consequences. On reading the book, human experiences, feelings, worries and desperation of those who were involved and their reactions and behaviour become understandable.

Erhard Nippa
Bellheim, 4 March 2003

(Sadly, Ernhard Nippa passed away 27 June 2003)

Introduction

"...I was walking up the main street in Torquay, when we heard the noise of gunfire and then saw Focke Wulf 190s coming line astern overhead, firing as they went. Two girls were crossing the road and my friend Ben grabbed one and I the other and literally threw them into the arcade of Rockey's department store. The window shattered and there were fires; my uniform was torn and the girls must have wondered what had happened. When it was all over, they went on their way and then Ben and I went down to the promenade. It was like a battlefield with all the First Aid dressings on the ground and many RAF recruits injured; some were in fact killed..."
Leonard Brock

"...I started to walk along the seafront when the air raid sirens sounded and immediately planes swooped low over the hills from the Babbacombe direction. I thought they were Spitfires but then I saw a black dot leave one of the leading planes and an explosion threw a column of debris into the air behind the church. An RAF sergeant leapt onto a mound of sandbags and shouted to everyone to lie down. The skies seemed full of low-flying aircraft, strafing the ground. Hundreds [sic] of people, many of them RAF, were lying on the ground and it was surprising that a lot more were not killed..."
Terry Stevens

These two accounts graphically illustrate what it was like to be on the receiving end of what was called by the British a 'tip and run' attack – a bombing raid carried out at very low-level and at a great speed by German single-engined fighters normally carrying either a 250 or 500 kg bomb, sometimes four 50 kg bombs. In March 1942, the *Luftwaffe* had commenced a bombing campaign against Allied shipping and coastal military and industrial installations on the southern coast of England. By fitting bombs to the Messerchmitt 109 single-seat fighters of 10 (*Jabo*)/*Jagdgeschwader* 2 '*Richthofen*' and 10 (*Jabo*)/*Jagdgeschwader* 26 '*Schlageter*'†, these fighter-bombers, or in German *Jagdbomber*, nearly always shortened to *Jabo*, began attacking targets as far east as Kent †† and as far west as The Lizard in Cornwall. These attacks continued until 6 June 1943 by which time the *Luftwaffe* had increased its strength of fighter-bombers on the western front from in the region of 28 to 118. All this had prompted the following phlegmatic British comment:

"...for the first three months of the year [1943], the position with regard to enemy fighter-bomber activity was not satisfactory...the problem was to get adequate warning of these low flying raids as, though enemy casualties were

---

†For simplicity, these units will be referred to as 10/*JG* 2 and 10/*JG* 26
††In 1943, this extended as far east as Great Yarmouth

high, these casualties mostly took place after the bombs had been dropped…"†

Without warning, 'tip and run' attacks ceased altogether following the highly successful attack on Eastbourne on 6 June 1943. The majority of German fighter-bombers were then transferred to the Mediterranean, leaving just 42 fighter-bombers which were used solely for attacks at night.

I have always had an interest in 'tip and run' attacks, which probably goes back to my school days when I remember a teacher telling us that at some stage during the last war, she had been walking in a seaside town when without warning, a German aircraft had appeared, had bombed and machine-gunned the town and then disappeared in the direction of France. As a schoolboy, one could only imagine what these attacks were like – one moment, a normal day, the next the scream of an aircraft engine, the sound of a bomb exploding and machine-gun fire. Minutes or even seconds later, the aircraft had gone leaving death, destruction and terror in its wake and a fear that an attack like this might happen again; for many southern seaside towns such as Eastbourne, Brighton, Bournemouth and Torquay, the fear of another such attack was well-founded.

Both my German co-researcher, Bernd Rauchbach, and I started researching these raids about four years ago and we were lucky in contacting a few surviving German aircrew who freely gave us an interesting insight into what it was like being a 'tip and run' pilot. However, contacting the brother of, Leopold 'Poldi' Wenger, who was killed in action on 10 April 1945 aged just 23, was instrumental in convincing us that we had enough material to write a book on the subject. Wilhelm Wenger still held all of his brother's letters and logbook from the period he was a *Jabo* pilot over southern Britain, covering the operations he flew from 31 May 1942 to 4 June 1943. Furthermore, he still had his brother's photographs, including many taken by him during a number of the 'tip and run' attacks in which he had participated – an amazing feat for a lone pilot, flying at low-level and high speed and running the gauntlet of the British ground and air defences.

Understandably, this book will rely heavily on this source and also relies heavily on the memories of many civilians who were unfortunate to be in towns or near to targets attacked by German fighter-bombers; many memories are still vivid and portray exactly what it was like to be on the receiving end of a minor bombing campaign which lasted 15 months but the effects of which, physical and otherwise, were out of proportion to the numbers of German aircraft involved. I only hope that this book is a tribute not only to those British servicemen, service women and civilians whose memories ended so suddenly 60 years ago but also to those German pilots whose part in the Second World War has generally been forgotten.

Lt *Leopold Wenger, Spring 1943* (Wenger)

Chris Goss, Marlow, 2003

† Royal Observer Corps Narrative 1943 p.101

1
Origins of 'Tip and Run'

1914 – 1918

Prior to the start of the First World War, it was generally accepted that, in the event of hostilities with Imperial Germany, only airships would pose an immediate threat to mainland Britain. Any possibility of air attack by German aeroplanes was thought unrealistic as it was firmly believed that aircraft lacked both the necessary range and performance to reach England from their bases in Germany.

In the event, and to the profound relief of many, the anticipated raids by fleets of *Zeppelins* failed to materialise. During the opening months of the war, the German Army quickly lost five of its six *Zeppelins* and therefore lacked sufficient airship numbers to mount an offensive against England. The German Navy did, however, have airships that could be made available but most of them were already committed to scouting the North Sea in support of the German High Seas Fleet and few could be spared on such risky endeavours as attacking mainland Britain. Nevertheless, it was mainly reluctance on the part of *Kaiser* Wilhelm II, who refused to sanction any air offensive against Britain, that would frustrate German naval ambitions for such attacks in the months to come.

As early as August 1914, with the German Army already advancing beyond Brussels, *Konteradmiral* Paul Behnke, Deputy Chief of the German Naval Staff, had proposed bombing England from *Zeppelin* bases to be set up on the Belgian and French coasts, saying:

> *"In general, air attacks with aeroplanes and airships ... promise considerable material and moral results. [They] may be expected ... to cause panic in the population which may possibly render it doubtful that the war can be continued."*

Intense rivalry between the German Army and Navy to be the first to open the bombing offensive against England, as well as the *Kaiser's* continued reluctance to sanction such attacks, hampered preparations and would continue to thwart any plans for joint operations. With the Imperial High Command unable to agree a strategy for attack, enterprising German pilots soon seized the opportunity to launch individual raids.

The first reported air attack on Britain took place on 25 October 1914 when two Gotha-Taubes of the German Army's *Feldflieger Abteilung 9* set off to attack Dover. Experiencing poor visibility, one was forced to turn back before reaching the Channel but the other, crewed by *Lt* Karl Caspar and *Lt* Roos, claimed to have reached and bombed the target. This audacious act, a local initiative by the unit concerned, was much heralded in the German Press although British records do not confirm it.

What can be confirmed is that from December 1914, small German floatplanes of *See Flieger Abteilung 1* (*SFA* 1) regularly ventured across the Channel from their recently occupied new base at Zeebrugge in Belgium to drop bombs on England. Appearing without warning, they could attack and be well on their way back across the Channel before the inadequate British defences had any chance of response. These early attacks bore every hallmark of what would soon come to be termed 'tip and run' raids.

Dover Harbour was particularly favoured as a target for these incursions – an undeniable military objective with the double advantage of its prominence and proximity to the enemy coast. *SFA* 1, soon to be dubbed 'The Hornets of Zeebrugge' by the German Press, launched its first daylight attack on Dover on 21 December 1914 when a solitary Friedrichshafen FF29 floatplane dropped two bombs into the sea off Admiralty Pier before retiring back across the Channel. Three days later another FF29 of *SFA* 1 appeared over Dover at 1030 hours and dropped a single 22 lb bomb that exploded in a garden near Dover Castle leaving a crater 10 feet wide and four feet deep – the first enemy bomb to fall on British soil.

On Christmas Day 1914, another FF29 crew made their foray against England. Crewed by *Oblt zS* Stephan Prondzynski and *Fähnrich zS* von Frankenburg, the floatplane followed the River Thames as far as Erith before it was eventually intercepted by a 7 Squadron Vickers Gunbus from Joyce Green, crewed by 2nd Lt Montagu Chidson and Cpl Martin. In what would become the first air combat over Britain, Cpl Martin fired several bursts from his Maxim machine-gun, causing damage to the seaplane's fuselage and floats before the machine-gun suffered a stoppage. It is possible that, ambitiously, Prondzynski intended to reach London but on sighting the Gunbus, he prudently retired down the Thames and unloaded two bombs which fell in a field near Cliffe railway station in Kent. He later claimed to have attacked the oil storage tanks at Sheerness, his Observer apparently mistaking the mouth of the Thames for that of the River Medway. Nevertheless, both German airmen were welcomed back to their base as heroes and awarded the *Eiserne Kreuz* next day.

Many people witnessed this raid and the thrilling spectacle of what was the first air battle over Britain naturally received wide Press coverage, though general comment on the raid was fairly dismissive: *"the visit may have disturbed digestion but it did not interrupt the feasting"*. One Press account even described *"the intrepid enemy ... an airman of quite exceptional skill"* – an opinion presumably based on the fact that he had avoided all efforts of the British defences to shoot him down and made good his escape. At this stage in the war, public sentiment toward enemy airmen had yet to harden and such feelings would persist for some time. Even when a *Zeppelin* dropped about 20 bombs on Ramsgate on the night of 16 May 1915, one report described how the town *"revelled in the novelty of the whole affair"*.

However, attitudes soon began to change when the frequency and severity of German air attacks increased and people came to recognise the seriousness of their position with the failure of the British defences to counter such attacks. Typifying many of the coastal towns attacked, at Ramsgate *"the local public were in a state of perpetual apprehension throughout 1916, 1917 and the war months of 1918"*, many families having moved away, halving the town's population in the process, whilst visitors simply stayed away.

With German aircraft now seemingly able to attack Britain's coasts at will, the inadequacies of Britain's coastal defence system came under scrutiny and questions were soon raised in Parliament. It is true to say that bombs had so far caused little damage but with no effective counter-measures or adequate defence against such 'tip and run' raids, the Government could do little more than hope that these attacks would soon come to be accepted as a routine nuisance. In any case, given the overall scale of carnage reported daily from the Western Front, the civilian population had to simply stiffen its resolve!

However, such trifling raids were soon to pale into insignificance. On 7 January 1915, *Admiral* Hugo von Pohl, Chief of the Imperial Naval Staff, finally persuaded the *Kaiser* to approve limited air attacks on England and, three days later, von Pohl signalled orders to the Commander-in-Chief of the German High Seas Fleet; *"Targets not to be attacked in London but rather docks and military establishments in the Lower Thames and on the English coast"*. Within 10 days, the long-expected *Zeppelin* offensive began when, on the night of 19 January 1915, two German Navy airships attacked Great Yarmouth and King's Lynn. Four people were killed and another 16 injured, with damage estimated at over £7,000.

During 1915, as more airships reached German Army and Navy units, the scale of *Zeppelin* attacks on England steadily increased with London suffering its first attack on the night of 31 May 1915. Between April and October that year, there were 19 airship raids on England while there were only four attacks by aeroplanes, mostly of the 'tip and run' variety. One such raid took place in the late afternoon of 13 September 1915 when a solitary seaplane from *SFA* 1 dropped 10 bombs on Margate in Kent. Two BE2Cs gave chase but were unable to close on the enemy machine as it withdrew across the Channel. Two civilians were killed and six more injured – the first recorded 'tip and run' casualties.

Just along the coast, Ramsgate experienced its first raid:

> *"...by a couple of low-flying aeroplanes which, at 1530 hours on the bitterly cold afternoon of 9 February 1916, made a deliberate attack upon the tramways and conspicuous buildings on the East Cliff. One bomb fell near the tramlines and buried itself deeply in the ground, the passengers in a car having narrow escapes. Three other bombs fell in a field. When all danger had passed,*

thousands of people assembled to see the effect of the bombs. Many managed to secure pieces as souvenirs…".

Described by witnesses as Taubes, the aircraft were in fact a Friedrichshafen FF33e and a Hansa-Brandenburg NW seaplane, once again from *SFA* 1, the latter piloted by *Lt der Matrosen Artillerie* Friedrich Christiansen†. A mixed bunch of 24 RFC and RNAS aircraft from Dover, Eastchurch and Grain rose to meet the attack but despite an early warning from the North Goodwin lightship, the message was delayed and no aircraft made contact. Another four RNAS fighters from Dunkirk in France were similarly unsuccessful in intercepting the enemy floatplanes on their way back to Zeebrugge.

On the morning of 20 February 1916, in a successful attempt to confuse and split the defences, *SFA* 1 floatplanes made two widely separated attacks at Lowestoft in Suffolk and Walmer in Kent. Shortly before 1100 hours, two aircraft appeared over Lowestoft and dropped 19 bombs from about 5,500 feet before vanishing back out to sea. Five British aircraft sent up from Yarmouth saw nothing but, to add insult to injury, were shot at by their own guns. Half an hour later, a Friedrichshafen FF33e dropped six bombs on Walmer, killing one person, before making good its escape. From Dover, Eastchurch and Grain, 24 British aircraft took to the air in response to the threat from this solitary raider but all failed to make contact. In all the confusion, several were reported as hostiles on their return, prompting stories of air combats over Thanet in Kent and relative calm was not restored until mid afternoon.

The following month, the sirens again sounded in Ramsgate on 19 March 1916, when the town, together with Dover, Deal and Margate, was again attacked from the air. Paying their almost customary weekend visit to the Kent coast, seaplanes of *SFA* 1 were again involved – a Hansa Brandenburg NW, a Gotha Ursinus WD and four Friedrichshafen FF33s. Leading the attack and flying as observer in *Lt* Friedrich Christiansen's Hansa-Brandenburg was *Oblt zS* von Tschirschky und Bogendorff, the Zeebrugge station commander. The German aircraft approached the Kent coast in two formations, three approaching Dover at 5,000 feet, where they spent five minutes casually bombing the town before departing for Deal where they dropped yet more bombs prior to retiring out to sea.

Soon after this brazen display, three more floatplanes arrived over Margate and Ramsgate where crowds gathered to witness events:

"Shortly after two o'clock, two German seaplanes … appeared over the town from different directions and dropped ten bombs, all of which exploded.

† *Kapitanleutnant* Friedrich Christiansen ended the war with 21 accredited victories, including a British coastal airship and the British submarine C25. He was the first of only three naval airmen to receive the coveted *Pour le Merite*, awarded on 11 December 1917, the only seaplane pilot to do so. He reached the rank of *General* in the following war and died in December 1972

The greater part of the loss of life occurred outside St. Luke's church, where an explosive bomb fell on a motorcar, which was blown to atoms. The driver ... was killed, and a number of children on their way to Sunday school were killed and injured."

Four children and the driver of the car were killed, another nine children and a woman being seriously injured. One bomb fell on the Canadian Hospital at Chatham House – damage was done to the roof and to the top of the hospital but there were no casualties.

30 British aircraft took to the air from the air-stations at Dover, Eastgate, Westgate, Grain and Lympne but they were an ill-assorted lot and for most it was the same familiar story – they returned without even sighting an enemy machine. Even those that did, lacked sufficient performance to close within firing range and abandoned the fruitless chase over the Channel. One Nieuport 10 piloted by Flight Commander R J Bone, Commanding Officer of RNAS Detling, did make contact and after a 40-minute chase delivered three attacks on a retreating Friedrichshafen FF33, forcing it to land on the sea 30 miles off the North Foreland with its engine smoking and stopped. The crew, *Flugmeister* Ponater and *Lt* Herrenknecht, suffered minor injuries and the floatplane, one of those that had attacked Deal, was later towed back to Zeebrugge. The enterprising Bone, who had taken his aircraft to Westgate that day, had correctly anticipated a raid and was awarded an immediate DSO.

One more engagement took place as the German aircraft retired across the Channel but it owed more to good fortune than any alertness on the part of the defences. An FE2b, airborne from Lympne and en-route to France on a delivery flight, saw the Dover guns in action and spotted an enemy aircraft heading for Deal. 2nd Lt Reginald Collis, was experienced enough to continue gaining height over the Channel, planning to intercept the enemy seaplane as it returned. Keeping it in sight, Collis reached 12,000 feet before diving to the attack and closed to within 150 yards astern of Christiansen's floatplane before his gunner, Flt Sgt A C Emery, opened fire, emptying a complete drum of ammunition into the German aircraft which immediately spiralled away to starboard, its engine spouting steam.

With cooling system damaged and one cylinder out of action, Christiansen now had little hope of reaching Zeebrugge. In the front cockpit, von Tschirschky had been wounded in the shoulder but somehow managed to clamber out onto the wing and make running repairs to the damaged engine. This plucky action enabled them to stay aloft for another hour but eventually they were forced to alight on the sea 20 miles off Ostende. After taxying for some time to allow the engine to cool down a little, they managed to take-off again and finally struggled back to base at 1720 hours.

This raid was widely condemned as *"a ghastly outrage"* and provoked general revulsion, with an outcry for reprisals that resulted in a mass meeting addressed by the 'first air member' of Parliament, Noel Pemberton Billing MP. The *"wholesale murder of Sunday school children"*, together with the bombing of a military hospital, prompted a special meeting of the Ramsgate Council that sought to make immediate improvements to the town's warning system. In total, 14 people had died, including those casualties at Ramsgate, and a further 26 were seriously injured in what had been the most successful 'tip and run' raid to date.

It was now becoming increasingly evident, even to the public, that these daring raids were almost impossible to intercept. Despite the best efforts of such defences as lightships and picket boats, wireless intercepts and giant sound locators, coastal observers, aircraft standing patrols and anti-aircraft guns and balloons guarding key points, German aeroplanes continued to attack with seeming impunity. The official stance was another healthy dose of rhetoric as the Government, showing remarkable resolve, firmly resisted growing public clamour to increase fighter strength for home defence. Such attacks could easily drain defence resources, which was clearly the enemy's main intention, and there was a feeling in some official quarters that the defence effort was already too high – particularly since the Home Secretary, as early as December 1914, had asked the Cabinet to *"reconsider the policy of leaving the civil population to take its chance of death or injury from enemy aircraft"*.

British citizens did exactly that from 1915 to 1918 and ultimately 1,414 of them died and another 3,416 were injured while the air defences continued to improvise and evolve to meet the growing challenge. The *Zeppelin* menace was, however, finally laid to rest on the night of 27 November 1916 when two of the hated raiders fell to defending fighters. It was a turning point in the air offensive on Britain. German Navy airships now continued to raid England, on a much reduced scale, until 1918 when, with better airships and improved tactics, they mounted a final and costly assault, lasting until August of that year.

No sooner had the defences began to meet the *Zeppelin* threat, than a new danger emerged in the continuing air offensive against England. In the Spring of 1917, twin-engined Gotha G.IVs of the German Army High Command's *Kampfgeschwader* 3 [*Kagohl* 3], launched a series of devastating day and night attacks on England by formations of around 20 bombers, striking hard at strategic targets including London. *Kagohl* 3, dubbed the '*England Geschwader*', was based in Belgium where, in August 1917, the unit was joined by the giant four-engined *Riesenflugzeugen* of *Rfa* 501. Equipped with Staaken R.VIs, these aircraft were able to carry bomb-loads of up to 4,000 lbs. Their attacks in conjunction with those of *Kagohl* 3, heralded such concepts as round-the-clock bombing, and were the true genesis of what would later become recognised as strategic air offensive.

So potent had been the *Zeppelin* threat and so enduring the image, that it is surprising to learn that most German air raids on Britain in the First World War were by aeroplanes rather than airships; the day and night attacks mounted by aircraft between May 1917 and May 1918 being the most effective. Yet post-war figures reveal another surprising, yet often over-looked fact. Of the 61 German aircraft despatched on 'tip and run' or small-scale nuisance attacks against England during the First World War, not one was lost to the British home defences. Official statistics over the four years of conflict make it clear that, whilst both airships and large bombers could expect to suffer losses of more than 8% in raids against England, attacks on coastal targets by small formations or single aircraft experienced no casualties at all.

Clearly, there were several factors that influenced this remarkable outcome. Yet the simple fact remained that such attacks, even accepting the minimal damage and casualties they caused, tied down British defences disproportionate to the tiny German forces employed, were quick and easy to organise (with little or no disruption to other operational demands) and were undertaken at very low or no cost. However, they were over-shadowed by other, more devastating forms of air attack with the consequence that, a quarter of a century later, British and German air strategists would find themselves having to relearn the experiences gained from this first 'tip and run' campaign.

2
Birth of the Jabo

1937 – 1940

It was in Spain in 1937 that the idea of 'fighter-bombers' was resurrected, this term stemming from when a few German fighters in the First World War were fitted with bombs as a crude way of trying to stem the Allied advance in the Summer of 1918.

In August 1936, Nazi Germany, concerned that the Communists would get a foothold in western Europe when civil war erupted in Spain, began supporting General Franco's Nationalist army. The *Legion Condor*, a semi-autonomous German air component, would play an important part during the civil war, allowing German aircrew to gain vital combat experience for the coming Second World War and for *Luftwaffe* senior officers to devise and prove a concept of air operations. It was in Spain in March 1937 that 'fighter-bombers' first proved to be an effective weapon.

The Heinkel 51

The Messerschmitt 109s arrive in Spain

The single-seat Heinkel 51 biplane fighter was, until the arrival of the Messerschmitt 109 monoplane, the *Legion Condor's* principal fighter. However, it was becoming increasingly obvious that by February 1937, the Heinkel 51 was inferior to the Soviet fighters being used by the Republican forces. Faced with the inferiority of its principal fighter, the *Legion Condor* decided to enhance its offensive capability, particularly for the battle for Bilbao, by fitting the Heinkel 51s of *Jagdgruppe* J/88 with fragmentation bombs and on 31 March 1937, these aircraft were used to bomb and strafe Republican front positions with considerable success. In the days that followed, J/88's fighter-bombers proved ideal at neutralising those targets that medium to high-level bombers found harder to destroy.

Paradoxically, it was the success of the fighter-bomber that ultimately spelt its demise. Impressed by the concept of close air support and pinpoint bombing accuracy, the Junkers 87 *Stuka* and Henschel 123 dive-bombers were quickly brought to Spain and used with even greater success. It was this concept of operations that, following refinement in Spain, was used with great effect from 1 September 1939 when Germany invaded Poland and again on 10 May 1940 when Germany invaded France and the Low Countries. The *Stuka* suited the *Blitzkrieg* concept and with the air superiority achieved by the *Luftwaffe* in the first nine months of the Second World War, there was no need for a fighter-bomber. This was to change dramatically during the Battle of Britain.

A Junkers Ju 87 A-1 of the 'Jolanthe Kette", Spain

The Henschel 123

With the *Luftwaffe* anticipating the same air superiority it had enjoyed in previous campaigns, it was thought that the *Stuka*, as the *Luftwaffe's* premier ground-attack weapon, would enjoy similar success. However, when first committed en masse against a Channel convoy on 8 August, it became evident that against Spitfires and Hurricanes, the *Stuka* was extremely vulnerable and required a strong fighter escort. In bitter combats over the English Channel that day, eight *Stukas* of I/*StG* 3 and II/*StG* 77 were shot down and a further

'Stukas' over the Channel, Summer 1940 (Grahl)

Messerschmitt 109s in Spain

seven returned with damage; the cost in aircrew was 13 killed, three captured, and seven more wounded. The casualties included three executive officers; *Hptm* Waldemar Plewig, *Gruppen Kommandeur* of II/*StG* 77† and *Oblt* Martin Müller, *Gruppen Adjutant* of I/*StG* 3 were both taken prisoner and *Hptm* Horst-Hennig Schmack, *Staffelkapitän* of 4/*StG* 77, who was killed.

Nevertheless, limited *Stuka* successes in the days that followed lulled German commanders into sending them against inland targets – with catastrophic results. In a series of disastrous attacks on the airfields at Tangmere, Lee-on-Solent, and Gosport, and Ventnor radar station on 16 August, followed by Thorney Island, Ford and Gosport airfields and Poling radar station two days later, a total of 25 aircraft were shot down and five more seriously damaged.

Again, the loss of experienced crews was critical – 14 killed, five captured and five more wounded on August 16, and a further 26 killed, six captured, and six wounded on August 18. Casualties included *Hptm* Heinrich Brücker, *Gruppen Kommandeur* of III/*StG* 2, and *Oblt* Heinrich Eppen the *Staffel Kapitän* of 1/*StG* 3 both wounded on 16 August, and *Hptm* Herbert Meisel, *Gruppen Kommandeur* of I/*StG* 77, *Oblt* Fritz Sayler, *Staffel Kapitän* of 2/*StG* 77, *Oblt* Heinz Sonntag, *Gruppen Technisches Offizier* of II/*StG* 77 and *Oblt* Heinz Merensky, *Staffelkapitän* of 5/*StG* 77 amongst those killed on 18 August††. These losses were of such magnitude that the *Stuka* units were immediately withdrawn from front-line operations. Practically on the eve of the planned invasion of England, the *Luftwaffe* had no aircraft that could fulfil the close-support role.

In the Spring of 1940, the German Air Staff had requested that the *Luftwaffe* Technical Office explore the possibility of adapting the Messerschmitt 109 E to carry bombs. Design engineers produced a centrally-mounted bomb rack, contained in a streamlined fairing, bolted to the belly of the aircraft between the undercarriage legs. This bomb rack was designed to carry a single 250 kg bomb and the tests and performance trials showed that a single SC250 bomb could be carried with little appreciable loss in performance. The ETC500 bomb rack was therefore put into production and issued in kit form for retro-fitting to aircraft already serving with fighter units in the field. Orders were also placed to switch existing factory assembly lines of Messerschmitt 109 E-1s and E-4s then in production to Messerschmitt 109 E-1/Bs and E-4/Bs.

As a consequence, a total of 110 Messerschmitt 109 E-1/Bs were produced while production of the E-4/B variant totalled an additional 226 machines. Delivery of the new 109E fighter-bombers started in July 1940, the first being issued to 3 *Staffel* of the newly formed *Erprobungs Gruppe* 210 (*Erpr.Gr* 210).

---

†The experienced *Hptm* Plewig would be awarded the *Ritterkreuz* 14 December 1940
††Brücker would later be awarded the *Ritterkreuz Mit Eichenlaub* and by 1943 would have become a fighter-bomber pilot. Eppen would also be awarded the *Ritterkreuz* whilst one of those wounded on 18 August 1940 was *Oblt* Karl Henze who would also be awarded the *Ritterkreuz Mit Eichenlaub*

One of the victims-a Stuka of 3/StG 2 shot down 16 Aug 40 (Watkins)

An ETC 500 bomb rack fitted to a Bf 109 E-4/B (Sauer)

Erpr.Gr 210 was formed at Köln-Ostheim on 1 July 1940, under the leadership of *Hptm* Walter Rubensdörffer; the first two *Staffeln* equipped with Messerschmitt 110s and 3 *Staffel* with Messerschmitt 109s. Intended as a specialist ground-attack unit, the *Gruppe* was charged with operational development of ground-attack and dive-bombing techniques and equipment. It was hoped to equip the *Gruppe* with the twin-engined Messerschmitt 210 as a successor to the *Stuka,* acting in a close-support role and capable of defending itself against fighters in air-to-air combat. However, the introduction of the Messerschmitt 210 continued to be plagued by technical problems so *Erpr.Gr* 210 pressed ahead developing the fighter-bomber concept with the twin-engined Messerschmitt 110 and the Messerschmitt 109 E.

The *Gruppe* immediately set to working-up its new equipment and instituted a rigorous regime of dive-bombing practice. This training came under the direct supervision of *Hptm* Karl Valesi, a leading exponent on the use of the Messerschmitt 109 as a dive-bomber, who was seconded to the *Gruppe* to share his expertise.

Walter Rubensdörffer (Hintze)

On 10 July 1940, the *Gruppe* moved to Denain in France. Here dive-bombing practice continued and once the pilots had mastered the rudiments, they progressed to dropping cement bombs and it was during one such flight in the following month that Karl Valesi was killed.

It was found that for low and medium altitude dive bombing attacks a dive speed of 373 mph was most effective, with 403 mph being the ideal dive speed for higher altitude attacks. Bomb-aiming was rudimentary given the degree of expertise and limited training available at the time, but by trial and error a means of using the standard *Revi* gun-sight was developed, as the *Staffel Kapitän* of 3/*Erpr.Gr* 210, *Oblt* Otto Hintze, recalls:

> *"The angle of dive from a height of 3,000 metres was 45°, holding the target in the centre of the sight. At 1,000 metres, you started pulling out of the dive to resume level flight, releasing your bomb after about two seconds, when the target had reached half – way down the vertical line of the sight. Also, the wind must be taken into consideration."*

A Bf 110 C fitted with a bomb rack

Oblt *Otto Hintze, flanked by* Lt *Horst Marx and* Lt *Peter Emmerich* (via Cornwell)

Pilots of 3/Erpr.Gr 210. Front l to r: Oblt *?,* Oblt *Otto Hintze,* Hptm *Heinrich Seeliger,* Lt *Peter Emmerich. Back:* Fw *Wimpahl,* Ofw *Vogel,* Fw *Büttner,* Ofhr *Paul Drawe (+ 1 May 41),* Fw *Otto Rückert (+ 3 Jan 42),* Uffz *Volz (+ 8 Jul 40)* (Hintze)

Typically, most pilots spent two to three weeks gaining experience of their new aircraft and practising dive-bombing. It was around this time that a red line was painted on the side of the cockpit canopy at a 45° angle – aligned with the horizon, it helped pilots maintain the correct angle of attack. Anything steeper than that and they risked taking off their propeller when the bomb was released.

By the third week of July, the *Gruppe* was flying armed reconnaissance sorties and regular attacks on shipping off the south and east coasts of Britain. On 19 July 1940, 3 *Staffel* mounted two attacks on shipping in Dover Harbour; during the first, which involved the entire *Gruppe* with a fighter escort from III/*JG* 51, an armed trawler was hit. During the second mission mid-afternoon, the Admiralty oiler *Sepoy* was sunk and several near misses caused damage to the destroyer *HMS Griffin*; a tug and a drifter was also damaged.

In the following week, 3 *Staffel* flew a further 13 anti-shipping attacks, averaging almost two sorties a day, most of them against convoys of colliers, coasters, and merchantmen protected by minesweepers and destroyers. The German strategy of closing the English Channel to British shipping was starting to bear fruit.

By the end of the month, in the 16 days since it first started operations, *Erpr.Gr* 210 claimed to have sunk 89,000 tons of shipping, which included four warships, besides shooting down three RAF fighters, at a cost of three Messerschmitt 110s lost in action and two Messerschmitt 109s in accidents. This result prompted personal congratulations from *Generalfeldmarschall* Kesselring who visited them at Denain on 30 July. The 'flying artillery' had cleared the way across the Channel for a German invasion fleet. Now, he told them, they could start hitting targets further inland.

*Bf 109 Es of 3/*Erpr.Gr *210, Denain, August 1940* (Hintze)

During early August 1940, 3 *Staffel* continued to seek out shipping targets, a convoy off Harwich probably being a victim on 5 August when the trawler *Cape Finisterre* was sunk. Then on 12 August 1940 the entire *Gruppe* made simultaneous strikes on the crucial radar stations at Dover, Pevensey, and Rye on the Kent coast and the inland station at Dunkirk. 3 *Staffel* attacked Dover with eight aircraft, where their bombs fell amongst buildings within the compound and made the radar mast sway but caused no lasting damage. All aircraft returned to France leaving three of the vital radar stations temporarily out of action with just Dunkirk remaining operational. Then shortly after midday, *Erpr.Gr* 210 returned leading I/*KG* 2 to attack Manston airfield. The attack was a complete success and once the bombing was over, the Messerschmitt 109s returned and machine-gunned the airfield.

Fighter-bombers had demonstrated their ability to successfully deliver precision air-strikes on targets of tactical importance. The main ground-attack weapon in the *Luftwaffe's* arsenal, the *Stuka*, had already proved itself too vulnerable to British fighters and would soon be withdrawn after disastrous losses. The bulk of German medium bombers, the Dornier 17s and Heinkel 111s, lacked the speed to penetrate the British defences with any hope of surprise, and required increasingly heavy fighter escorts to battle their way to and from the target; they also lacked the bomb-aiming precision to hit pinpoint targets. Apart from *Erpr.Gr* 210, there were few units with relevant ground-attack experience. Only II(S)/*LG* 2, then back in Germany re-equipping with Messerschmitt 109 E-4/Bs, and the Dornier 17s of 9/*KG* 76, whose crews were low-flying specialists, fitted the bill. The problem for *Luftwaffe* planners was too many targets and not enough fighter-bombers.

However, the bubble was about to burst for *Erpr.Gr* 210. On 15 August 1940, they attacked Martlesham Heath in Suffolk. They had taken off from Calais-Marck, skirted the north Kent coast and crossed the Thames Estuary, their intention still being unclear to British fighter controllers even when the formation headed inland. In a characteristic lightning attack, the raid lasted no more than five minutes, the fighter-bombers delivered their attacks leaving many buildings badly damaged and two hangars destroyed. A Fairey Battle was also set alight and its 1,000 lb bomb load exploded adding considerably to the overall damage inflicted.

The second attack on that day would be disastrous for the Germans. Briefed to attack Kenley airfield, the *Gruppe* actually bombed Croydon two miles to the north of Kenley. Little major damage was caused even though 62 people were killed and a further 37 injured. However, Hurricanes from 32 and 111 Squadrons were quick to intercept and it was left to 3 *Staffel*, after they had delivered their bombs to try and protect the Messerschmitt 110s which were now forming a defensive circle. Without the advantage of height and faced with superior numbers of Hurricanes, it was a desperate situation. As individual aircraft broke away from the circle to head for the coast, they were pounced upon by more waiting

Lt *Horst Marx in front of 'Yellow 3'* (via Cornwell)

British fighters. *Lt* Horst Marx of 3 *Staffel*, sticking close to *Hptm* Rubensdörffer's aircraft as they made off south, flew into the path of a 32 Squadron Hurricane flown by Plt Off 'Polly' Flinders.

> *"An Me 109 came towards me from the starboard side. I throttled back completely and he passed in front of me and into my sights. I fired for about two seconds and a stream of white smoke came from his engine. The aircraft dived towards the ground. I realised that he could not get home and continued chasing the bombers. A minute later I saw a parachute open at about 6,000 feet, south of Sevenoaks."*

Horst Marx had baled out over Frant in Sussex. The wreck of his aircraft, the first Messerschmitt 109 fighter-bomber to crash on British soil, attracted little attention. There was not enough left to warrant close inspection and nothing to suggest that it was anything but a standard German fighter. Later, under interrogation, Marx convinced his captors that he had been on pure escort duties and the RAF Intelligence report on his capture was even noted to the effect that *'This Me 109 had no bombs, and could not carry any'*.

*A Stab/*Erpr.Gr *210 Bf 110 shot down on 15 Aug 40* (via Saunders)

The attack had cost the bulk of their officers, including the *Gruppen Kommandeur, Adjutant* and *Technischer Offizier*. Six Messerschmitt 110s and one Messerschmitt 109 failed to return. It was now becoming clear that, against modern single-engined fighters, the Messerschmitt 110 was too slow and cumbersome, its early successes achieved mainly through the skill of its more experienced and aggressive pilots. Furthermore, *Erpr.Gr* 210's operations were starting to indicate that low-level attacks by *Jabos* against shipping were generally most successful, whilst attacks against mainland coastal targets, although successful, could result in higher loss rates. Raids against targets further inland were proving very costly in terms of aircraft and crews lost and also carried little guarantee that the intended target would be destroyed or indeed even badly damaged. It was apparent that, of the two aircraft being operated, the Messerschmitt 109 was the better fighter-bomber and far better able to defend itself after delivering its load.

Nevertheless, the *OKL* had already decided to expand the fighter-bomber effort against England by ordering the re-equipment of two further *Gruppen*. One of them, I(*J*)/*LG* 2 commanded by *Hptm* Herbert Ihlefeld, was a conventional fighter unit and one of the first to receive the Messerschmitt 109 E on its introduction to service pre-war. This unit had been responsible for the operational development of the new fighter during the Polish Campaign. Now, it was to start taking delivery of the new Messerschmitt 109 E-7 fighter-bomber version then coming off the production lines, each aircraft equipped with an ETC 500 bomb-rack with the facility for an optional auxiliary belly tank containing 300 litres of fuel to extend the range. They could now operate as *Jabos* or longer-range escort fighters as operational demands dictated.

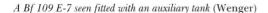

A Bf 109 E-7 seen fitted with an auxiliary tank (Wenger)

First examples of the Messerschmitt 109 E-7 were delivered to I(*J*)/*LG* 2 at Calais-Marck during August 1940 and by the end of the month, the entire *Gruppe* had been re-equipped and serious training could begin. Some pilots were sent to Denain where they would also benefit from the combat experiences of the 3/*Erpr.Gr* 210 pilots but it was not until the end of September that I(*J*)/*LG* 2 was declared fully operational flying their first sortie on 4 October 1940.

Meanwhile, 3/*Erpr.Gr* 210 was joined by an entire *Gruppe* of Messerschmitt 109 E fighter-bombers of *Hptm* Otto Weiss's II *(S)/LG* 2, one of the premier *Schlacht* units in the *Luftwaffe*. Originally formed as an operational development unit for the evaluation of ground-attack with fighter-bombers, its pilots had already gained experience in the campaigns in Poland and France. After the fall of France, the *Gruppe* had been withdrawn to Braunschweig-Waggum where, in late July, it began exchanging its elderly Henschel 123 biplanes for the new Messerschmitt 109 E-4/Bs then coming off the assembly lines. After four weeks re-equipping and gaining experience of the new aircraft they were declared ready for action and moved to Calais-Marck, flying their first *Jabo* mission against England on 2 September 1940.

A Henschel 123 A-1 of II(S)/LG 2 (Wenger)

That same day, Göring had issued a document detailing a number of suggestions for tactical changes in the on-going offensive against Britain. He wanted precision attacks on the British aircraft industry and nuisance raids on industrial targets in the far north of the country using single aircraft crewed by experienced volunteers. Any targets within range of the Messerschmitt 109 E were to be attacked with fighter-bombers – and so the Messerschmitt 109s of one third of all *Jagdgeschwadern* were to carry bombs.

The Messerschmitt 109 was available in large numbers and the results of 3/*Erpr.Gr* 210 were impressive. *Geschwader* were to receive the Messerschmitt 109 E-4/Bs now becoming more widely available and pilots were to receive the appropriate training. With immediate effect, every *Jagdgruppe* was ordered to equip and operate one *Staffel*, a third of its strength, as *Jabos*. Reaction to the order amongst the fighter pilots was mixed.

For most fighter pilots, retraining as a fighter-bomber pilot was not at all popular as *Gefr* Heinz Zag of 8/*JG* 53 recalls:

> *"I did not think it was a good idea – we had short enough flying range without being weighed down by a bomb!"*

'Only a cloud of dust was left'-a laden Messerschmitt 109 E (Griehl)

An alternative – four 50 kg bombs (Griehl)

Obstlt Adolf Galland, then *Geschwader Kommodore* of *JG* 26 and who had experience as a ground-attack pilot flying Henschel 123s prior to the Battle of France, expressed the majority view:

> *"We fighter pilots looked upon this violation of our aircraft with great bitterness. We had done everything possible to increase our performance ... We had discarded everything dispensable in an attempt to squeeze another ounce of speed out of them ... Instead of that, they now gave us bomb-release gadgets and we were forced to see a third of our aircraft drop out of air combat.*
>
> *"The fighter was ... made into a fighter-bomber as a stop-gap and a scapegoat. We started from the premise that the fighter was apparently unable to give sufficient protection to the bombers. This was true. If the fighter arm is unable to protect the bombers, it must deliver the bombs to England on its own account. The raids on England had become a question of prestige, and as day bombing could not be continued and night raids were only in preparation, this gap was to be filled by fighters transformed into fighter-bombers. Not military expedience but a momentary political demand ..."*

Adolf Galland

II*(S)/LG* 2 suffered its first losses four days after commencing operations when on 6 September, two of its *Jabos* ventured too close to naval anti-aircraft fire over Chatham during an evening sortie against shipping in the Estuary. *Lt* Herbert Dültgen of 4*(S)/LG* 2 was forced to abandon his aircraft over the sea off The Nore whilst the aircraft flown by *Fw* Werner Gottschalk of 6*(S)/LG* 2 was hit in the fuel tank and he was forced to land at Hawkinge airfield in Kent. Both pilots were captured unhurt but revealed little of interest, though Gottschalk's aircraft provided the British with first firm evidence of a factory-built Messerschmitt 109 E-4/B. Not surprisingly, it underwent a thorough inspection and technical evaluation. So by early September 1940, with many German fighter units in northern France still in the process of re-equipping with the new Messerschmitt 109 E fighter-bomber, the RAF was already well aware of its existence and capabilities.

JG 26 was one of the first units to respond to Göring's order of 2 September with 4/*JG* 26 flying practice *Jabo* flights from 5 September. Two days later, *Oblt* Hans Krug the *Staffel Kapitän* of 4/*JG* 26, force-landed at Pluckley, in Kent. His aircraft, a Messerschmitt 109 E-4/B was relatively undamaged and in due course, the RAF noted a red line painted on the cockpit perspex, auxiliary bomb-fusing and selector panel mounted directly below the oil temperature gauge, and red bomb-release handle, evidence enough that the long-anticipated Messerschmitt 109 E fighter-bomber was starting to make an appearance.

Evidently, a degree of autonomy was being allowed (or simply taken) in the execution of Göring's order for not every *Gruppe* had a dedicated *Jabostaffel*. Surviving records show that the 9/*JG* 54 received three of the new fighter-bombers on 20 September and these were allocated to *Oblt* Günter Fink, *Lt* Waldemar Wübke and *Uffz* Karl Kempf who formed a *Jaboschwarm* within the *Staffel*. Over the next three weeks, the *Jaboschwarm* flew 17 missions against targets in England until 12 October 1940 when they exchanged aircraft with 8 *Staffel* which was to become the *Gruppen Jabostaffel*. Five more *Jabo* sorties followed, all of them to London, until 21 October when III/*JG* 54 was transferred to Holland and took no further part in the 1940 fighter-bomber offensive against England.

With most *Jagdgeschwadern* still fully committed to bomber escort duties, while others were only just starting to re-equip with fighter-bombers, *Jabo* sorties in September 1940 were limited. Throughout the month a total of 19 attacks were mounted by formations of between 20 and 25 aircraft – a total of 428 sorties, 264 of them with London as the target. Losses were minimal, the *Jabo* units losing only four aircraft, (less than 1% of the total force deployed) – three to *Flak* and one to fighters.

However, the increasing switch of emphasis to night bombing by the German medium bomber units based in Holland, Belgium and France meant that the *Luftwaffe* now lacked any real means of maintaining pressure on the British defences during the day. The ratio of bombers to fighters in

A Jabo of III/JG 54 (Griehl)

Fitting a 250 kg bomb to a 3/JG 53 Bf 109 E-4/B, October 1940 (Sauer)

*A 250 kg bomb on a Bf 109 E-4/B,
of 3/JG 53 October 1940* (Sauer)

the formations being sent over England gradually dwindled and any modest bomber presence usually favoured the faster Junkers 88 which were still limited in numbers.

High-level sweeps over England now featured large formations of fighters accompanied by a few fighter-bombers; tactics that the British were finding difficult to counter. Radar detection and ground observation were problematic at the heights these raids came in and, unhindered by bombers, *Jabos* could be over London within 20 minutes of the first warning of their approach. British controllers had no way of knowing which formations included any bombers and, consequently, which to intercept. At heights above 20,000 feet the Messerschmitt 109 E, thanks to its two-stage supercharger, enjoyed far better performance than both the Hurricane and the Spitfire and with such a disadvantage the RAF was not going to be tempted to challenge German fighter formations. Without any bombers, they posed little real threat. Another way would have to be found to bring the RAF fighters to combat.

General lack of dive-bombing skills in the *Jabo* units was another decisive factor in the choice of London as the main target for such attacks. Apart from II(S)/LG 2 and 3/Erpr.Gr 210, now operating together as a single *Gruppe*, the majority of the *Jabostaffeln* were low on expertise and limited in experience of the fighter-bomber role. Most of the pilots had received perfunctory training in dive-bombing techniques and many of them lacked any real enthusiasm for what they widely viewed as an unwelcome change in role. As Adolf Galland confirms:

> *"The fighter-bombers were put into action in so great hurry that there was hardly time to give the pilots bombing training, and most of them dropped their first live bomb in a raid over London or other targets in England."*

With a target the size of London, and little apparent risk of interference from RAF fighters, all pilots had to do was reach the target area and drop their bombs but this wearisome task, day in and day out, simply increased many *Jabo* pilots' resentment and had a seriously adverse effect on their morale, already low due to pure exhaustion.

Adolf Galland, clearly no advocate of the *Jabo* strategy adopted over England in 1940, has expressed the view that the attacks, *"apart from their nuisance value, ... achieved very little of any military value"*. He further acknowledged that such missions had an adverse affect on German pilots' morale:

> *"...it is disconcerting for a fighter pilot to have to fight without being able to take the initiative. The morale of fighter pilots was affected; they had to carry bombs, release them at great altitude on an enormous target without being able to observe the effect and then had to adopt a passive attitude towards enemy fighters..."*

An attack against important railway junctions by II(S)/LG 2 *Jabos* on 15

September 1940, received petulant coverage in the British Press. In emotive language, reminiscent of the outbursts provoked by air raids during the previous war, the report condemned the use of fighter-bombers as 'unfair'. As *Oblt* Viktor Kraft recalls:

> "*A British newspaper wrote when our Gruppe flew for the first time over Kent: 'Today a group of German fighters flew over Kent and London. Nobody had expected they were carrying bombs but they did so. It is not fair to fly like a fighter and then to drop bombs like a bomber'. I should say that we didn't do it because we were unfair. It was just a new development as is usual in war.*"

Bad weather over the Channel and southern England in early October reduced the scale of operations which allowed more units to complete their conversion training in readiness for a break in the weather and a resumption of large-scale attacks. It was now that many units made their debuts over England as fighter-bombers.

Jabo pilots of 3/JG 53, October 1940. Standing l to r: Uffz *Alexander Bleymüller,* Fw *Walter Seiz,* Lt *Wolfgang Tonne,* Oblt *Walter Rupp* (St Kap). *Sitting:* Lt *Karl Leonhard,* Uffz *Alfred Baumer* (Sauer)

For some, introduction of the fighter-bombers would prove a costly business. On their first *Jabo* mission on the morning of 2 October 1940, *Hptm* Wolf-Dietrich Wilcke's III/*JG* 53 lost four aircraft including one *Staffel Kapitän*. Experiences like this did little to bolster *Jabo* pilots' confidence in their new role or convince them of any value in such missions. Many fledgling *Jabo* units experienced similar losses on their first fighter-bomber sorties early that month. On 7 October 1940, it was the turn of I/*JG* 51. Leading the *Jabostaffel* was *Oblt* Victor Mölders, brother of Werner Mölders, the *Geschwader Kommodore* of *JG* 51.

> "My Staffel, eight aircraft armed with 250 kg bombs, were to take off from Pihen, climb to 6,000m, fly north to London and attack the Docks. We were to be protected by the Stabschwarm and eight (other) aircraft.
>
> "As we approached the Thames Estuary, my brother informed me that he would remain at this altitude and return to Pihen as they were running low on fuel. I then dived with my Staffel and flew at rooftop height over the streets of London. It was funny to see the flak bursting above me! We dropped our bombs on the docks and proceeded to return to France. Suddenly I heard the radio call, 'Indians behind you!' and on looking saw about thirty aircraft at 6,000m diving towards us. I waited until they were close, then turned and flew towards them. All that I can remember after that is that I was hit in the radiator, I began to leak glycol and the engine temperature rose.
>
> "I decided to remain low as the engine was not capable of climbing. I was too low to bale out so I began to look for a suitable field to land in. All the fields had old cars in them or other anti-glider obstacles. I eventually had to crash-land on top of an anti-tank ditch ..."

The attack on London that morning cost 2/*JG* 51 two aircraft to the Hurricanes of 501 and 605 Squadrons, another of their *Jabos* only just making the French coast where it crash-landed with an injured pilot. *Oblt* Heinrich Vogler's 4(S)/*LG* 2 also lost two *Jabos* with two more from 5 *Staffel* returning severely damaged.

On 12 October 1940, the *Luftwaffe* launched 12 waves of *Jabos* against England, a total of 217 aircraft with 175 heading for London. Three days later, the capital was again the main target with close to 300 *Jabos* in 15 waves crossing the English coast throughout the day, again, with 175 of them heading for London where they caused serious damage and severe disruption to the rail system. On 17 October, the scale of attack reduced, only eight *Jabo* attacks being recorded; once again, London was the main target attracting 110 of the 186 *Jabo* sorties launched that day.

A different strategy was now being adopted with large formations of 50 plus *Jabos* being despatched along with medium bombers, these mixed formations accompanied by a strong fighter escort. On 25 October, four waves of *Jabo* attacks were launched against England, in all 237 *Jabo* sorties, with 186 targeting London. In a further effort to confuse and split British

Maj *Werner Mölders*, Lt *Erich Meyer (also POW 7 Oct 40)*, Oblt *Victor Mölders* (Mölders)

defences, 41 conventional bomber missions were also flown that day, the whole effort protected by 634 fighters.

First official acknowledgement of the use of the Messerschmitt 109 E fighter-bomber in surviving RAF Intelligence records is a report dated 21 October 1940, which summarises all they had managed to glean on the subject from inspection of captured aircraft and interrogation of prisoners. This document confirms that the RAF had by then discovered that a single German unit, 3/*Erpr.Gr* 210, had had been 'practicing' bombing with Messerschmitt 109 Es armed with 250 and 500 kg bombs from early July 1940. The report also reveals that they knew that one third of all German fighter groups were retrained as '*Me 109 bombers*'. From this they could have readily estimated the number of fighter-bombers deployed in northern France and the likely scale of the offensive but by the time the report was circulated, the fighter-bomber phase of the Battle of Britain was coming to an end.

Larger *Jabo* formations interspersed with conventional medium bombers were again employed on 27 October, when another four waves of *Jabos* totalling 234 aircraft attacked England, 169 of them again targeting London. Some 76 conventional bomber sorties were also flown on the day, with escort fighter protection being reduced to 566 sorties due to lack of serviceable aircraft.

Two days later and making full use of prevailing low cloud cover, II(S)/LG 2 delivered a textbook *Jabo* attack on another Fighter Command airfield, showing what they could do. Reported as 50 plus, the formation was tracked by radar as it crossed the Thames Estuary and approached the Essex coast around 1630 hours, as the light was beginning to fade. The RAF was unclear of their intentions; Hornchurch and North Weald were both possible targets but it was equally possible that the enemy formation would suddenly swing south to attack the capital. In an effort to divide and confuse the defences, the raid had been timed to coincide with several attacks over Kent and, on this occasion, the British fighter control system was shown to be fallible as the *Jabos* slipped the defences and struck at North Weald.

Two squadrons of Hurricanes, 17 and 46, had already been ordered up from Martlesham Heath to cover North Weald as a precaution but at North Weald itself, the Hurricanes of 249 and 257 Squadrons were ordered off too late and were still taking-off when about 20 *Jabos*, diving from 3,000 feet, swept over the boundary at 500 feet and carpeted the runway with bombs. One exploded directly under Yellow Section of 249 Squadron, the Hurricane of Fg Off Keith Lofts being so badly damaged he was forced to land. 257 Squadron was also caught, Sgt Alexander Girdwood being hit by bomb splinters and his aircraft crashing in flames near 249 Squadron's dispersal hut.

Released from duty that afternoon, Plt Off Tom Neil of 249 Squadron was resting in his room in a hut alongside the mess when the attack took place:

> "... I heard the far-away noise of engines and concluded that the Squadron ... was being sent off on patrol. I was barely interested. Then with rapidly growing intensity, the noise of more engines and every hair on my neck stood on end. Rising quickly to my feet, I crossed to the window, just in time to see the first of a stream of 109s flash across the top of my head, low enough even for me to pick out the black crosses on the wings.
>
> "Thereafter it was bedlam. As the bombs began to drop, the air was thick with the sound and fury of explosions, the ripping burp of machine-guns and the roar of engines. I flung myself to the floor ... expecting every moment to hear and feel the roof collapsing about my ears. On and on it went for an eternity – probably no more than twenty seconds! Then, after the briefest of intervals, a monster bang made the floor lift as though we were all about to become airborne. After that, a period of comparative silence in which the despairing clump – clump – clump of a distant Bofors gun and the diminishing buzz of fast retreating aero-engines seemed almost intrusive."

The remaining Hurricane pilots, recovering their composure fast, reformed and chased the *Jabos* who were now climbing hard and heading due east for the coast where III/*JG* 26 was waiting for them. After a running fight, 249 Squadron finally caught up with them over the Blackwater Estuary near Maldon in Essex and a series of bitter combats spilled out over the Essex coast.

Flight Lieutenant 'Butch' Barton claimed one *Jabo* which crashed alongside the Maldon to Goldhanger road after its pilot baled out; *Fw* Hans-Joachim Rank of 4*(S)/LG* 2, badly burned and wounded in the thigh, died of his wounds later that day. Sgt 'Micky' Maciejowski claimed another which forced-landed close to the shore at Langenhoe, with lateral controls damaged and engine about to seize. Its pilot, *Ofw* Josef Harmeling also of 4 *Staffel*, was captured slightly wounded. Sgt George Stroud chased a third out to sea and shot it down 12 miles off-shore. This was the aircraft of *Oblt* Bruno von Schenk, *Staffelkapitän* of 5*(S)/LG* 2 whose body was later recovered from the sea.

Back at North Weald, they started to assess the extent of the damage. Tom Neil recalls:

> *"By nightfall, the full extent of the action was becoming known. A considerable amount of fairly superficial damage had been done all over the camp but not sufficient to halt or even suspend operations. Casualties though had been heavy with between 15 and 20 people killed and a further 40 wounded, including one of 249's ground crew. Also, the station guardroom, ... which had just been rebuilt at great expense, had been flattened for the second time."*

A hangar was also destroyed and the Motor Transport yard hit but most of the bombs had dropped on the runway. It had been a classic example of just the sort of attack that fighter-bombers flown by skilled pilots could have been making for weeks past; low-level, pin-point attacks that the British most feared and would have found difficult to counter. Repeated and sustained attacks of this nature, on key targets such as RAF airfields, would have quickly made some of them untenable and severely reduced the capacity of Fighter Command. However, by late October 1940 it was too late.

By the end of October 1940, 186 of the new Messerschmitt 109 E-7s had been produced, so at the height of the fighter-bomber offensive against England, over 550 factory-built *Jabos* were available to the *Luftwaffe*; additional aircraft being field-modified as fighter-bombers at unit level. That month, with the daylight *Jabo* offensive on London at its peak, a total of 2,633 *Jabo* sorties were launched against the capital in 140 separate attacks. Post-war statistics show that 60% of them reached the target, the RAF forced to concede that *'a fairly high proportion of small bomb-carrying formations reached their targets without serious interference'*. Analysis shows that 37% of the *Jabos* that took-off to bomb London were forced to drop their bombs on alternate targets (either due to bad weather or interference from the defences), while less than 3% broke off their attacks. Losses amongst the *Jabo* units had been minimal, 29 aircraft lost, a mere 1% of the total force deployed.

Even at this late stage, some *Geschwader* had yet to re-equip. It was not until 9 November 1940 that 2/*JG* 2 arrived at Denain for a short introduction to their new aircraft. According to the diary of their *Staffel Kapitän, Oblt* Siegfried Bethke:

"Some cement bombs were dropped. Apart from that there was no training. After that there was a lot of cursing and grumbling about the bomb-racks under the fuselage."

The cursing and grumbling grew widespread and loud enough to reach the higher echelons of command. As Adolf Galland later wrote:

"We had an outspoken antipathy for the order to act as fighter-bombers. The Luftwaffe High Command countered our negative attitude sharply. Göring declared angrily that the fighter arm had failed to give adequate protection to the bomber squadrons and was now opposed to acting as fighter-bombers, a job which had resulted entirely from its own failure. If it was to prove unfit for this task as well, it would be better to disband the fighter arm altogether.

"In young flying officer circles the leadership was passionately and bitterly criticised. This was the first serious crisis in the relations between the fighter arm and the Luftwaffe Command."

Junior officers were not alone in voicing their criticism. An exasperated *Generalmajor* Theo Osterkamp, who as *Jafü 2* was responsible for all fighter units in *Luftflotte 2*, belaboured *Generaloberst* Hans Jeschonnek, then *Chef der Luftwaffe General Stab*, with the view that *'thanks to these senseless operations'* it would not be long before the entire fighter arm was grounded. Clearly, the general introduction of the *Jabo* was proving no success for the *Luftwaffe*. Measured in both terms of military gains and pilot morale it was in fact a notable 'own goal' and as part of the perceived failure of the fighter arm during the campaign against England it resulted in a crisis of confidence within the *Luftwaffe* that would rumble on for years.

Meanwhile, *Jabo* missions continued whenever the weather permitted, and the *Luftwaffe* continued losing experienced pilots it could ill afford to waste on such increasingly futile operations. Arguably one of the most experienced, *Oblt* Otto Hintze, the *Staffel Kapitän* of 3/*Erpr.Gr* 210 had been shot down and taken prisoner after yet another attack on London on 29 October 1940 – his 52nd *Jabo* sortie. His award of the *Ritterkreuz 'for outstanding leadership'* would be announced on 24 November 1940.

On 5 November, *JG* 26 suffered their first *Jabo* losses in almost a full month of operations when two 9 *Staffel* aircraft collided over Dungeness. *Oblt* Heinz Ebeling, the *Staffel Kapitän*, and his *Rottenflieger Fw* Walter Braun both baled out to join the swelling ranks of *Jabo* pilots held in British POW cages; Ebeling's award of the *Ritterkreuz* had been announced the same day for *'18 air victories, numerous ground attacks, and the successful and rapid conversion of the 9 Staffel to the fighter-bomber role'*.

However, on 11 December 1940, *Oblt* Viktor Kraft of *Stab* II/*LG* 2, who had flown 65 *Jabo* missions, was destined to be the last *Jabo* casualty of 1940:

"The target for myself and another Messerschmitt 109 were the docks in London Port. Over France and over the Channel, we had thick cloud and bad visibility. We were also told that the same weather conditions could be expected over Kent so we did not fly at our normal height of 7,000-8,000 metres. After we had crossed the Channel, we arrived over England at a height of 2,000 metres and found the sky bright and blue! We should have turned back for France immediately and my Rottenflieger did so. I flew on and after a few minutes, realised that I would be foolish to continue on to London so I looked for a target and dropped my bomb and turned back eastwards. I hoped to make the clouds over the Channel in order to escape the fighters which I saw coming from the direction of Rochester.

Oblt *Heinz Ebeling (2nd from right) with, from l to r:* Lt *Willi Fronhöfer,* Lt *Wolfgang Ludewig &* Lt *Hans Naumann* (Ebeling)

"Then there was another flight of fighters which I could see right over my plane – six vapour trails convinced me that they were on their way to shoot me down. I could do nothing but disappear as quickly as possible into clouds near Dover. However, they were too far away. One of those vapour trails dived, gaining enough speed to catch me. I didn't see him in time, he opened fire and my plane caught fire. The seat of the Messerschmitt 109 was armoured and I felt the bullets but they didn't penetrate the armour plating. A second burst of gunfire from the port side wounded me – it was now time to bale out…"†

In December 1940, with the onset of winter gales and worsening weather over the English Channel and southern England, many Luftwaffe fighter units were being withdrawn to Germany for rest and refit. The *Jabo* offensive gradually petered out and by the time the weather improved enough for missions to continue, RAF fighter aircraft were already flying their own offensive fighter operations over the French coast. The *Luftwaffe* was forced to commit those fighters still remaining on the Channel coast to combat increasing RAF incursions and found itself forced onto the defensive.

†*Oblt* Kraft's Messerschmitt 109 E-7 *Wk Nr* 5941 coded Green D was shot down by Plt Off Hubert Allen of 66 Squadron and crashed at Baddlesmere, Kent at 1040 hours

Oblt *Viktor Kraft in the cockpit of a Bf 109 D-1 during training* (Kraft)

The Battle of Britain had witnessed the advent of the true fighter-bomber, exemplar of the high-performance ground-attack aircraft which later came to form so critical a part of any modern air force. However, its introduction had been marred by lack of strategic vision and clear understanding of its potential; its tactical deployment as offhand and trivial as the results it finally achieved. Yet, evidence of the capabilities of the *Jabo* was abundant enough, even in 1940, had the *Luftwaffe* High Command seen fit to acknowledge it.

Ground-attack aircraft used as a tactical weapon in support of ground troops was something the *Luftwaffe* well understood from its earlier campaigns in Poland and France but thanks to the English Channel, the campaign over southern England in 1940 was quite different. They failed to recognise the strategic value of *Jabos* striking at key targets deep in enemy territory using their speed and pin-point accuracy. This was well within the grasp of the *Luftwaffe* in 1940, even with the limitations of their Intelligence department. Had they done so, as the British anticipated they might, the potential damage they could have inflicted on Fighter Command's control system and fighter airfields would have seriously reduced their effectiveness and even threatened its continued ability to resist.

By the end of 1940 the fighter-bomber was discredited and most of the pilots heartily glad of the fact, welcomed a return to pure fighter operations. Nevertheless, a few, who could master the necessary skills of low-flying, navigation, and dive-bombing accuracy, and who recognised the true potential of the *Jabo*, would continue to champion the concept in the months ahead.

The threat remained – the *Jabo* had yet to come into its own and mainland Britain would not be free from them for another three years.

3
The Liesendahl Process

By the start of 1941, the *Luftwaffe* had considerably reduced the number of its fighter aircraft based on the Channel coast. *Jafü* 2, with its headquarters at Wissant, now commanded all three *Gruppen* of *JG* 3, I(*J*)/*LG* 2 and all three *Gruppen* of *JG* 26 as well as the *Jabos* of *Erpr.Gr* 210 and II (*S*)/*LG* 2. *Luftgaukommando* Holland, based at Rotterdam, commanded just one *Staffel* of *JG* 1 and the first two *Gruppen* of *JG* 52. Further to the west in *Luftflotte* 3's domain, IV *Fliegerkorps*, based at Rennes, commanded II and III/*JG* 77 whilst V *Fliegerkorps* commanded all three *Gruppen* of *JG* 2. Even three months later little had changed – all three *Gruppen* of *JG* 51 and *JG* 53 had replaced *JG* 3 and I(*J*)/*LG* 2 and *JG* 26 had temporarily moved west to V *Fliegerkorps*, replacing *JG* 77. *Erpr.Gr* 210 was still based at Abbeville but II(*S*)/*LG* 2 had already moved eastwards. In *Luftflotte* 3, the only fighter units were *JG* 2 and *JG* 26 and there was no change to the *Luftgaukommando* Holland fighter force. All of this would change dramatically in June 1941 with the German preparations for *Operation Barbarossa* – the invasion of Russia.

Attacks by *Jabos* did occur during the early months of 1941 but at a much reduced frequency. The attacks now took place either early in the morning or at dusk, by smaller numbers of aircraft flying at low-level and against military or industrial targets in eastern England close to the coastline – different to the *Jabo* attacks of the latter part of the Battle of Britain. However, many attacks attributed to fighter-bombers were in fact armed weather reconnaissance or armed reconnaissance flights as well as *Tiefangriff*, low flying strafing attacks with cannon and machine-guns, or *Störangriff*, nuisance attacks by fighters aimed at irritating the British defences. A good example of the latter type of attack is best given by *Lt* Günther Pöpel of *Stab*/*JG* 3:

> "I had been posted to Stab/JG 3 just a fortnight before I was shot down on 8 May 41. During the period April to June 1941, we had been ordered to cause as much trouble as possible in the skies over Great Britain, partly to hide the concentration of German forces on our eastern border, ready for the war on Russia. Consequently, we flew over southern England three times a day in small flights attacking air bases, shooting captive balloons etc.
>
> "On 8 May 41, three Messerschmitt 109s of Stab/JG 3 led by Maj Günther Lützow, were on such a mission†. After reaching the outskirts of London, we turned southwards and coasted to conserve fuel, soon reaching the Channel. Halfway across the Channel and having flown through a fog bank, we were

†The third aircraft was possibly flown by *Oblt* Friedrich-Franz von Cramon

attacked by Spitfires [sic] coming from behind one of these fog banks. I saw them first and signalled to my comrades and at once, all three of us turned hard to port and climbed – I was the right hand aircraft, Maj Lützow in the lead. The Spitfires, having seen us, dived below us, turning left as well and it was now that I made my big mistake. As I turned to port and climbed, the Spitfires behind Maj Lützow turned to port and dived. Briefly I was in a very good position to attack so I tipped over to the left and followed the Spitfire. I guess the pilot had been warned by another because he started to turn sharply – no chance for me to hit him. He then flew a long curve to port and as I was getting into a good position to fire, I saw smoke trails to my left wing – a Spitfire was shooting at me! I immediately pushed the joystick forward and dived but a few seconds later, my fighter exploded. I blacked out but soon recovered consciousnes, could open my parachute and came down in a field…"†

Pure *Jabo* attacks still occurred and popular targets were airfields, such as Manston and Hawkinge in Kent. For example, mid-afternoon on 8 February 1941, two Messerschmitt 109 E-7/Bs of 5(S)/LG 2 attacked Hawkinge at low-level and high speed. No RAF fighters were able to intercept and two of 91 Squadron's Spitfires were damaged. However, one of the *Jabos*, flown by *Lt* Werner Schlether, made the mistake of carrying out a second pass over the airfield. The light anti-aircraft guns were ready this time and the fighter was hit and crashed shortly afterwards, killing its pilot. A more successful attack took place against Manston on 4 May 41 as Sgt Frank Jensen of 601 Squadron remembers:

"On the morning of 4 May 1941, I took off with my wingman for a Channel patrol, myself leading and feeling a little peeved with the Germans. Swept well out over the Channel at 11,000 feet and as near as we dared to Boulogne to spot three ships which were lying outside the harbour. Apart from these, there was nothing to report on the French Coast and no enemy aircraft in the clear blue sky. Came back to base from the direction of Calais and heard 'ops' nattering on about two bandits. My wingman did a covering circuit whilst I came in to land. Touched down and was rolling along the ground thinking what an uneventful trip it had been and how peaceful was the day when there came upon my gaze three aircraft approaching very rapidly and very low from the sea. I remember thinking how stupid it was for Spitfires to beat up the aerodrome when another nine came into view and they all opened fire…"

It would appear that *Jabos* from I/JG 51 carried out this attack with an unknown number of aircraft from the rest of the *Geschwader* acting as escort. The two Hurricanes that replaced Frank Jensen's patrol had the misfortune to be bounced and were therefore unable to prevent the attack, Flt Lt

†*Lt* Pöpel was flying a brand – new Messerschmitt 109 F-2, *Wk Nr* 5467 coded <<<+. He was shot down by Hurricanes of 302 Squadron (either Sgt Marian Rytka, Fg Off Zygmunt Kinel or Plt Off Waclaw Krol) and crashed at 1245 hours near Tenterden, Kent

Howard Mayer being shot down off the Kent coast, becoming the 66th kill of the *Geschwader Kommodore* of *JG* 51, *Major* Werner Mölders. Meanwhile, back at Manston, things were not much better for Frank Jensen:

> *"...one singled me out as an easy target no doubt and never have I felt so helpless as when I caught the momentary glimpse of the 109 diving towards me, its evil intentions confirmed by the flashes from its guns. I ducked down in the cockpit and hoped for the best. Felt bullets and shells ripping into poor old 'I' and the bombs bursting in front and behind me. In a flash, the 12 109s had gone and I thought it high time I found myself a safer spot. By this time, the starboard aileron had caught fire but there was nothing I could do about it so I*

Werner Mölders (centre) seen here just before he took command of JG *51 in the Summer of 1940* (Bezner)

> *made a very hasty exit before the 109s came back again. Fell out of cockpit, snapping the oxygen tube. Picked myself up off the ground, observed the apparent departure of our visitors and therefore climbed back into the cockpit and taxied thoughtfully in, evidently to the relief of all who knew that I had been stuck in the middle of the deck during the fun and games. Very little damage done by this attack – a few aircraft shot about..."*

It would be in March 1941 that what were to become recognised as 'tip and run' attacks first started to be developed. *JG* 2 had been only minimally involved in the *Jabo* missions of the Battle of Britain, possibly because of where the *Geschwader* had been based for much of the Summer of 1940. Flying escort missions from its base of Beaumont-Le-Roger in Normandy, the Messerschmitt 109 E would have been flying at the limit of its range with very little time for air-to-air combat whilst carrying a 250 kg bomb would limit its endurance even further. Accordingly, it would therefore appear that *JG* 2's tasks for the early part of 1941 were defence of their *Jafü* 3's area from the RAF, escort duties for shipping and preparations for full operations when the weather improved, such operations being greatly enhanced when it had re-equipped with the Messerschmitt 109 F.

Nevertheless, like the other *Jagdgeschwadern*, it was decreed that one *Staffel* from each of the three *Gruppen* of *JG* 2 would re-role to be *Jabostaffeln*.

Messerschmitt 109 Fs of III/JG 2 (Jahner)

The first *Staffel* to comply, *Oblt* Werner Machold's 7/JG 2, was apparently detached to Denain on the French/Belgian border to be taught the rudiments of *Jabo* operations by *Erpr. Gr* 210. The remaining two *Jabostaffeln* were *Oblt* Siegfried Bethke's 2/JG 2 and *Oblt* Frank Liesendahl's 6/JG 2. However, all three *Staffeln* continued to fly pure fighter operations, 7/JG 2 and Werner Machold in particular, with Machold shooting down five of his *Staffel's* six kills prior to June 1941; *Jabo* missions still appear to have been secondary to pure fighter operations.

JG 2's commitment towards and use of *Jabos* is best related by 2/JG 2's *Oblt* Siegfried Bethke:

> "*Someone had the idea to hang bombs under our planes to cause some trouble on the other side. As a trial, one Staffel in each Gruppe was re-equipped. A rack was fixed to the fuselage of the aircraft which could carry a 250 kg bomb. This was only unwillingly accepted by the pilots because the bomb-rack reduced the speed. My Staffel was ordered the first to be re-equipped. We had to transfer to Denain in Belgium and between 9–14 November 1940 and after the installation of the bomb-rack we practiced bombing attacks by using cement bombs.*
>
> "*[Jabo attacks were a] kind of martial art which had been completely new to us. Similar to Stukas which, at a steep angle of 70° and about 350 km/h [212 mph], dived down from a great altitude, we had to dive at an angle of 45° but from a much lower height. After reaching a certain minimum height the bomb was dropped on the target by pushing the button on the joystick – and then you had to show them a clean pair of heels. It was simple to maintain the 45° angle of dive: black lines had been painted on both sides of the canopy glazing so that, when you were diving at the correct 45° angle, these lines were parallel to the horizon.*
>
> "*Between occasional half-heartedly flown fighter missions, we did a lot of practice flights and dropped cement bombs on shipwrecks in the Seine Estuary off Le Havre. According to my Flugbuch, I carried out 35 practice flights altogether. After some time we even scored more hits and eventually we had some fun – but only until we were put into action. I would also like to add, that as a consequence of the severe criticism expressed by all the fighter unit's commanding officers, this re-equipment was carried out only half-heartedly. Most units escaped re-equipment.*"

2/JG 2's first mission was not flown until 26 April 1941. Escorted by a *Schwarm* of Messerschmitt 109s and in very hazy weather, *Oblt* Bethke and *Lt* Rudolf Schleicher were briefed to attack shipping south of Portsmouth. Flying at low-level towards the Isle of Wight, they stumbled across two patrol boats, which were protected by balloons. These were attacked and hit by machine-gun and cannon fire but the bombs missed.

The next raid took place on 11 May 1941 when all eight aircraft from 2/JG 2 were tasked to attack the airfield at Warmwell, north of Weymouth. Siegfried Bethke vividly remembers what happened:

"The whole Staffel was to attack an airfield north of Weymouth about 50 kms from the coast. A folder with details and aerial pictures of the target was pressed into my hand. The photos showed a large number of Spitfires lined up in front of big hangars. It was assumed that this place was the final assembly of these 'kites'. What we had to do was cause an inferno.

"For three weeks I walked around with these documents under my arm because they were declared top secret. I even had to keep them next to my bed at night. Because of the weather situation and other reasons the date of the mission was postponed a few times. Correspondingly my fellow pilots and I myself became a bag of nerves. We had talked about the sortie several times and we all knew about the risk involved in flying this attack – the Staffel had to meet the English coast at a certain spot having flown low-level over the sea for about 150kms. We had often seen the place from a higher altitude, but now we had to find it while flying just a few metres above the sea!

"On 11 May 1941, the time came. The short entry in my diary reads as follows: 'The sortie began in the evening – and was a complete flop. Haze and the setting sun on the flat, reflecting surface of the sea meant that we did not find the airfield. We attacked a large ship which was hit by two or three direct hits, probably in Brixham. The escorting Bf 109 Fs shot down 6 planes. About 80 of our fighters had been in action. This was the first big operation down here. Perhaps it will be repeated."

"However, this [attack] was unique and exciting. The orders were to take off in the evening without considering that we had to fly into the low sun. In addition there was no wind and so the surface of the sea in the Channel was like glass. Under these conditions the half hour flight at a height of 10 metres became a torture. Also, the blinding light made it difficult to read the compass. There was yet more haze just over the water as we approached the coast. The estimated flying time passed but we could not make out the place we were looking for – Portland Bill. In the haze and from our height it remained invisible.

"We were still flying over the sea. If we had made Portland Bill on time we had planned to climb rapidly to 2,000 metres and then get our bearings. Then we would have quickly reached the target to carry out the attack. We had often gone through this plan in theory. After dropping our bombs we were expected to return and strafe the target to destroy aircraft which had escaped damage.

"But I now realised that we had flown past our objective without having seen it and found ourselves over the wide bay off Torquay. Our plan was now useless. We should have climbed and looked for the target, but if we had done that the Spitfires would have quickly spotted us. So the only alternative was to look for a secondary target at the coast. Eventually we reached and followed the coastline, still flying very low.

"Suddenly, I was able to make out some buildings and docks in the distance and the haze. I gave the order to attack the ships and docks by radio and at the same time I climbed to 300-400 metres. Then we were over the target and dived

to attack. In front of us, at right angles to our direction of flight, was a big ship behind a mole. I dropped the bomb like the others – some had to fly through the blast but there was no damage to the aircraft. Then, we headed for home, flying low-level but this time the formation looked more like a 'bunch of layabouts'. Unmolested we returned and landed after 2100 hrs. At the same time, Spitfires and Me 109s tried to shoot each other down†.

"I was really depressed and felt shattered when I gave a report on the action to the officer responsible for the whole mission, Obstlt Galland, Kommodore of JG 26. He only replied that he had not expected anything else that I should calm down and remember that I had done my best. He was one of those officers who had vehemently crusaded against the re-equipment of fighters into bombers. Fortunately the fighters had not suffered any losses. I soon calmed down and had a bottle of wine brought to me after dinner."

Two days later, 2/*JG* 2 was in action again when a *Rotte* unsuccessfully attacked a convoy off Portland. The following day saw a change in tactics with a raid by a *Schwarm* led by Siegfried Bethke against warehouses in the harbour of Swanage. The second *Rotte* in the formation had to fly through the blasts of the first bombs and the radiator of *Lt* Erich Rudorffer's plane was hit by pieces of cement. Luckily they did not cause permanent damage and he returned home safely. Another attack took place against a convoy south-west of Portland in the mid-morning of 17 May 1941, one pilot, *Fw* Josef Niesmann, reporting hitting a 6,000 BRT ship with a 250 kg bomb. It is believed that this convoy was attacked again by *Jabos* of 6/*JG* 2 that same evening, this time south of Shoreham; *Oblt* Frank Liesendahl was credited with damaging a 2,500 BRT ship but *Uffz* Helmut Ries was shot down by *Flak* into the Channel and was killed.

Erich Rudorffer (right) seen here with Obstlt *Walter Oesau, 1943* (Mende)

†In the ensuing air battle, Spitfires were claimed by *Fw* Pfeiffer of 3 *Staffel*, *Lt* Jakob Augustin of 7 *Staffel* and *Uffz* Theodor Zingerle of 8 *Staffel*. The only RAF casualty was a Hurricane of 504 Squadron flown by Flt Lt B E G White which was damaged. Sqn Ldr M V Blake and Sgt R Martin of 234 Squadron each claimed a Messerschmitt 109 – there were no German losses

What was to be 2/*JG* 2's penultimate *Jaboangriff* took place on 19 May 1941 – an attack against another convoy off Portland. Bethke again:

"Another idiotic attack on reported naval targets was carried out by eight aircraft of the Staffel. The sea was smooth like oil. Off Portland there were three ships, balloons and flak. Lt Erich Rudorffer and his wingman attacked a diving submarine. Both bombs fell very close. It was said that the sub went down vertically. Reconnaissance planes later observed a large film of oil and a fire on one of the ships. On our way back Uffz Kuno Dollenmaier had to bale out just before reaching the coast when the the throttle linkage of his Messerschmitt broke and the engine overheated bringing danger of fire. Fifteen minutes later he was pulled out of the water by French fishermen. A Rotte from 1 Staffel had taken off soon after our aircraft in order to reconnoitre our successes. Both planes were shot down by Spitfires. Five hours later Ofw Rudolf Täschner was rescued about 40 kms north of Cherbourg. His wingman [Uffz Kaspar Amhausend] could not be found. †A search and rescue mission as far as the English coast was flown without success. On his return flight the Kommodore, Maj Wilhelm Balthasar was able to shoot down a Blenheim over the Seine estuary near Le Havre. We did not know it at that time but this was the last mission with bombs the Staffel had to fly. In the evening, after this failure and needless losses, I wrote into my diary: 'That is enough in times of otherwise quiet air defence sorties.' "

Although Siegfried Bethke did not fly any further *Jabo* missions, it is believed that 2/*JG* 2's final fighter-bomber attack took place on 30 May 1941. According to the logbook of *Fw* Josef Niesmann, he took part in an attack on barracks at Portland in the evening; British records report Portland being attacked at 1905 hours.

Despite *JG* 2's apparent reluctance to have pure *Jabostaffeln*, by June 1941, the *Luftwaffe* had credited 2 and 6/*JG* 2 with sinking two freighters between 3,000 and 5,000 BRT and a tanker of 2,500 BRT as well as damaging a submarine, a cruiser of 10,000 BRT and a freighter of 3,000 BRT. It is also alleged that the 5,000 BRT freighter was sunk by 6/*JG* 2's *Oblt* Frank Liesendahl south of Portland on 9 June 1941 but no firm evidence of theses claims has been found.

About now the name of one man starts to be mentioned more and more in respect of the development of *Jabo* attacks. Frank Liesendahl has always been an enigma and little is known about him or his achievements. Born in Wuppertal-Barmen on 23 February 1915 he joined the *Wehrmacht* as a gunner in a *Panzer* battalion in 1934, transferring to the *Luftwaffe* in the

---

†Two Spitfires were claimed in this combat by *Oblt* Werner Machold of 7/*JG* 2 which tally with the Spitfires of Sgt Barker and Plt Off A S Harker of 234 Squadron. 234 Squadron, Flt Lt E B Mortimer-Rose, Plt Off E W Wootten and Plt Off G T Baynham, claimed a total of five Messerschmitt 109s; only the two mentioned were lost in combat

Autumn of 1936. On 1 December 1937, Liesendahl was promoted to *Lt* and at that time it was stated that he was a member of II/JG 334 (later II/JG 133 and then on 1 May 1939, II/JG 53). On 1 July 1939, he was posted to II/ZG 1 where it is believed that he participated in the Polish Campaign that September. Moving once more on 15 November 1939 to 6/JG 2 he was promoted to *Oblt* on 1 April 1940. He was then transferred to be the *Gruppen Adjutant* of II/JG 2 and participated in the French Campaign. Although no formal records exist, he was shot down, wounded and taken prisoner over Dunkirk on 26 May 1940 whilst carrying out a *Tiefangriff* against

Frank Liesendahl (Arnold)

ground targets, a tactic that he was destined to develop just over a year later. The following account, taken from a typical German Press report of the time, gives an idea of what happened:

> "At the end of May 1940 the Gruppe carried out low-level attacks on English troops. After having finished this task Oberleutnant L., flying as the Adjutant of the Kommandeur, again attacked a squadron of Spitfires while the rest of the Gruppe turned back because they were short of fuel and ammunition. Shortly after he was following his comrades when his 'crate' was suddenly hit from above, behind and the side.
>
> "All at once he felt a blow against his upper arm, he was hit! Then a second hit in the lower leg and finally a bullet shot through his hand. More and more bullets hit the aircraft and suddenly Oberleutnant L., already dazed and sitting in his own blood, noticed that the Me had begun to burn. He jettisoned the canopy roof with difficulty and tried to straighten up in order to bail out. Being semi-conscious he pressed the parachute release button but at the very last moment realised his mistake and sat down again. Below him was enemy held country and, severely wounded in a burning plane, he felt a paralysing feeling creeping into his heart: this was it, everything was lost, this was his fate and he could not do anything about it. Again he pulled himself together and looked for a place to land. He spotted a small meadow, close to an English anti-aircraft position which looked promising. Hardly able to operate the Messerschmitt's control, Oberleutnant L. dived down and, nearly unconscious, pushed the gun-button and fired at the ground. The Englishmen thought it was a low-level attack and fired back.

"*Luckily he made a safe belly-landing in a very small meadow but his Messerschmitt was riddled with bullets and burning. Balancing on his uninjured leg he moved out of the seat, hobbled a few metres and lay down next to his burning plane. The Englishmen seemed afraid and began shooting at him with pistols and rifles. Only when he stood up and waved during a break in the firing did they carefully come nearer and quickly took away his pistol. He was carried into a farmhouse and from then on he was treated excellently; the Belgian doctor who cut open his flying suit dressed his wounds and gave him cigarettes and schnapps.*

"*In the course of the day Oblt. L. was taken to a military hospital in a church. Earlier in the day a Hauptmann der Infanterie had died from his injuries, so Oblt. L. was the only German among all the Englishmen. He was amazed at the friendly and obliging treatment and later that day was told that he would be taken to Canada. That evening, as the Germans came nearer everybody left the church and the Englishmen tried to take their injured soldiers back home. But there was no transport at Dunkirk harbour so they returned to the church again. On the second evening this happened again. Later Oblt. L. had a fright when he noticed four Allied soldiers bending over him. As it was dark he could not see if any of the nursing staff were there so he began to moan loudly and when a German-speaking doctor moved closer he was able to persuade them to leave him alone. On the third day a rumour went through the church that the English, although still trying, could no longer reach the coast.*

Göring visits JG 2, 28 Oct 1940. To Göring's right are Lt Heinz Dudeck, 4/JG 2, Oblt *Helmut-Felix Bolz, 5/JG 2, Oblt Frank Liesendahl, 6/JG 2, Ofw Siegfried Schnell, 6/JG 2, unidentified. Just visible to Göring's left is* Maj *Helmut Wick* (Arnold)

"When the news became certain the British became depressed and all the excited talking stopped. The doctor was the only person to approach Oblt. L. and asked him how many of them would be shot and how many would be taken prisoner. 'Not one, of course', L. assured him. The doctor left, smiling in disbelief.

If he had been able to move, Oblt. L. would have flung his arms around the neck of the Rittmeister of the German advanced forces, who entered the hospital next day. The Englishmen were astonished and could not believe that they were permitted to keep their doctors. The Oberleutnant was relieved when the hospital train took him home to convalesce."

Released from captivity, Liesendahl spent at least eight weeks in hospital recovering from his wounds before he returned to *JG 2*. The *Staffel Kapitän* of 6/*JG 2*, *Oblt* Edgar Rempel, had been shot down and killed on 11 August 1940 to be temporarily replaced by *Hptm* Hans-Joachim Gerlach and then by *Oblt* Karl Müller. Karl Müller lasted a matter of days, possibly a week before he too was shot down and killed on 4 September 1940. Command of 6 *Staffel* was then passed to the recently returned Frank Liesendahl either on 5 September or 15 October 1940.

Liesendahl was therefore there at the start of *JG 2*'s involvement with *Jabo* attacks and it is believed that he quickly proved to have a natural flair for fighter-bomber, as opposed to fighter, operations. This appears to be

Frank Liesendahl on his return to JG 2, *Autumn 1941, with his new* Kommodore, Maj *Walter Oesau* (Arnold)

Helmut-Felix Bolz (2nd from left), the Gr Kdr *of II/JG 2; to the left is* Hptm *Karl-Heinz Greisert, his predecessor; to the right, newly promoted* Maj *Helmut Wick, Geschwader Kommodore JG 2, killed in action 28 Nov 40* (Puttrich)

reinforced by the fact that although some records state he had an unknown number of air combat victories, no positive proof of this has emerged whilst photographs of the rudder of his aircraft show only shipping as opposed to aircraft victories.

On 10 July 1941, Liesendahl was again shot down and wounded in combat with RAF fighters (not on a *Jabo* mission) and again it is believed that he spent the next eight weeks in hospital putting his experiences as a *Jabo* pilot onto paper and developing new tactics. He returned to *JG 2* in late Summer 1941, by which time command of 6/*JG 2* had passed to the highly successful *Lt* Erich Rudorffer (Rudorffer had moved from 2/*JG 2* to be *Adjutant* of II/*JG 2* on 1 June 1941 only to be given command of 6/*JG 2* five days after Frank Liesendahl had been shot down and wounded). It is then believed that Liesendahl persuaded the current *Geschwader Kommodore, Major* Walter Oesau, of the benefits of a dedicated and independent *Jabostaffel* and so it was that 13/*JG 2* was created on 10 November 1941, subordinate to *Hptm* Helmut-Felix Bolz's II/*JG 2*.

The Jabostaffel *in training, Spring 1942. L to r:* Lt *Erhard Nippa,* Oblt *Frank Liesendahl, ?, Lt Josef Fröschl (?), ?, Fw Gerhard Limberg, ?, ?, ?* (Arnold)

Liesendahl's new *Staffel* soon began to receive those pilots who had flown with 2, 6 and 7/*JG* 2 who showed greater flair as *Jabo* as opposed to fighter pilots as well as less experienced pilots posted to *JG* 2 straight from training. It is not known exactly what form this training took but from 10 November 1941 to 18 February 1942, Liesendahl's *Staffel* trained and perfected the tactics they would employ against British shipping, suffering just one accident when on 8 February 1942, *Lt* Josef 'Sepp' Fröschl suffered engine failure during a training flight, force-landing and writing off his Messerschmitt Bf 109 E-7 at Quillebeuf-sur-Seine. During the months of training, Frank Liesendahl devised what was called the '*Liesendahl Verfahren*', the 'Liesendahl Process', and this was quickly adopted as the preferred method of *Jabo* attack. Approaching the target at 450 kph and at an altitude of five metres, 1,800 metres from the target the fighter-bomber would climb to a maximum height of 500 metres before levelling off and diving at an angle of 3° and a speed of 550 kph then pulling up and lobbing the bomb at the target.

L to r: ?, Hptm *'Assi' Hahn*, Gr Kdr *III/*JG 2, Oblt *Frank Liesendahl*, Lt *Josef Fröschl. Remaining pilots are unidentified* (Arnold)

Although the Winter months were spent on the theoretical training of the pilots and ground crews and practice flights, it is believed that 13/*JG* 2 did undertake a number of trial attacks. According to British records†, the first recorded 'tip and run' attack was made against an unspecified target at Fairlight in Sussex on Christmas Day 1941 and then in January 1942, 'tip and run incidents' were mentioned as having occurred in Kent (three), Sussex (nine), Dorset (two), Hampshire (one), Cornwall (28) and the Isle of Wight (one). However, no evidence has been found to prove 13/*JG* 2's involvement and it is possible that some of these could have been carried out by the Dornier 217s of *KG* 2.

Nevertheless, it would appear that Liesendahl was still trying to convince senior officers of the value of *Jabo* attacks and this proof finally came on 10 February 1942 when the 3,000 BRT steamship *Lieutenant Robert Mory* was badly damaged in an attack off the Cornish Coast. Eight days later, *JG* 2 declared that 13/*JG* 2 was fully operational and on 4 March 1942, *Jafü* 3 authorised *Jabo* missions with *JG* 26 being ordered to form its own *Jabo Staffel* with effect from 10 March 1942.

The die was cast and for the next 15 months, southern Britain was about to experience a new and terrifying form of air warfare.

†Royal Observer Corps Narrative 1942 p.85

4
The New Offensive

MARCH – JULY 1942

Erwin Busch, seen here after being commissioned (Storsberg)

From the start of the new campaign, it was clear that *JG* 26 was at a distinct disadvantage when it came to *Jabo* operations, not having *JG* 2's three month work up period and a *Staffel Kapitän* as dedicated to such operations as 13/*JG* 2's Frank Liesendahl. Pilots who had limited *Jabo* experience from 1940 and early 1941, such as *Ofw* Erwin Busch of 9/*JG* 26 (one of *JG* 26's original *Jabo Staffeln*), were transferred to *JG* 26's new *Staffel* whilst a number of pilots who were either unsuitable as fighter pilots, ill disciplined or had incurred the wrath of their *Staffel Kapitän* made up the remainder.

For example, despite having shot down five RAF aircraft, *Fw* Hans-Jürgen Fröhlich of 2/*JG* 26 was described as 'wildly undisciplined' whilst *Uffz* Oswald Fischer had upset his *Staffel Kapitän* by laughing at him when he had fallen off a horse! Command of the *Jabostaffel* was given to 28 year-old Austrian *Hptm* Karl Plunser – little is known of this officer and his abilities but it is believed that he had flown with II/*JG* 2 before becoming a *Staffel Kapitän* in the *Ergänzungsgruppe of JG* 26.

With the apparent unsuitability or unwillingness of some of *JG* 26's pilots for 'tip and run' missions coupled with a lack of formal *Jabo* training, the initial effectiveness of 10/*JG* 26 (as it soon was designated) was questionable, despite it being claimed that they started flying *Jaboangriff* almost immediately with an attack by four Messerschmitt 109s on Folkestone†. British analysis of 'tip and run' attacks supports the imbalance of missions between 10/*JG* 26 and 13/*JG* 2 in March 1942, the first month of authorised operations. 17 'tip and run' attacks were carried out in 10/*JG* 26's area of operations (Sussex and Kent) whilst 13/*JG* 2's area of operations (Hampshire westwards) reported 49 such attacks. Admittedly 10/*JG* 26 was operating in an area heavily defended by anti-aircraft guns and the fighter aircraft of the RAF's Number 11 Group but the successes of 13/*JG* 2 were impressive and an instant concern to the British. Furthermore, it cannot be confirmed whether these attacks were carried out by fighter-bombers or by pure bomber aircraft.

*A Messerschmitt 109 F-4/B of 10/*JG 26 *seen at Arques* (Feiger)

The first clear evidence of a 'tip and run' attack took place at 0925 hours on 7 March 1942. Four Messerschmitt 109s succeeded in reaching the Devon coast undetected and then roamed unmolested in the Exmouth-Teignmouth area with houses in Exmouth and Teignmouth Pier being machine-gunned. When RAF fighters were ordered to take off and intercept, one Polish pilot Sgt Kazimierz Sztramko found himself a potential target as the Operations Record Book for 317 Squadron stated:

†Folkestone's first recorded attack took place at 0836 hours on 24 April 1942 when a gas holder was set alight, 600 houses damaged and one person killed

A Messerschmitt 109 F-4/B of 10/JG 26 seen at Arques (Feiger)

Sgt Kazimierz Sztramko, 317 Squadron (via Matusiak)

"At 0935 hours, White Section (based at Bolt Head) was ordered to scramble base. The first aircraft, Sgt Sztramko, on becoming airborne, had just completed the first circuit when he was attacked by 2 Me 109s which dived on the aerodrome from the north. Our aircraft was hit and while trying to complete a circuit, was forced to make a pancake landing on the 'drome. The bandits made their escape as the other pilot of the Section was unable to hear the Sector Controller owing to low altitude. Sgt Sztramko only sustained a slight superficial wound in the leg†."

Sztramko's Spitfire Vb, AB215, seen early in 1943 and after its repair (via Matusiak)

†Sgt Kazimierz Sztramko was an experienced pre-war Polish Air Force pilot who had shot down a number of enemy aircraft before joining 317 Squadron in April 1941

To add insult to injury, the German aircraft remained in the area for nearly 40 minutes before machine-gunning Exmouth again as they headed for home. It would appear that this attack, if it was 13/*JG* 2, was very much a precursor raid as for much of March 1942, coastal areas appeared to be 13/*JG* 2's preferred target with initially convoys and then harbours being attacked. For the coastal resort of Torbay, the first of many such raids over the next 14 months occurred at 1150 hours on 18 March 1942 when two Messerchmitt 109s approached Torquay from the north-east, machine-gunned the town and dropped two bombs near Torquay Pier extension before streaking off southwards. This certainly fits Frank Liesendahl's *modus operandi* even if the identity of the unit cannot be positively identified. Six days later, Liesendahl claimed to have damaged a ship and then on 27 March, he led a *Schwarm* to attack Torquay and Brixham simultaneously. It would appear that Liesendahl's handiwork was witnessed by AC Gordon Collinson:

> "*Between 15 March and 29 June 1942, I was with 4 Initial Training Wing Paignton and witnessed three 'tip and run' incidents. In the first, the date of which I cannot remember, a lone [sic] Me 109 machine-gunned Torquay Harbour and sank a small single-funnelled ship at anchor. I was in the amusement arcade which fronted onto the harbour when it happened – not particularly amusing!*"

At 1650 hours, two Messerchmitt 109s approached Torquay from the north-east whilst simultaneously, two more approached Brixham from the north. At Torquay, the town was machine-gunned before four bombs, all believed to be 50 kg, were dropped and sank the blockship *Staghound* which was anchored near to the harbour entrance. At Brixham, two bombs were dropped on the outer harbour and the Royal Observer Corps post, oil depot and the Coastguard Station at Berry Head were machine-gunned. All four aircraft then headed off to the south at about 400 feet. Four days later, 13/*JG* 2 carried out a repeat performance but just against Brixham with almost the same results except this time, the Germans were destined to lose their first aircraft and pilot on a 'tip and run' mission. What happened was recorded by war reporter Karl Klaus Krebs in a typical piece of German propaganda:

> "*The portable telephone in the command post of the Rote Füchse†† is ringing. The officer in charge takes the receiver and recognizes the voice of the Ia of the Jafü 3 operations staff who orders a mission against a harbour in the western part of the Channel. The weather could be better. Low clouds and heavy showers reduce the visibility and fierce gusts of wind throw the aircraft back and forth – there are heavy seas. Under the lead of their Hptm†, a Schwarm of the Rote Füchse is going to carry out the attack. Despite the weather conditions and heavy*

---

†It is believed that this account was written later in 1942 by which time Liesendahl had been promoted to *Hptm*

††This refers to the *Staffel* badge designed by Liesendahl's fiancée which showed a red fox carrying a broken ship in its mouth

Flak defences the sortie is carried out according to plan. Hptm Liesendahl and Lt Nippa drop their bombs on a freighter of about 4,000 tons at its mooring while Oblt Schröter and Uffz Weiser blow up a group of thirty landing craft. Flak is firing from the shore and the ships. After he has dropped the bomb, Nippa pulls his Me 109 out of the dive and, evading the Flak, flies into a layer of low clouds. He looks back but all around him it is looking very grey. Where is the Hauptmann? There is a discussion on the radio but he cannot understand it very clearly. He only wants to get out of the clouds and so he turns his Me 109 homewards and races towards the French coast at low-level. Hptm Liesendahl creeps south, the engine is not running smoothly so he has to try every trick to keep it running. A hit must have destroyed the radio because he cannot hear anything. But where is the second Rotte?

The 10/JG 2 'red fox' (Wenger)

"Only a moment after the attack on the landing craft Oblt Schröter hears the excited voice of Uffz Weiser on the radio: 'Received hits in the engine, have to bale out!' Then he can see his wingman's Messerschmitt climbing steeply southwards so decides to stay close to his comrade. Uffz Weiser climbs as high as

Lts *Kurt Eckleben, Erhard Nippa and Leopold Wenger resplendent in their Red Fox emblazoned pullovers* (Wenger)

he can manage with the damaged engine, then he jettisons the cabin roof and pushes the control column forward so that he is thrown out of the aircraft. Twenty-one, twenty-two, twenty-three – now he pulls the ripcord and the parachute quickly opens. Oblt Schröter, flying narrow circles around his downward floating comrade, has found the position on his map and sends out radio signals. The air-sea rescue command has to be alerted. A few metres above the surface of the water the Uffz unfastens the parachute harness and opens the compressed air bottle to fill his rubber dinghy – the landing is successful. Once again the Oblt checks his position and sends a second series of radio signals. Then he turns back and races towards the French coast. He is running short of fuel now and has to get back to the airfield.

"In the meantime Hptm Liesendahl has informed the direction finding station and asks them to listen hard for radio signals from the direction of the crash. After 10 minutes it is confirmed that they have been able to take a bearing. The Staffel Kapitän calls the air-sea rescue service: 'Seenot Cherbourg, please, urgent!' He gives them the necessary details and they immediately start the rescue operation using two aircraft and an E-boat. At the command post everyone sits together without saying a word. They can do nothing else. At their own base 'QBI' is in force which means the weather is too bad to permit flying. They can only wait and pin their hopes on the air-sea rescue service.

"The weather has deteriorated. Uffz Weiser is drifting in his tiny rubber dinghy in the middle of the Channel. It is cold and nobody knows if the air-sea rescue service will find him. The crews in the seaplanes search tirelessly. They fly in large circles just above the water. The weather is terrible, the visibility lousy, but they do not give up and search one grid square after the other. They fly to the west and a few kilometres to the east. They fly to the north – although there they face the danger of being caught by the 'Tommies' – and turn back to the south again. They can't see a yellow rubber dinghy and there's no flare signal. The crew of the Dornier 24 strive to find their comrade, but are forced to turn back to their base as it is getting dark. It is very stormy and they can only land the seaplanes at their base with great difficulty.

"Nobody knows when and how Uffz Weiser died. The Channel took him, the ocean will never give him back. The Rote Füchse Staffel paid the first bitter toll of lives..."

On returning from the attack on Torbay, where they succeeded in sinking the 3,000 ton collier *London City* off Brixham, 21 year-old *Uffz* Gottfried Weiser baled out some 30 kms north of Alderney and even though he was seen to get into his dinghy, he was never seen again.

Frank Liesendahl in his Messerschmitt 109 F-4/B, Wk Nr 7629, Blue 1, Beaumont-Le-Roger, 31 March 1942 (Arnold)

In April 1942, 'tip and run' raids increased dramatically, with British intelligence reporting 156 such attacks. April also saw a shift to land targets, particularly gas holders as these were such prominent targets, easily visible whilst approaching the coastline at high speed and low level. The *Luftwaffe's* intelligence during the last war has been criticised as being inaccurate or misguided but many 'tip and run' targets attacked from April 1942 onwards

Frank Liesendahl strapping in for another mission (Arnold)

did show a high degree of good planning (or possibly luck). For example, the Germans were aware of an underground explosives store inland from Poole at Holton Heath, as an interrogation debrief of a 10/*JG* 2 pilot captured in May 1942 reported:

> "...*the Jabostaffel had been informed that the Ritterkreuz would be awarded to the first pilot who successfully bombed what was described as a large store of nitro-glycerine at a position 21 miles inland from Poole Harbour – presumably Holton Heath. It was stated that the Jabostaffel had made five attempts against this target. On two occasions, the attack was abandoned owing to unsuitable weather and on the three remaining occasions, the defence was so good that the aircraft failed to reach the objective...*"

Of greater concern were two attacks carried out, presumably by the newly re-designated 10/*JG* 2, against the Telecommunications and Research Establishment (TRE) at Worth Matravers in Dorset. Described as '...*one of the country's single most important defence research related establishments during the whole of the Second World War...*', much of Britain's radar and radar-related research and development was being carried out at the TRE. In April 1942, the TRE was studying the effect of the ionosphere on 'Gee' transmissions, 'Gee' enabling RAF bomber crews to fix their position by using pulse signals from three widely separated transmitters and could also be used to find targets when they were obscured by cloud. At 1909 hours on 6 April 1942, three Messerschmitt 109s attacked the site causing unrecorded damage; at lunchtime two days later, another attack killed two and injured six, whilst a bomb passed through the 350 foot tall 'Gee' tower, causing slight damage. The raids were remembered by Plt Off Cyril Halstead who was serving at the TRE at the time:

> *"On 6 April 1942, there were a few thuds and on the 7th, we found out that these were bombs. The CO now issued us with identity discs and kept us off 'E' Site. On the 8th, the attack took place during our lunch time and I distinctively remember sheltering under the wooden table in our rest room – 1328 hours would be a good time for this raid. We were certainly kept off 'E' Site until at least 12 April according to my diary. The nature of the target was obvious. At the time, we were studying the effect of the ionosphere on 'Gee' transmissions and were radiating signals northwards from the 350 foot tower on 'E' Site. I understood that one of the bombs travelled through our aerial without damaging it but hit the site across the road to the south so at least that pass must have been from the north (inland)."*

Sadly, the cookhouse was hit, killing AC1s Ivor Mitchell and William Richardson and wounding AC2 Samuel Rix. The site was unoperational for four days and because of the risk of a further more devastating attack and German reprisals for the Bruneval Raid†, the TRE was moved to Malvern in Worcestershire in May 1942.

In addition to an increase in 'tip and run' attacks, April 1942 saw the first loss for 10/*JG* 2 when on 21 April, *Ogefr* Franz Langhammer was shot down by *Flak* off Portland; the attack which resulted in his death was witnessed by nine year-old Scott Sedwell:

> *"I was playing with friends in the quarries behind my Dad's pub (he was the landlord of the Mermaid Inn in Wakeham, Portland). I heard the sound of aircraft approaching and because of the fear of enemy aircraft, I was under strict instructions from my Mother to make for home immediately. This I did, to the jeers of my companions – 'Go on Scott run – it's the Jerries!' they shouted. I was running along the rough quarry road as fast as I could because I had heard the uneven 'grunt' of the approaching aircraft's engines. Suddenly, an aircraft was coming up fast behind me and was firing its machine-guns! Dust and bits of stones were flying everywhere but luckily none of us were hit. The plane was so low that we could see the pilot in his cockpit and he had to climb to clear the pile of quarry waste across the road from the Mermaid Inn. This aircraft dropped a bomb, presumably aimed at the nearby railway line, but it exploded harmlessly in the quarry."*

†This took place on 28 February 1942 when British commandos captured German radar equipment from a site at Bruneval near Le Havre in northern France

"Further to the north, another aircraft strafed the centre of Wakeham, the road in which the Mermaid Inn stood. It had been seen to drop a bomb but there had not been an explosion. A search by local Police and Civil Defence revealed an unoccupied house with some minor damage to the road. The house was immediately checked and a bomb was found wedged in the upper floor – not immediately found because it had wrapped itself in the bed and bedclothes!

"Most of Wakeham was cleared and the Army Bomb Disposal arrived and worked well into the night to defuse and then steam out the bomb's explosive. My Dad entertained the team once they had completed their work and I remember seeing the fuses and detonators laid out on the public bar counter for us to see. We were told that the attack had been carried out by Messerschmitt 109s and one had been shot down..."

Three days later, it was the turn of recently operational 10/JG 26 to suffer its first loss. During a particularly successful attack on Folkestone, the Messerschmitt 109 of the experienced yet 'ill disciplined' *Fw* Hans-Jürgen Fröhlich was shot down by *Flak* into the Channel; his body was washed ashore on a Dutch beach nearly three months later.

It should be emphasised that during 1942, the combined strength of 10/JG 2 and 10/JG 26 was rarely more than a maximum of 28 aircraft† but their effectiveness was keenly felt by the British who quickly voiced concern as to means of combating 'tip and run' attacks. The official narrative produced after the war by the Observer Corps was quite specific as to the threat and the difficulties posed, saying:

"...In view of the persistent attacks made by the enemy using very low flying aircraft on coastal targets along the south coast of England, various methods were tried to facilitate interception. The difficulties were great as, in view of the low altitude, RDF [Radio Direction Finding or radar] information was seriously limited with the result that anti-aircraft defences were frequently unable to come into action until the attack had been delivered..."

The speed of such attacks and the helplessness of British defences to effectively counter the fighter-bombers is graphically related by Peter Montgomery who witnessed the attack by 10/JG 2 on Cowes on the Isle of Wight at 0700 hours on 28 April 1942:

"No air raid siren heralded the arrival of seven Messerschmitt 109s and two of the first people to know of their arrival must have been Jock Leal and Ted Pardey. Jock, about to enter the industrial spotting post on Mount Joy in Newport, overlooking the valley in which Newport is situated, and Ted, reporting for duty in the adjacent Royal Observer Corps post. As they threw themselves flat on their faces, the 109s skimmed the Post's telephone wires before diving across Newport to follow the River Medina to Cowes.

†Balke, U (1997) p.389

"Surprise was so complete that not a gun was fired at the raiders. I heard the aircraft go over and my parents, who were lying in bed with the curtains open, saw them and thought they were some of ours. They were disillusioned when, about three minutes later, the aircraft returned and shot up the streets as they passed! This time, the light AA guns around the town opened fire and I made one of my fast exits from my bedroom, rushed downstairs and dived into our reinforced cupboard under the stairs.

"This attack was one of the few occasions when enemy aircraft were in range at low level and the machine-gunner on the nearby Drill Hall roof stitched a line of holes across the gable end of a nearby house..."

By the end of April 1942, the value of the raids must have been increasingly clear to the *Luftwaffe* especially against shipping. Post-war analysis shows that between July 1941 and February 1942, German aircraft had sunk or damaged just 32.35% of the ships they attacked in daylight but in the period March-October 1942, this increased to 64.4%†. It was clear that this new tactic was having the desired effect yet still, the *Luftwaffe* did not expand its two units but at the end of May 1942 did co-locate both units and subordinated them to the *Luftflotte 3's* Fighter Headquarters for operational, and later administrative, command and control. This was a clear indication that greater direction in fighter-bomber operations was at last being realised.

However, it was also clear to the British that the quickest and easiest way of countering these 'tip and run' attacks was by light anti-aircraft guns – predominantly 40mm calibre, fighter aircraft having failed so far to account for a single attacker. When the 'tip and run' attacks commenced, Anti-Aircraft Command only had forty-three 40mm calibre guns in position on the south coast and these were assigned to protect military installations, the sort of targets that the fighter-bombers were not attacking. Even then, these calibre guns had their failings as another brazen attack on the airfield at Bolt Head in Devon on 1 May 1942 shows:

"The aerodrome was attacked from the north by five Me 109s which came in at 1,000 feet, stepped down from the leader. They dived at about 300 mph to 50 feet, dropped two 500 lb bombs which fell, one 60 yards west, the other 60 yards north, of the dispersed aircraft. Apart from one Spitfire damaged by stones thrown from the crater, little damage was done. The Me 109s also shot up our aircraft, slightly damaging two (Category AC) and one hit an engine mounting and oil pipe (Category B)††.

"The enemy aircraft then turned east, two of them banking and returning from the south-west, opening fire on 'B' defended area, dispersed aircraft and the Army compound. One more bomb was dropped which fell north of the aerodrome and caused no damage. Fortunately, there was only one casualty – Sgt Marchewicz, who was standing by for a scramble and was slightly injured by flying splinters.

†Neitzel, S (1995) p. 127
††306 Squadron Spitfires R6776 and AA858/UZ – D were Cat AC, AB862/UZ – B Cat B

"The RAF 4 AA Flight twin Lewis gun posts and one Bren gun† were in action firing 304 rounds. Hits were claimed on all aircraft but no damage was observed. The Bofors guns made a rather poor showing. Number Four gun fired only two rounds before the traverse gear jammed and Number Two gun fired one round, the case of which could not be ejected…No warning was received until 0650 hours when Black Section was ordered to scramble. It was too late and the pilots and ground crew were lucky to escape."

The sole casualty of this attack, Sgt Henryk Marchewicz of 306 Squadron, would disagree that he was 'slightly injured':

"We were billeted in a public house in Hope Cove and two of us arrived very early in the morning while it was still dark. Having checked our aircraft, we sat on camp beds in our trailer awaiting sunrise. Shortly afterwards, the telephone rang and I was told 'Red Section scramble!' and virtually at the same moment, there was machine-gun fire. We ran to our aircraft, mine nearest was being strafed and dive-bombed. However, before reaching it, I was hit in my face by something which left my nose hanging on one side. What caused it, I will never know. Their ammunition expended, the attacking Me 109s departed a few minutes later leaving me the only casualty. Then followed a frantic ride to Babbacombe Hospital in Torquay, driven by a

Sgt Henryk Marchiewicz (left) (Marchiewicz)

†Both .303 calibre machine-guns

beautiful female driver who frequently shared her brandy with me and often took sharp road bends on two wheels. Superb surgery then restored my nose to its rightful place but unfortunately it prevented me from using an oxygen mask therefore ending my operational flying…"

The remainder of May 1942 saw little change to German tactics and targets with both units carrying out in the region of 25 known 'tip and run' attacks. However, May 1942 is notable for a number of events in respect of this campaign. First of all, 10/JG 2 had particular success against shipping, two of them sinking a Motor Launch off Brixham on the 6th of the month, four of them sinking a trawler and damaging another two in Brixham Harbour on the 15th and another trawler, this time in the Solent, on 27 May. Commensurate with an increase in raids was an increase in losses, the majority being suffered by to 10/JG 2. One occurred on 16 May 42 when six aircraft from 10/JG 2 attacked warships in Plymouth Sound. This was a change to previous targets as there were heavily defended military establishments both in and around Plymouth; the Plymouth Command Diary of Events recorded what happened:

"At 1252 hours, six Me 109s made a low-level attack on Plymouth Sound. Two bombs near missed SS TORKEL and one near missed BV 7. HMS BROCKLESBY was machine-gunned and HMS WOLVERINE near missed

Damage caused by a 'Tip and Run' attack at 0617 hrs, 9 May 1942 – St Barnabas Vicarage, Bexhill (Saunders)

by two bombs. HMSs CLEVELAND, BROCKLESBY and WOLVERINE opened fire and the former shot down one Me 109 and seriously damaged another which probably crashed in the sea later†. One rating on the WOLVERINE was killed and three slightly injured in the BROCKLESBY. One dead enemy airman was picked up from the crashed aircraft."

20-year old *Lt* Hans-Joachim Schulz had only been with his *Staffel* a few weeks and was buried with full military honours by RAF personnel from the seaplane base at Mountbatten. Plymouth and similarly well defended naval targets were very rarely attacked again by *Jabos*.

Schulz's burial (via Irwin)

Schulz was the first of many German casualties from the 'tip and run' campaign to be buried on British soil but he and his aircraft were unable to give the British any insight into German intentions, equipment or tactics. Four days later, 10/*JG* 26's only loss of the month gave the British something they wanted, as *Uffz* Oswald Fischer recalls:

†Only one Messerschmitt 109 was lost

"I was ordered by Hptm Plunser to lead a mission. I planned a raid to Brighton since we had not visited that area for some time and few wanted to fly there because of the long flight over water. I found a Fw who was willing to accompany me as my wingman. I planned to go inland about 20 miles before we hit the harbour and this we did. All worked out fine – low flight over the Channel and hedgehopping over the British countryside right into the harbour at Brighton. I saw a large ship and told my wingman 'Let's hit it hard!' In we went. The Flak sprayed like a fire hose but we made it and struck the ship with both bombs.

Oswald Fischer's Messerschmitt 109 F-4/B (via Watkins)

"As we exited, I got hit. I could hear the impact but everything seemed to be alright. As soon as we were over the water, my temperature gauge shot up to 'hot' and I could smell the coolant so I told my wingman to keep going low-level towards home. My engine started to smell very bad. I turned around and belly-landed in a field. I tried to blow it up but the explosive charge would not go off. I became a POW. I regretted my fate but it was better than drowning in the Channel!"

British luck continued when they were able to get far more information from a second *Jabo* pilot captured six days later. *Lt* Josef Fröschl of 10/*JG* 2 was the second 'tip and run' casualty attributable to an RAF fighter, the first occurring on 8 May 1942 when *Uffz* Bruno Görendt from the same *Staffel* was shot down by Adjutant André Debec of 340 Squadron during a *Jaboangriff* against Worthing. On 27 May 1942, Spitfires from 41 Squadron were on patrol off the Isle of Wight and happened to be in the right place at the right time when 10/*JG* 2 attacked, as Flt Lt Derek Wainwright† reported afterwards:

"I was proceeding on patrol to St Catherines Point when I noticed a large column of smoke rising from a ship in the Solent. Almost immediately I saw an Me 109 F coming towards me slightly below, followed by a Spitfire which was presumably Plt Off J J Allen. I gave the tallyho and chased it to the starboard of the Spitfire. After the 109 had dropped its bomb close to a cruiser lying in the mouth of the Solent, he gained speed but soon pulled up in a right hand turn,

Adj André Debec (via Rohrbacher)

†Flt Lt Wainwright was shot down on 10 Jun 42 by *Fw* Karl Nowak of 9/*JG* 2 and despite crash-landing on the Isle of Wight, suffered a fractured skull and died in hospital later that day

bringing me into range. I fired a two second burst after which it turned away again to port. Soon after that, we again pulled up to starboard in a climbing turn, this time I was about 100-200 yards away and practically astern. I gave it a good burst and saw strikes on the fuselage and pieces falling off. He then turned for land and I closed to very close range, overshooting eventually when the pilot baled out and landed on Isle of Wight, his 'plane crashing into a field."

Josef Fröschl was leading a *Schwarm* of *Jabos* on what was ostensibly labelled as an armed shipping reconnaissance off Spithead. They had flown low over Spithead, attacked a small trawler and climbed from 30 to 100 metres to overfly a warship. It was only then that they spotted and were spotted in turn by 41 Squadron's standing patrol – the first burst of gunfire apparently damaging Fröschl's engine but did not prevent him from dropping his bomb, almost hitting another warship. The Austrian pilot realised that his engine was so badly damaged that he had no chance of getting back to France so climbed, jettisoned his canopy and baled out, ensuring that his fighter-bomber was totally destroyed.

23 year-old Fröschl was an experienced pilot who in his debrief boasted he had flown with I/*JG* 2 from early 1941, had then apparently transferred to 4/*JG* 77 on the Eastern Front before returning to 2/*JG* 2 in the Autumn of 1941. By the time of his capture, he claimed to have shot down at least 22 enemy aircraft, mostly Russian, and had been nominated for the *Deutsches Kreuz in Gold,* which he expected to receive shortly, and was hopeful of being awarded the *Ritterkreuz.*

Frank Liesendahl, now a Hptm *and wearing the* Deutsches Kreuz in Gold *(Arnold)*

It would appear that Fröschl took great delight in misleading his interrogators as no evidence has emerged of his air combat victories in either *JG* 77 or *JG* 2. However, it is clear that he was an able pilot who volunteered to be a *Jabo* pilot, presumably to further his career, and that he had been involved in a number of successful 'tip and run' attacks, namely against Cowes in the Isle of Wight on 28 April 1942 and Eastbourne on 4 May 42, and he was indeed awarded the *Deutsches Kreuz* in *Gold* on 10 July 1942, a month after the same award was given to his *Staffel Kapitän,* Frank Liesendahl.

Fröschl's interrogation, added to the interrogation of Oswald Fischer of 10/*JG* 26, did reveal useful information on what was now confirmed as being 10/*JG* 2 including its base, recent operations, strength, aircraft armament and bomb loads. However, what was revealed gave no clues as to effectively combating 'tip and run' attacks. More worryingly, Fröschl revealed that *JG* 2 was re-equipping with the Focke-Wulf 190 but because the *Jabostaffel* operated close to the British mainland and in order to therefore minimise the chances of a Focke-Wulf 190 landing on British soil, 10 *Staffel* would continue to operate with the Messerschmitt 109 for the time being but the intention was that they too would be one of the last *Staffeln* to receive what would then be a very potent fighter-bomber.

This was a great concern for the British. The Focke-Wulf 190 was superior in all flight parameters, except turning radius, to the best Allied fighter at that time, the Spitfire Mark Vb. It was 25 to 30 mph faster at all altitudes up to 25,000 feet and had the highest rate of roll of any fighter of the last war. As a fighter-bomber, it could carry a single 500 kg bomb under the fuselage or four 50 kg bombs, more than doubling the bomb load of the Messerschmitt 109. Furthermore, if the Messerschmitt 109 had been hard to shoot down, the Focke-Wulf 190 was faster, more suited, because of its air cooled engine and robust construction, to fighter-bomber operations and far more capable of taking care of itself when confronted by RAF fighters.

Caen-Carpiquet: One of 10/JG 2's last sorties using the Messerschmitt 109 F. L to R: Ofw *Gerhard Limberg, ?,* Lt *Leopold Wenger* (Wenger)

Frank Liesendahl looking at the rudder of Wk Nr 7629 showing successes on 17 May 1941, 9 Jun 1941, 23 Mar 42, 27 Mar 42, 31 Mar 42, 2 May 42, 7 Jun 42 (Arnold)

In mid-June 1942, both *Jabostaffeln* were withdrawn piecemeal to Le Bourget near Paris where they began re-equipping with the Focke-Wulf 190. Accordingly, 'tip and run' attacks decreased, dropping from 105 in May, to 77 in June and 37 in July 1942.†

Nevertheless, 10/*JG* 2 was able to fly its first attack with the Focke-Wulf 190 on 7 July 1942, when *Oblt* Fritz Schröter and *Lt* Leopold 'Poldi' Wenger claimed to have sunk or damaged three ships off the Isle of Wight; two days later, Schröter and *Lt* Erhard Nippa did the same again, claiming to have sunk two ships and damaged one west of Portland. 10/*JG* 26 returned to Caen-Carpiquet on or about 10 July 1942 with its new fighter-bombers and soon commenced operations. From now on, at least one 'tip and run' attack a day was planned or flown and as yet, the British had no means of effectively countering them.

The future for southern Britain now appeared bleaker than ever.

†Analysis of South Coast Tip & Run Incidents (7/43)

10/JG 2 converting to the FW 190 at Le Bourget, June 1942; Lt *Leopold Wenger and* Ofw *Gerhard Limberg* (Wenger)

Le Bourget, June 1942 (Wenger)

*A new FW 190 A of 10/*JG 26 (Storsberg)

5
Butcher Birds and Rats

JULY – SEPTEMBER 1942

10/JG 2, 9 July 1942. L to R: Oblt *Fritz Schröter, Lt Gerhard Limberg, Lt Leopold Wenger, ?, ?, believed to be* Obstlt *Karl Hentschell,* Ofw *Werner Magarin,* Hptm *Frank Liesendahl,* Uffz *Kurt Bressler, Lt Erhard Nippa. To the front is 'Bim' the dog* (Wenger)

Aptly nicknamed the *Würger* or Butcher Bird, the Focke-Wulf 190 quickly proved itself a potent weapon in the hands of 10/*JG* 2 and 10/*JG* 26's pilots. Leopold Wenger had been transferred to the *Jabostaffel* from 3/*JG* 2 on 27 May 42 and flew just one *Jabo* mission in the Messerschmitt 109 F-4 before he and the rest of the *Staffel* converted to the Focke-Wulf 190. His first *Jabo* mission with the new aircraft was on 7 July 1942 when, as mentioned previously, he and Fritz Schröter had successfully attacked shipping off the Isle of Wight for which Wenger was immediately awarded the *Eiserne Kreuz II*. Five days later he and an unnamed pilot attacked shipping in Brixham harbour as local records make mention:

> "*...1347 hours, 2 FW 190s approached from the south-east and were engaged by AA. They dived on the harbour and dropped two bombs there. Aircraft continued north for 4,000 yards then turned back south towards Brixham. Engaged by another AA site, the aircraft turned south-east. A claim of a hit to the tail of one was made. Minesweeper No. 174 damaged...*"

Leopold Wenger's award of the EK II, Chateau Louvigny, 9 July 1942. L to R: Oblt *Fritz Schröter,* Lt *Erhard Nippa and 'Poldi' Wenger* (Nippa)

Wenger's view of the attack was far more vivid:

> "*...We broke through the balloon barrage out of a marvellous blue sky and completely took them by surprise. We fired at the ships with all of our guns. While I was shooting, I could see that there were already flames coming out of my ship's superstructure. The rest was done by the bomb and my ship leaned over with a broken keel. The other ship began to sink stern first. Then the Flak began firing very strongly so we had to give up our observing. Anyway, I was very pleased with this success. It was the first ship I had finished off alone...*"

Lt *Leopold Wenger* (Wenger)

Whilst 10/*JG* 2 was meeting with considerable success, it has been hard to ascertain what success 10/*JG* 26 was having but it was felt necessary to replace *Hptm* Karl Plunser as *Staffel Kapitän* on 12 July 1942. No suitably experienced officer was found to replace him from within 10/*JG* 26. It has been assumed that his natural successor would have been *Oblt* Hans Ragotzi but he had been shot down on a *Jabo* mission against East Wittering in Sussex by Plt Off Keith Mason of 131 Squadron late in the evening of 9 June 1942†. Command was therefore temporarily given to the successful deputy *Staffel Kapitän* of the sister *Jabostaffel* – Fritz Schröter††. In view of the successes by a number of pilots of 10/*JG* 2, it is thought that this move could have been beneficial to 10/*JG* 26 but this is pure supposition. Nevertheless, Fritz Schröter's time as temporary *Staffel Kapitän* would be short, the reason why occurring five days after he transferred.

Further west, 10/*JG* 2 continued its war in and around Devon. On 13 July, Leopold Wenger scored his second success against enemy shipping.

†Although he survived the ditching, he was never seen alive again and his body was washed ashore in northern France some time later
††Some records state that an *Oblt* Schröfter took over as *Staffel Kapitän* but no evidence of the existence of such an officer has been found

The Free French Submarine Hunter CH 8 *Rennes*, captained by *Enseigne de Vaisseau 1er Classe* Guy Perrault was preparing to escort in the French submarine *Rubis* which was returning from a mine-laying operation off the coast near Bordeaux. The *Rennes* was not destined to make the rendezvous; Wenger describes what happened:

> "*I wanted to attack the port of Dartmouth but the clouds were thick on the coast so I approached a single escort vessel with my Rottenflieger, Uffz Max Meixner and attacked it. The ship was sailing at full speed in the direction of the coast and my bomb hit the ship amidships, in front of the stern. My Rottenflieger's bomb exploded just short of the stern. Then everything happened very fast. There was a gigantic blast – it was probable that the ship's boilers had exploded. When the smoke and steam had dispersed, you could see a long track of spray at the end of which many ship's parts, boards and a lifeboat were floating. There was no trace of the crew. The escort vessel was about 800 tons and looked exactly like the one I had sunk in Brixham the day before. During the attack, I was hit in the wing by machine-gun fire. Everything happened very quickly and I hardly had time to machine-gun the ship during the attack. I was sure that no radio message was made – the attack had taken place about 5-10 kms south-east of Dartmouth.*"

Guy Perrault and 25 crew were all killed.

On 17 July 1942, disaster struck 10/*JG* 2, as Leopold Wenger related in a letter home four days later:

> "*I was on duty in the Command Post where it is most unpleasant to sit and wait. Occasionally you get a radio message – you look at the clock and realise that the attack is taking place at that very moment. Then you wait for the return and get worried when not all of them are back at the same time. No, I would rather fly every mission than wait at the Command Post.*
>
> "*Our Kapitän that did not return from this sortie, and now, four days later we still cannot comprehend that he is no longer with us. He had sunk a British destroyer just a few days ago [11 July 1942] and now he was probably shot down by Flak. I flew my first bombing sorties with him and learned the trade, so to speak, from him. He already had the Deutsches Kreuz in Gold and should receive the Ritterkreuz in a few days. We all hope that he is in captivity – that is not nice but nevertheless better…*"

At about 1145 hours on that day, four Focke-Wulf 190s lifted off from Caen-Carpiquet to carry out an 'armed reconnaissance in and around Torquay'. Frank Liesendahl with his *Rottenflieger Lt* Erhard Nippa formed one pair, *Fw* Josef Niesmann and another unknown pilot the second pair. What exactly happened during the attack was never explained by the surviving German pilots – Erhard Nippa recalls that during the attack on a tanker off Brixham, he observed both a bomb exploding and another splash in the water whilst Josef Niesmann in his logbook just notes that he dropped his bomb in a barracks south-east of Brixham and that he and the other pilot from his *Rotte* landed at Théville at 1250 hours. British records are far clearer:

> "At 1225 hours, four enemy aircraft, 2 Me 109s [sic] and 2 FW 190s approached Berry Head from SE at 100 feet. A tanker accompanied by two MLs due east of Berry Head and only just offshore was attacked by at least two e/a with bombs and machine-gun. Near misses but no hits. One e/a brought down into sea, remainder split up by AA fire from Bofors and ships, spread out, two turning west along north side of Berry Head and then receding north towards Torquay, the east and SE out of view, one turning west, then south over Brixham and eventually SE out to sea, dropping one bomb in open country SE of Brixham.
>
> "Spitfires were patrolling at low altitude just prior to the attack…Ships guns first to open fire, immediately followed by Bofors at sites EL2 and EL 3, all of whom claim hits and destruction of one aircraft destroyed. Observer Corps confirm Bofors hit…"

The report filed by the Royal Navy's Plymouth Command confirm what happened but also credit a ship with shooting down the Focke-Wulf 190:

> "At 1245 hours, four Focke-Wulf 190s attacked tanker DAXHOUND escorted by MLs 118 and 157 in position one mile SE of Berry Head. Two planes attacked the tanker and one plane each ML. ML 118 undoubtedly shot down her attacker.
>
> "The tanker suffered minor damage from two near misses and ML 157 was hit by a bomb which passed through the bridge and burst in the water alongside. Two casualties were sustained by ML and returned to harbour. Both MLs put up a determined fire with their Lewis Guns."

The identity of the shot down aircraft was not known at the time and no wreckage was apparently recovered†. However, on 6 September 1942, a badly decomposed body was found in the sea six miles east of Berry Head. The body was of a *Luftwaffe Hptm* who had been awarded the *Eiserne Kreuz I* and *Deutsches Kreuz in Gold*. Further investigation of the body revealed an identity disc in the name of 'Liesendahl'. With due respect but sadly for his family, it was then decided to bury Frank Liesendahl's body at sea.

The loss was understandably a great one to both his *Staffel* and the *Luftwaffe*'s small yet potent *Jabo* force. Nevertheless, the tempo of attacks did not falter. Fritz Schröter returned to 10/*JG* 2 and assumed command of the *Staffel* whilst command of 10/*JG* 26 was given to 26 year-old *Oblt* Joachim-Hans Geburtig. Geburtig had been a member of 8/*JG* 26 in 1941 and had been shot down and wounded on 21 June 1941. On returning to *JG* 26 almost a year later, it would appear that success as a fighter pilot still eluded him and by volunteering to be a *Jabo* pilot, he saw a chance to get noticed.

†In the 1970s, fishermen off Brixham brought ashore parts of an aircraft, including a cannon and propeller boss purporting to have come from this aircraft

Oblt *Joachim-Hans Geburtig, seen here when he was with 8/JG 26 in 1941* (Geburtig)

Unfortunately for him, success still was hard for him to come by. After being in command for just 12 days, he and *Fw* Emil Bösch took off from Caen-Carpiquet to attack shipping in the Channel. What happened was clearly documented in Geburtig's intelligence debrief:

> *"This aircraft was one of two which attacked a stationary collier† with bombs and machine-guns from a height of 140 feet. The bombs were near misses and caused slight blast damage while two members of the crew were wounded by MG bullets.*
>
> *"The collier returned fire with twin MGs and claims to have shot this aircraft down. It hit the sea and sank immediately but the pilot managed to struggle to the surface and was picked up by a launch. He maintained that he had not been hit by the ship's fire but that he had failed to pull out of a dive."*

Command of 10/*JG* 26 now passed to *Lt* Paul Keller. Like Frank Liesendahl, very little is known about this enigmatic pilot. Born in Gelsenkirchen in 1918, Keller had been shot down over Dunkirk on 1 June 1940 whilst flying with 6/*JG* 26. His wounds prevented him from flying for nearly a year and he then returned to *Stab* II/*JG* 26 in 1941, shooting down two RAF aircraft in the Summer of 1941. When or why he became a *Jabo* pilot is not known but he was soon to earn the nickname '*Bombenkeller*'. However, curiously, surviving German records list Keller as a *Staffel Führer*, a position also occasionally undertaken by the more experienced *Jabo* pilot *Lt* Erwin Busch, as opposed to *Staffel Kapitän*, suggesting that his appointment was temporary pending official confirmation or the appointment of another permanent *Staffel Kapitän*.

†Believed to be the SS Newglen

Bombenkeller (seen here in early 1943) (Storsberg)

'Tip and Run' attacks were still proving to be a headache for the British defences and as radar was rarely able to detect the approaching high speed and low level fighter-bombers, the tried and tested first line of defence still had to be the personnel of the Observer Corps who were based at various points along the south coast. It was soon obvious that new tactics had to be introduced. Selected posts were now ordered to fire a rocket (known as 'Totter') as soon as low-flying aircraft were seen and to continue to fire them whilst they remained in their vicinity. Furthermore, in order to speed up the reporting of low-flying fighter-bombers, the Observer Corps post would immediately pass the code word 'Rats' to the Observer Centre before passing any plot. Passed immediately to the Sector Controller, such messages had full priority to then scramble, or if already airborne, direct RAF fighters to intercept.

The 'Totter' and 'Rats' systems were still inadequate. It took until November 1942 before standing patrols of two fighters (with another two on standby on the ground) were introduced at anticipated vulnerable points and even then, successful interceptions were infrequent. Furthermore, the existing spacing of the Observer Corps posts still made it possible for enemy aircraft to fly for appreciable distances overland at very low altitude without their tracks being maintained sufficiently to enable fighters to intercept and air raid warnings given.

All of this was made worse for the British at the start of August 1942 when the *Jabos* changed their tactics. 10/JG 26 moved back under the control of *Luftflotte 2's* Fighter Leader and again started carrying out more attacks on Britain's south-eastern coast, stretching British defences to their limit, even if during their first attack of the month, they suffered another loss to an Allied fighter. *Lt* Arnd Flock had only been with his *Staffel* just over a month when he and the more experienced *Ofw* Karl-Heinz Knobeloch were tasked to attack Newhaven. Unluckily for them, a pair of Spitfires from 412 Squadron had taken off from Merston near Chichester at 0910 hours and were on patrol flying at 1,000 feet 20 miles south of Shoreham. At 1000 hours, two aircraft were spotted by Canadians Fg Off George 'Dusty' Davidson and Plt Off Ken Robb flying north at high speed and at low level. Turning to investigate, the low-flying aircraft were identified as Focke-Wulf 190s, each carrying a single bomb, so the Spitfires went immediately into attack. The following combat report was related to the Sector Intelligence Officer at RAF Tangmere on their return:

Ofw *Karl-Heinz Knobeloch* (Storsberg)

Plt Off Ken Robb (2nd from right) with Sgt Stew Pearce (+12 Dec 42), Sgt Joe Richards, Sgt Dave Boyd, Flt Sgt 'Red' McCrimmon, Robb, Plt Off Andy McNaughton (+1 Jun 42) (Richards)

Fg Off 'Dusty' Davidson, 412 Squadron (Richards)

"Yellow 2 (Plt Off Robb) was unable to keep up with Yellow 1(Fg Off Davidson) and slowly fell behind. Yellow 1 closed to within 100 yards of the nearest e/a apparently without being seen, firing a 2½ second burst of cannon and machine-gun astern. Strikes were seen all over the e/a and black smoke was coming from the engine as it crashed sideways into the sea approximately 10-15 miles south of Brighton. Yellow 2 reports that the e/a exploded on striking the sea and afterwards dense smoke up to 300 feet and flame was seen for three or four minutes. After the e/a hit, Yellow 1 then attacked the other e/a which was still flying north and apparently unaware that his No.2 had been attacked.

"Yellow 1 closed to within 100 yards astern firing several bursts and using up all his ammunition. During the first burst, Yellow 1 saw strikes along the fuselage and tail unit and small pieces coming off the latter after which the e/a started a climbing turn to port, Yellow 1 still attacking. After Yellow 1 had used up all his ammunition, the e/a turned south, went down to sea level and then started to climb. This was the last seen of the e/a…"

Meanwhile, further west, in addition to shipping and coastal targets, the pattern of targets attacked by 10/*JG* 2 now showed a shift towards specific inland targets starting with Yeovil in Somerset on 5 August. Whether this was as a result of the initiative of the new *Staffel Kapitän* or an order from *Jafü* 3 as revenge attacks for Bomber Command's attacks on smaller German cities is not certain. However, the rationale for this change in targets was hinted at by a German war reporter who wrote about the Yeovil attack:

"…until now, every mission flown by the Red Foxes has only been aimed at the south coast of England. They have not yet made an attempt to attack the English hinterland. Special preparations are in hand for Operation Ypsilon which will hit industrial works on the other side of the range of hills which stretch behind the south coast. Only two planes are going to carry out this difficult mission but first of all they have to wait for appropriate weather. Up to now, those designated for this attack had to turn back twice because they had not been able to break through the line of English fighter patrols…"

The task was given to two experienced non-commissioned pilots, *Fw* Karl Blase and *Uffz* Kurt Bressler; their account of the attack was given to the same war reporter:

"…As soon as the weather gives a chance of them breaking through, they are going to take off. The morning passes – nothing! The same in the afternoon – nobody will give permission to take off. Eventually in the evening, the time has come. 'Good luck!' the Staffel Kapitän shouts after them. Then the canopy roofs are closed and the engines roar. Both Red Foxes, completely used to each other in many sorties, have worked out precise details. They want to outflank the fighter defences and make up the kilometres they have lost by flying a detour further inland.

"They soon reach the coast at exactly the point they have chosen as an approach path. Flying low-level, they race over the British soil. It is a daring hedgehopping flight. Rivers and streams are crossed, trees and hills jumped. There is the railway line…"

What happened next is best told by those on the ground who experienced the attack first hand:

"I was an impressionable boy of nine. My mother and I were returning from Sherborne, about six miles away, where we had been visiting my Grandparents. We were on the outskirts of Yeovil and I was looking out of the window on the right hand side of the bus when I saw two aeroplanes flying low and which to me at the time almost seemed to be no higher than the bus. In my youthfulness, I pretended to shoot at them and very much to my surprise, they started to shoot back! At this time, there had not been any sirens sounded so it was a complete surprise attack. In his wisdom, the bus driver stopped the bus right in the middle of the bridge that crossed the railway line, we piled out onto the road and all the passengers were led to the pavements either side of the bus as two Focke-Wulf 190 fighter-bombers flew so low overhead that I could distinctly see the markings on the wings and the heads of the two pilots. They proceeded to attack Yeovil and we boarded the bus again and eventually got off and my Mother and I ran to where we lived. We could not see the road as it was completely blanketed by smoke and dust. When we got to our house, the windows were all shattered and the weather boards on the doors blown off.

"At the time of the attack, my Father was working in his allotment and was suddenly swept off his feet and carried through the air about 100 yards to find himself sprawled out in the middle of a cabbage patch with the fin of one of the bombs besides him. He was very fortunate…"

Graham Toms

"I was three weeks off my ninth birthday. I had not long been put to bed when the sirens went. My Father came up either to reassure me or to take me downstairs and when he entered the room, we heard planes fly over the house low and fast. Almost at once there was a loud bang and the thing that I remember clearly was that the pictures on the wall appeared to swing away from the wall…"

Michael Pittard

"I was looking out of the window and my Mother was about to draw the black-out curtains when an aeroplane went by at roof-top height, approximately 120 feet away. My Mother shouted 'Get under the bed quick!' – we dived under the bed and there were two loud explosions. The house shook and the windows rattled. Mother then said 'Get downstairs quick and get in the shelter!'. I tried to move but my trousers were caught on the bed springs – I pulled hard on the bed and tore them. Mum was not pleased!"

Tony Robbins

"They came up the Taunton Yeovil Railway Branch line and we saw these two planes travelling very low. They took everyone by surprise, the sirens sounded and the Barrage Balloons started to rise at the same time. The planes travelled over the Railway Station and on up towards Penmill Station. They then turned and came down towards where we were in the town centre and dropped two bombs ..."
C M Randall

Three civilians were killed and 25 suffered varying degrees of wounds. 15 buildings were totally destroyed and a further 972 suffered varying degrees of bomb damage, a further 67 were damaged by gunfire. Some have stated that the target was the Westlands Aircraft Factory on the western outskirts of Yeovil but both fighter-bombers had apparently approached from the west, passing the airfield before turning to port, attacking the town centre from the north and streaking back south. The only target close to where the bombs dropped was Yeovil Railway Station but if the town centre was the intended target, this would accord with the notion that the attack was a revenge attack. Both German aircraft returned unscathed and each pilot was awarded the *Eiserne Kreuz* I the following day for what was an audacious attack.

Two days later, 10/*JG* 2 tried to emulate the success of the Yeovil attack by targeting Bodmin and Constantine in Cornwall. The four aircraft involved moved from Caen-Carpiquet to Morlaix in Brittany and just after 1300 hours, took off for Cornwall. It was a difficult flight in more ways than one as Leopold Wenger, who was briefed to attack Constantine, later wrote:

"Today I flew a sortie which exhausted me more than any I have flown before. First of all, I flew with my Katschmarek to the area around Falmouth on the western corner of England. The long flight over the water was certainly very demanding. I could hardly see the horizon. Then we flew into very bad and misty weather over England – you could hardly see the hand in front of your face! In retaliation for the attacks on German cities, we attacked two small towns. Then on our return flight, we again flew into dense fog. On top of this, a couple of electrical instruments failed so I had no control over my aircraft's attitude. Suddenly I saw some telegraph poles shooting past my cockpit. Instinctively, I put my kite into a steep climb and found a couple of barrage balloons in front of me. I was able to avoid them just in time but whilst doing this, I lost my Rottenflieger – I was sure he had flown into a hill; he had thought it had happened to me. When we landed back at Morlaix, we were very pleased to see each other again!"

Wenger was very non-committal about this attack but yet again, the effect on those on the receiving end at both the attack near Coverack and at Bodmin as the following accounts show:

"We used to go to Cadgwith when my father, a lighthouse keeper on the Lizard, had his days off. One day, I was standing outside my Great Aunt's

house when the familiar sound of a single-engined aircraft was heard. Suddenly, there was an almighty explosion and an FW 190 roared very low down the valley, over the fishing cove and out to sea. I clearly saw the pilot and the familiar German markings. Later we heard that he had dropped his bomb which had landed in a field and a nearby cottage had its windows broken. A remarkable escape for the family crockery that was on the dresser in the kitchen – not one piece was broken, so it was said at the time…"

Aubrey Jane

"I was playing with a boy when we saw two FW 190s coming in from the south-east at no more that 1,000 feet. We clearly saw the crosses and as both of us were model makers, we identified the planes easily. Both had a bomb slung under the fuselage. A few minutes later, we heard explosions and saw two clouds of smoke from the direction of Truro, some four or five miles, as the Crow flies, to the west. We heard gunfire from the retreating 'Jerries'. I know that the two bombs were dropped on Truro railway station…"

Don Pyatt

The devastation in the centre of Bodmin 7 Aug 42 (Cornwall county Library)

"There was no air raid warning! Two FW 190s came very low over Bodmin firing cannon and each aircraft had one bomb. I never saw the first plane but I saw the second one, also the pilot, and just below the pilot was a yellow <. That raid killed nine people and injured 32, set the gas works on fire and put it out of action for eight weeks…"
Mike Lyne

"My home was just outside Bodmin below the flight path of the attacking planes and I witnessed at very close hand one of the FW 190s as it approached the town. The sight of this aircraft flying so low that it seemed to climb to clear the trees lining the road filled me with amazement. Although only 11 years of age, I could not but admire the skill of the pilot. Speed and surprise was obviously the key of the operation as the attack was completed and the planes clear of the area before the air raid siren was sounded. After machine-gunning the barracks, they attacked the gas works. Unfortunately, a residential area close by was hit killing nine people, eight of whom were from one family."
Edwin Renals

"I was involved in this attack as an ARP Messenger Boy, aged 15, and was the first person to arrive at ARP HQ. The fighter-bombers scored direct hits on the local gas works, several homes and a dairy. They might have tried to attack the Duke of Cornwall's Light Infantry barracks. It was midday (I recall having my lunch the moment the first bomb exploded) and two fighter-bombers were involved, flying very low over the town…"
George Vaughan-Ellis

There would be one more attack by 10/*JG* 2 against targets well away from the coast in August 1942. At 1630 hours on 11 August, Leopold Wenger with another unnamed pilot carried out a raid on the cathedral city of Salisbury in Wiltshire. Taking off from Cherbourg-East at 1700 hours, he and his *Rottenflieger* landed back safely just 55 minutes later flying so low and fast that British records stated the attack was plotted but was so fast they were unable to scramble fighters to intercept, even if Wenger did report seeing 15-20 Spitfires north of Salisbury headed towards Portland Bill. Both aircraft flew exceptionally low along the A338 Bournemouth-Salisbury road, then swung east before crossing Salisbury east to west. One bomb landed in an allotment and the fighter-bomber, presumably flown by Wenger, machine-gunned the gasholder, rendering Salisbury without gas for four days. The second aircraft machine-gunned the railway station, its bomb skidding along the railway track before exploding harmlessly in some more allotments. The two aircraft then flew along the River Avon, close to the fighter airfield at Ibsley, and off home unscathed. Memories of this attack are suitably vivid:

"Two fighter-bombers strafed and bombed the railway station area. I didn't see them but I've never forgotten the sound of mixed armament being fired. The

railway services were operating that evening so I presume they missed. I saw one crater outside the station by a bridge. No warning was sounded."
Reg Hillyar

"As a keen aircraft spotter, I was given the task of roof spotter on the roof of the Dunn's Seeds store. Armed with a pair of the boss's binoculars, whenever the air raid sounded, I had to proceed to the roof where a button was installed which sounded the alarm on all the floors.

"On Tuesday 11 August 1942, the siren had sounded two or three times followed about 15 minutes later by the 'All Clear'. I had been dashing up and down to the roof like a monkey on a stick so after the third 'All Clear', I decided to stay up on the roof for a while and have a smoke. I was shortly joined by one of the store staff, Bert Safe, who said 'Let's have a look with your binoculars, Ev; I'll have a look around'. All of a sudden, Bert called out 'Hey, Ev, look at these two Harvards. I've never seen any as low as that before!' I grabbed the glasses from him and had a quick look. 'My God, Bert!' I shouted 'They're not Harvards, they're Focke-Wulfs!' and hit the panic button, sending everyone down to the basement. The two aircraft came in from the direction of Southampton Road and literally flew up Castle Street, so low in fact that I lost sight of them at times as they went past the buildings. One of the aircraft flipped round in a vertical bank and was so close I could look into the cockpit. He straightened up and opened fire with his cannon, hitting one of the gasholders. I was so busy watching the first machine that I lost sight of the second which I think carried on in the direction of Old Sarum..."
Don Evans

These attacks now only further reinforced the inability of the British defences to combat these 'lightning nuisance' attacks, as the Salisbury raid was described. The Observer Corps was now forced to form approximately 150 satellite reporting posts, connected to the nearest Observer Corps 'parent' post which would increase low coverage in a belt 30 miles width from the coast. These satellite posts were simply to report low flying 'doubtful' aircraft during the hours of daylight. However, it would be some months before the system was fully operational.

During the days that followed the Salisbury attack, the *Jabos* of 10/*JG* 2 and 10/*JG* 26 attacked the occasional coastal target without loss whilst noting an increase in Allied air and sea activity. The reason for this became obvious when just before dawn on 19 August 1942, a predominantly Canadian force carried out a raid on the French port of Dieppe. German twin-engined bombers, mainly from the Dornier 217 unit *KG* 2, were not in action until 1100 hours which was about the same time that the Focke-Wulf 190s of 10/*JG* 2 and 10/*JG* 26 were committed *en masse*. However, as the only bomber assets available during the early hours of the raid, a number of *Jabos* did carry out armed reconnaissance of the seas off Dieppe with unknown effect.

For *Lt* Leopold Wenger, 19 August 1942 was a memorable day for many reasons. He and the other pilots of 10/*JG* 2 had a rude awakening at their billets at the Chateau Louvigny near Caen when news of the raid came through and he, *Fw* Karl Blase and *Uffz* Werner Magarin were quickly ordered to carry out an armed reconnaissance. Eager to sink something, Wenger made sure that his Focke-Wulf 190 carried a 500 kg bomb; what subsequently happened on take off he had reason to remember well:

> *"I had lousy luck and at the same time a lot of good luck. Whilst opening the throttle on take off, the undercarriage collapsed and I slid along the grass on my bomb. It was not a very cheering experience, especially when you know about the explosive effect of the bomb or when you have been able to watch its effect during an attack. So I missed the first mission. I then flew a Messerschmitt 108 from Caen to Ste André to get a new FW 190 and then flew back to Caen again. Valuable time was lost and I was afraid that I would be too late and the whole fuss would be over!"*

The two NCO pilots managed to carry out an attack on an unidentified warship but Karl Blase's Focke-Wulf 190 suffered some damage from *Flak* whilst damage caused to Werner Magarin's fighter-bomber necessitated him force-landing at Paluel, to the west of Dieppe.

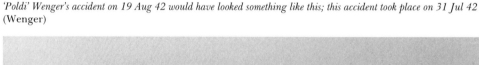

'Poldi' Wenger's accident on 19 Aug 42 would have looked something like this; this accident took place on 31 Jul 42 (Wenger)

Leopold Wenger had little to fear about missing the action. Shortly after the first attack, 10/*JG* 2 carried out another, this time flown by the *Staffel Kapitän*, *Oblt* Fritz Schröter, *Lt* Erhard Nippa and *Lt* Gerhard Limberg, and three hits were reported on another unknown ship. Then, at 1033 hours, Wenger, *Uffz* Walter Höfer and two other NCO pilots again took off from Caen, each armed with a single SC500 bomb.

10/*JG* 2 were in their element, being the more experienced of the two *Jabostaffeln* and having had much practice attacking British shipping. Leopold Wenger remembered his first successful attack of the day clearly:

> "When we arrived over Dieppe, the fighting zone was shrouded in mist, dust and dense smoke. The British [sic] fleet was completely hidden. Everywhere there were muzzle flashes and ashore you could see lots of fires from shot down aircraft and burnt out tanks which had hardly advanced more than 20 metres up the beach. Many aircrew were floating in the sea in their rubber dinghies.
>
> "At exactly midday, we began a low-level attack. At the same moment, a German bomber dived past us into the sea†. We advanced in the mist and got to the cause of the smoke screen. All our guns were fired and the bombs released at the same time. A bomb went off under the stern of a destroyer but then I was shot at by all kinds of Flak and because of the fireworks, I couldn't watch any more. The three other FW 190s flying with me damaged a few more ships and one shot down a Spitfire††. Still flying at low level, we fired into the packed landing craft. The effect was devastating."

10/*JG* 2 returned to Caen virtually unscathed whilst 10/*JG* 26, flying a similar mission at the same time, returned similarly unscathed to its airfield at St Omer, even though an escorting Focke-Wulf 190 of 2/*JG* 26 flown by *Ofw* Paul Czwilinski was shot down into Dieppe harbour and the pilot killed.

However, it was the next *Jabo* attack that was the most spectacular and successful. The only Allied airman to witness the attack from the air was Gp Capt Harry Broadhurst DSO DFC AFC. 'Broadie' was Deputy Senior Air Staff Officer at HQ 11 Group and not content with sitting in the 'Ops' Room at RAF Bentley Priory, flew four sorties that day. He took off from Hornchurch at 1230 hours on his third mission together with Wg Cdr Robin Powell and recorded the following:

> "The withdrawal was almost complete and with the exception of a few ships two or three miles off Dieppe, which included the destroyer Berkeley, the convoy was in full progress back towards the English coast.
>
> "After cruising around for a few minutes, Wg Cdr Powell separated from me and went down to sea level to see the situation from low altitude whilst I circled the Dieppe area gradually losing height down to 18,000 feet. I noticed one or two attacks by Dornier 217s whose bombing appeared to be extremely inaccurate, many of them jettisoning their bombs as soon as they were attacked by Spitfires.

†Almost definitely a Do 217 of 6/*KG* 2
††*Uffz* Walter Höfer was credited with a Spitfire in this attack

"I noticed that the rear of the convoy i.e. that part of it nearest to the French coast was being subjected to the most severe attacks and latterly the majority of these were being directed against the destroyer Berkeley which was apparently in difficulties. I called up Hornchurch Control and asked them to suggest to Group Operations that the patrols be concentrated over that area, at the same time calling up the ships control and suggesting that he moved the bottom cover squadron to the immediate vicinity of the Berkeley. The ship controller was continuously reporting the presence of Dornier 217s but I noticed that there were several Focke-Wulf 190s about, some of them carrying bombs. Towards the end of my patrol I saw two Focke-Wulfs dive towards the Berkeley. I dived after them but could not intercept them until after they had dropped their bombs, one of which appeared to score a direct hit on the stern of the Berkeley. I closed in to the rear of the Focke-Wulf as he pulled away from his dive and empted most of my cannon and machine-gun ammunition into him with good effect and then returned along the line of the convoy to Kenley where I had lunch."

Four Focke-Wulf 190s of 10/*JG* 2 had taken off from Caen at 1250 hours. This time the *Schwarm* was led by *Oblt* Fritz Schröter and with him was Leopold Wenger plus two unnamed NCO pilots. Again, Wenger's recollections were vivid:

" ...the English [sic] were withdrawing everywhere but the smoke screen did not help them much. I attacked a second destroyer and achieved a direct hit amidships with an SC500 bomb. During the attack, I was under heavy anti-aircraft fire from the destroyer but when the bomb went off, the guns stopped shooting. An explosion followed – simply disastrous. The whole ship was enveloped in black cloud but then I was chased and attacked by many Spitfires and unfortunately could not watch the complete sinking. In the course of this I had got a good thrashing from the Flak – wing, engine, cowling, undercarriage and tail unit were riddled with bullets. There were also two hits in the cockpit but three had ricocheted off the head armour plate. Of course the mission was worth it..."

The Hunt Class destroyer HMS *Berkeley*, commanded by Lt James Yorke RN, had been in almost constant action since the start of the raid, using its guns in the bombardment of the town and surrounding cliffs, laying smoke screens and shelling specific targets in the town. In addition to its normal ship's complement of 146, the *Berkeley* was also carrying a number of RAF, Army and USAAF observers and air controllers, the senior of which were Lt Col Loren Hillsinger USAAF and Wg Cdr Stanley Skinner. Skinner was a pre-war auxiliary pilot and one of the RAF's first night-fighter pilots, having flown with 604 Squadron during the Battle of Britain and the *Blitz* that followed. By the time he had been taken off operations for a rest, he had shot down one German bomber, probably destroyed another and damaged two more, his last combat being in May 1942. Sadly, he and the other air controllers were helpless to prevent the German air attack which was so quick and brutal almost all on the *Berkeley* never even saw the raiders. The following eyewitness accounts vividly tell what happened:

> *"...all I heard through the headphones was 'aircraft approaching!'; the next thing was an enormous cracking sound, the ship lifted up and we were flung in the air, my contact with the Director Control Tower was broken and I suffered a cut chin from the headset.*
>
> *"When we gathered our senses there was smoke and dust everywhere and we were in complete darkness. The ship had assumed a distinct bows down attitude and we thought she was going to drive herself under as we were still underway. Our natural instincts drove us aft towards the hatchway to the upper deck but on arriving, we found the ladder had disappeared! Fear enhances the adrenalin and I jumped up and managed to get my hands over the edge of the hatch, my two colleagues helped push me up and over. I then pulled them up in turn and we proceeded to the upper deck with great relief!"*

Ordinary Seaman Dick Venables

> *"...for something like the six hours that the raid lasted, the Berkeley was constantly engaged in supporting the landings and running the gauntlet of the Luftwaffe and German shore batteries. Eventually when it was decided that there was no point in continuing the action, the order was given to all participants for the general withdrawal. Berkeley together with other ships waited off shore for the last of the evacuees and was constantly under attack. The ship stopped momentarily to pick up a party of Canadian soldiers from a landing craft; many were badly wounded and all were suffering from shock and exhaustion. We made the walking wounded as comfortable as possible and handed round cigarettes and when this was accomplished, I grabbed a tea urn and made my way to the galley to make tea for them. It was just as I got into the galley and had turned on the tap of a large hot water tank that a bomb struck the ship just forward of the bridge, breaking its back. The blast from the bomb broke through the bulkhead and I was enveloped in boiling water. The cooking range on the opposite side of the galley disintegrated and I found myself on the deck of the galley amongst red hot metal. I eventually picked myself up in some pain from the scalds and burns and made my way to the upper deck.*
>
> *"I didn't realise it at the time but I understand that the Berkeley was going at full speed when she was hit and with the steering smashed, she continued to sail at high speed in a circle, heeling over so steeply that some of the crew were thrown off her decks.*
>
> *"Just as I reached the upper deck, the 'Abandon ship!' call was made and painfully I made my way to the Carley Float which was my 'abandon ship' post but the float was completely entangled in the broken structure of the bridge where it had been attached. The bombing of the ship had happened in the final moments of the evacuation and my first thoughts were now that there may not be any craft left to come to our rescue but fortunately Steam Gun Boat 8 had witnessed the bombing and quickly returned to pick up the survivors. Unfortunately all of the*

Taking off survivors from the Berkeley (via Cheshire)

*Canadian soldiers in the forward mess deck and 15 of the ship's company were
lost in the bombing. Incidentally, we had picked up a German airman earlier that
day and I vividly remember that after the 'abandon ship' was sounded, someone
recalled that he was still locked away and a rating was sent to release him..."*

Supply Assistant Tom Hare

In addition to the 15 ships company who were killed, an unknown
number of Canadian soldiers were also killed whilst Wg Cdr Stanley Skinner
simply disappeared and is still listed as missing believed killed. Mortally
damaged and with all the survivors and bodies taken off, the destroyer HMS
Albrighton was instructed to sink the *Berkeley* which she did with two
torpedoes. The second torpedo hit the forward magazine and following an
immense explosion, at 1338 hours, just 20 minutes after the German attack,
the *Berkeley* sank. Her remains now lie in 10 fathoms of water, about three
miles out from Dieppe, the final explosion having broken her in three.

HMS Albrighton torpedoes the Berkeley (via Cheshire)

It has been stated that the *Berkeley* was sunk by a Dornier 217 from either *KG* 2 or *KG* 40 but recent research proves that no claims for a destroyer were ever filed by those units. Furthermore, the reports filed by both Gp Capt Broadhurst and *Lt* Wenger and the times that they were airborne are now conclusive proof as to the identity of the successful German unit.

By mid-afternoon, the battles around Dieppe were over. However, one further *Jabo* attack is known to have taken place that day when 10/*JG* 2 sent five aircraft to add further insult to injury by attacking the retreating ships. Again, Leopold Wenger, flying a new Focke-Wulf 190, led the attack and his report sums up the feeling of elation that the *Jabo* pilots of 10/*JG*2 and 10/*JG* 26 must have felt, even if their claims were a little over optimistic and, after 60 years, his writing appears blood thirsty:

> *"At 1608 hours, I took off again on my third sortie against the fleeing fleet. Eventually we reached a force of big landing craft off Brighton. As a defensive measure there were barrage balloons. We attacked at once and after receiving hits, two ships sank immediately. Unfortunately my bomb went over the ship and exploded 10 metres besides it but I then shot at it and set fire to the superstructure to make up for it!*
>
> *"That ended our combat at Dieppe. Our Staffel had sent two destroyers, two big landing craft, two escort ships and in addition a Spitfire to the bottom. It had also damaged one destroyer, one cargo ship, one landing ship and two escort ships. The pilot of one of our planes that had force-landed near Dieppe† arrived back the next day and told us how it looked there. The English [sic] had been scythed down by the dozen in front of the barbed wire on the beach by heavy machine-guns and mines. Most of the armoured vehicles had been destroyed on the beach. In any case, this was a terrible defeat for the Tommies and hopefully they would repeat the whole lot again so that we did not get out of practice!"*

From a *Jabo* viewpoint, 19 August 1942 had been a success but still the *Luftwaffe* failed to increase its *Jabostaffeln*. *Luftwaffe* records state that 44 fighter-bombers participated in nine *Jabo* attacks throughout the day and in addition to the claims made by 10/*JG* 2, its sister *Jabostaffel* also claimed hits on numerous ships. Apart from aircraft returning with varying degrees of damage and the one Focke-Wulf 190 of 10/*JG* 2 which crash-landed near Dieppe in the morning, the only loss was suffered by 10/*JG* 26 when *Uffz* Heinrich Von Berg, after landing at Abbeville-Drucat to check on damage to his FW 190, then took off again only to crash four kilometres north of Hesdin.

It would be nearly 22 months before the Allies would carry out a much larger 'raid' in north-west Europe by which time Allied air, numerical and technical superiorities and a weakened Germany, helped ensure an Allied success. It therefore must have been an anti-climax when a few days later the *Jabos* of 10/*JG* 2 and 10/*JG* 26 recommenced their 'tip and run' war, the German pilots never again getting the 'practice' against Allied shipping that they so wished for.

†This was *Uffz* Werner Magarin who had force-landed after the first attack of the day

Following the excitement of the Dieppe Raid, there was a brief pause and German records state that Hythe was the next target to be selected on 21 August 1942 but this was probably in reference to an early morning reconnaissance flown by 5/*JG* 26. However, the following day, Bournemouth and Salcombe were both attacked with unrecorded results whilst the day after, two Focke-Wulf 190s targeted Swanage Gas works in the early evening.

However, an unusual incident occurred on 24 August 1942. Four fighter-bombers from 10/*JG* 2 took off from Caen mid afternoon on a *Jabo*/armed reconnaissance in the vicinity of Start Point. Bombs were dropped in Dartmouth and on their return, the German pilots recorded contact with two Spitfires and a Lysander but made no claims. At this time, a Lysander of the air-sea rescue unit 276 Squadron, on a training flight off Start Point, went missing. Rumours abounded afterwards that the pilot, Plt Off Jack Ernst, had defected, this apparently arising from the fact that he had a Germanic surname. However, neither the pilot or his crewman, AC2 Stuart Fleet were ever seen again and it would appear that in an attempt to avoid the Focke-Wulf 190s, the Lysander crashed into the sea.

Two days later, 10/*JG* 26 suffered another loss. *Ofw* Werner Kassa and *Ogefr* Richard Wittmann were briefed to attack industrial targets and housing in Eastbourne. Streaking in over the town from the east, they each dropped one bomb on the Roselands district, close to the commercial vehicle workshops of Messrs Caffyns Ltd. Caffyns carried out servicing and repairs to military vehicles and because of this, the workshops were defended – on the roof was a Bren gun manned by Private E G Johnstone of the Canadian Seaforth Highlanders. As the fighter-bombers banked away to starboard, they presented Private Johnstone with a much better target and he opened fire on the lead aircraft. It would appear that Werner Kassa was either hit by a burst of fire from the Bren gun or had lost control as his aircraft continued rolling to the right and then hit the ground inverted at Lottbridge Drove, killing him instantly. Richard Wittmann failed to see what had happened to his *Rottenführer* as he was too occupied in avoiding the *Flak* which slightly damaged his fighter-bomber. The demise of Kassa was witnessed by many people:

> *"I observed it all from a safe distance. I saw the bombs fall from the two planes and an FW 190 shot down immediately afterwards. Later that day I visited the crash site and saw that the plane had landed upside down in a ditch alongside an old drove road. It was reported at the time that a Canadian soldier had shot it down with a Bren gun but I still wonder if it had been hit earlier by Bofors or Lewis guns and he just finished it off. The coal and coking works and gasometer were the likely targets – one bomb destroyed houses in Marlow Avenue, the other fell on an electricity generating station."*
John Kingsley-Smith

> *"It was a lovely sunny summer holiday morning. Having just finished breakfast, I was sitting on the dining room window-sill looking south across the playing green. With that scenario, one could well imagine the shock of having*

Torcross under attack by 'Poldi'Wenger, 10/JG 2, 24 Aug 42 (Wenger)

Lysander T1696/AQ-H of 276 Squadron, lost on 24 Aug 42 (via Thomas)

The remains of Ofw Werner Kassa's fighter-bomber, 26 Aug 42 (Burgess)

The other 10/JG 26 pilot involved in the attack on Eastbourne – Uffz Richard Wittmann (Wittmann)

no warning when aircraft flying at 200 feet up and 400 mph towards me against the clear blue sky. I saw two aircraft, beautifully marked, side by side with the one nearer to me slightly in front, with the prominent black crosses on the underside of the wings and fuselage and the black swastika on the fin. The smart radial front of the BMW powered nose was new to me then. By the time I thought these FW 190s were lucky our Spitfires weren't around just then, the impudent intruders had gone, followed by a bang fairly nearby – the timber cooling tower of the works south of St Philips Avenue was hit.

"I was soon to discover that one of the FW 190s had turned clockwise and, passing the gasworks at Lottbridge Drove to turn south for home, was shot down by a Canadian Bren-gunner who fired a long burst from his parapet position on the flat roof over Caffyns armoured vehicle assembly workshops. I remember some days later, the dead pilot was stretchered away from the ditch he dived into. I also recall before these events, looking up at the Caffyns gun emplacement as I passed many times on returning home from playing on the Crumbles, hoping it would get many chances at target practice against the Hun whom I hated for so frequently disturbing my sleep and education!"

Basil Wootton

The bomb that hit the Eastbourne Corporation Electricity Works in Churchdale Road caused considerable damage and the Works was out of action for a number of days. The bomb that exploded in Marlow Road demolished a number of houses and damaged others. Three civilians either died in the attack or of their wounds and a further seven were injured.

For the remainder of August 1942, targets as far east as Folkestone and as far west as Falmouth were attacked, the attack against Falmouth on 29 August 1942 was the last of the month and resulted in the steamship *Jernfeld* being sunk in the harbour. September 1942 started badly for 10/*JG* 26. Shortly after attacking barracks at Lydd on the first day of September, white smoke was seen coming from the engine of *Ofw* Heinrich Wagner's aircraft, despite the German pilots reporting afterwards that they had not experienced any *Flak*. Wagner headed out to sea, jettisoned his canopy and ditched in the Channel but his fighter-bomber sank immediately, taking him with it. Three days later, it was 10/*JG* 2's turn to suffer their first casualty for nearly two months.

10/*JG* 2 had already attacked Ventnor on the Isle of Wight and Teignmouth on the first two days of September 1942. Then, an attack against Dartmouth on 3 September had been aborted due to weather and so on the evening of 4 September, six Focke-Wulf 190s led by *Lt* Leopold Wenger returned to one of their favourite targets – Torbay. Wenger wrote of the attack:

> *"On this day I flew with six aircraft to attack targets in the western Channel. We flew over the city of Torquay, which had already been bombed by us. The town of Paignton has had it this time. Trains, railway stations and large buildings were our targets. The British Flak was very intense and accurate..."*

There were many witnesses to this attack one of whom was Private Godfrey Riley, home on leave in Torquay:

> *"It was a lovely sunny evening and my aged aunt and myself were returning by bus from afternoon tea at Paignton when the bus suddenly stopped as three or four German planes swooped in from the sea, strafing the area. Everyone scrambled out of the bus and sheltered under or alongside a bus shelter. I well remember at that time that here I was, a fully trained soldier in uniform and how disappointed and helpless I was that I couldn't do anything about it! However, a big cheer went up as one plane was shot down and landed on the water's edge on the beach. I think it was shot down by a lone Lewis gun mounted on the cliff at Berry Head. The plane landed on the beach and was mostly burnt out except for one wing which was in the shallow water. I can well remember seeing the black cross on the wing as the waves lapped up against it. It was rumoured that a WAAF and her boyfriend were killed by the strafing whilst walking hand in hand and a few more were killed by the bombs† ..."*

†Section Officer Marjorie Hussey and her husband LAC John Hussey were killed in this attack and were buried together in Torquay Cemetery

Another witness was David Ince, a trainee at the Initial Training Wing who had the misfortune to be playing a game of rugby when the fighter-bombers attacked. In his book *Combat and Competition* he records having witnessed the last moments of 22 year-old *Uffz* Walter Höfer's life:

> "... as he pulled up, a flame appeared under the fuselage. He continued climbing and jettisoned the canopy, simultaneously rolling inverted but the nose dropped before he could get out. We learned later that a bombardier from the nearby coastal battery, armed with a single Lewis gun, had shot him down and probably saved our lives into the bargain."

Uffz *Walter Höfer* (via Irwin)

The remains of Walter Höfer's fighter-bomber burning on the beach (via Irwin)

'Tony' Liskutin (3rd from right) inspecting damaged inflicted on his Spitfire, 19 Aug 42 (Liskutin)

Yet again, the most effective way of shooting down 'tip and run' attackers was by light weapons and even if British fighters were scrambled chances of catching the Germans on the way home were slim. During this attack, two Spitfires of 312 Squadron were scrambled to intercept and even today, one of the Czech pilots involved, Sergeant Miroslav 'Tony' Liskutin, can remember every detail of the chase:

'Tony' Liskutin taxying in EP559/DU-V of 312 Squadron Harrowbeer, May 42 (Liskutin)

Fg Off Josef Pipa (Popelka)

"*...after scrambling with Joe Pipa [Fg Off J Pipa] from Bolt Head, we were directed to intercept four [sic] FW 190s in the Torbay area. Soon after settling on the given course, I spotted three aircraft low over the sea but already heading back towards France after a 'tip and run' attack against Torquay. I was puzzled why there were only three of them and why they were on the opposite course. I was not to know that one of the FW 190s was shot down over Torquay and flew into the beach just outside the Palm Court Hotel...*

"*At the moment of sighting, we were some five miles away from the enemy formation. After cutting the corner on them, the distance was reduced to well under a mile. My engine was at full power with the boost override beyond the gate and the propeller set at maximum revolutions. My Spitfire was gradually closing to about 700 yards when they spotted us. I was positioning behind the Number Three FW 190 and Joe was settling behind the Number Two. We needed just to halve the remaining distance and that would have been our day.*

"*Until then, we had no idea how the Spitfire Vb would compare in a real life race with an FW 190. Our pilots knew that there was no great difference in the performance between these two aircraft anyway, although the FW 190 would have been regarded as a marginal favourite. This occasion gave us the proof that at sea-level, we were exactly equal. Though it is difficult to believe, our speed was absolutely the same.*

"*The FW 190s were leaving a long trail of black smoke, as if their engines were on fire. This was a clear indication, if one needed it, that they were using their maximum power. So, all engines were labouring at their maximum but our distance remained constant. They were not pulling away, although I had the impression that we were gaining very slightly. However, despite my early optimism, my distance behind the Number Three FW 190 stabilised at about 650 yards. Without waiting any longer, Joe tried some shots at this distance while I was holding back my fire. It seemed that the only effect of Joe's firing was a temporary slight slowing down of his aircraft due to the recoil of his cannon.*

"*I was still hoping to close at least 100 yards to get a better chance of shooting. The black smoke pouring from their engines told me that they were labouring under a gross overload and would be unable to sustain it much longer. Although our Merlins were also restricted in the use of emergency boost, I felt confident we could stand it longer than the FWs. My engine temperatures and pressures remained constant and I was prepared to take the risk. In these conditions, my airspeed indicator was showing a steady 330 mph. There is no doubt that this was the true maximum speed of the Spitfire Vb and the FW 190 at sea-level in the Summer of 1942.*

"*Keeping up the pursuit, the minutes were ticking by and I realised that the distance between me and the Number Three FW 190 still remained steady at approximately 650 yards. Obviously there was nothing I could do about it. The conclusion eventually led me to the acceptance of having to shoot at this unfavourable distance. Under normal circumstances shooting at 650 yards with our 20mm cannons should be effective.*

"Then suddenly I realised I could not take aim. The Spitfire was not set up aerodynamically for this type of combat. My unusually high speed made the aircraft fly in a nose down attitude. This meant that the Spitfire was flying at sea-level with the nose pointing well below the horizon and, although I was sitting exactly behind the enemy aircraft, my gun sight pointed well below him into the waves.

"This was an extraordinary situation for which I had no answer. When I lifted the nose to place the gun sight onto target, my Spitfire started climbing and my engine covered the enemy from my view. There was also a small and temporary loss of speed with the gained height. Although I do not understand aerodynamics, at that time it hit me as a very strange and unexpected complication.

"Meanwhile our gaggle of aircraft was rapidly approaching the French Coast. The Cherbourg Peninsula appeared on the horizon and I knew that I could not go much further. Realising these limitations, I decided to play my last option: scatter shooting. Lifting the nose of my Spitfire up and down so that momentarily my gun sight was in the right position just above the nearest FW 190, I sprayed him with a long-ish burst from all my guns. It was unlikely to shoot him down but at least it was sure to cause some damage.

"At the same time as the enemy aircraft disappeared beneath my nose, I saw the first greetings from coastal batteries. Their flashes were pointing in my direction but it looked fairly inaccurate. In a harsh about turn, I disengaged and pushed the aircraft back down to sea-level on a course for home."

Despite the optimism of the Czech pilots, the remaining Focke-Wulf 190s landed undamaged at Théville.

It would appear that for the next two weeks, it was the south-west of England that was targeted and that these attacks were predominantly carried out by 10/*JG* 2. Unusually, on 17 September, 10/*JG* 2 carried out an attack on the gas works at Worthing, Worthing being almost in its sister *Jabostaffel*'s hunting ground. For the two German pilots involved, it almost ended in disaster for both of them as Fg Off Barry Needham of 412 Squadron remembers:

"'Pip' Powell [Plt Off Lloyd Powell] and I were sitting in our aircraft on readiness at Tangmere when we got the word to scramble. We immediately spotted two 190s and gave chase. Over the Channel, 'Pip' was able to catch up with his opponent while I chased mine more than half way across. Despite pushing the throttle though the gate, I wasn't able to get close. I fired my cannons at long range and observed some strikes warranting a damaged claim. I often wonder about how much damage I was able to inflict."

The interception was against two fighter-bombers flown by *Lt* Leopold Wenger and *Uffz* Hans-Walter Wandschneider. They had taken off from Caen each laden with a 500 kg bomb destined for Worthing but what they actually attacked was Bognor Regis, a popular target for the *Luftwaffe* and whose gasworks were bombed no less than seven times during the war. One bomb exploded on the rear of the West Parade Hotel in Goodman Drive in

Flt Lt Barry Needham (Needham)

Bomb damage at the rear of the West Parade Hotel, Bognor Regis, 17 Sep 42 (Burgess)

Damage to the gasworks, 17 Sep 42 (Hickman)

the town, killing one civilian and wounding seven, the other, dropped by
Wenger, passed through the gasholder and exploded on a mined bridge
behind it, the resultant explosion severing gas, water and electricity services.
A report written at the time stated what happened:

> "*At 1523 hours, the bomb landed at the bottom of an empty air seal-type
> centre gas holder, after losing two fins, one [of which] bent the iron ladder at
> side of eastern gas holder. It entered the centre gas holder, smashing a telescopic
> steel ladder inside, and emerged 50 feet up on west side, finally landing and
> exploding in the centre of the stream immediately under footbridge over gas
> mains on east side and causing explosion of land mines on main bridge.
> Damage: Two holes through large gas holder (empty), road-bridge destroyed,
> stopping all through traffic on A29. Destruction of three 12 inch gas mains,*

The effects of a 500 kg bomb and sympathetic detonations, Shripney Road, Bognor Regis, 17 Sep 42 (Burgess)

12 inch and 9 inch water mains, electric cable carried over bridge. Slight damage to gas works office. Water supply restored immediately via alternative route. Gas supply restored through temporary main on Saturday 19th. Shripney Road open to traffic on 25 September via temporary bridge…"

Again, 'Poldi' Wenger wrote home the following day and related what happened:

"Yesterday I flew a mission which unfortunately ended very tragically. Together with my Rottenflieger, a non-commissioned officer, I attacked the gasworks at Worthing. Flying at low level, I was able to place my bomb between the two gas holders where it detonated. All sorts of things were thrown into the air. My Rottenflieger meanwhile bombed the town. We made contact with British aircraft but managed to evade them and despite the heavy Flak, made it back out to sea. Mid-Channel we were completely surprised by Spitfires which attacked immediately. During the course of the dogfight, my Rottenflieger was killed. I saw him diving vertically into the sea. Then they hit my plane but I succeeded in making my escape. A 20mm shell tore the oil tank open and I lost so much oil that the whole plane looked like a sardine in oil. All was hideous – it went so quickly and I was not able to help [my Rottenflieger]."

The full combat report submitted by the two Canadian pilots match Wenger's account perfectly:

"...Green Section [Green 1 – Fg Off Needham, Green 2 – Plt Off Powell] *had been told to orbit base but shortly after being airborne, Green 1 saw two bombs bursting to the east and flew in that direction. They were then given a vector of 180 degrees and two e/a, identified as FW 190s which appeared to be orbiting were seen ½ a mile ahead in a position three to four miles south of Littlehampton. The e/a then turned south and Green Section gave chase, the e/a widening the gap to ½ mile but Green Section slowly closed with an Indicated Air Speed of 290-300 mph.*

"After approximately 10-15 minutes, both pilots had closed the range to 250 yards and each attacked one e/a. Green 2 opened fire with cannon and machine-gun from astern with a series of short bursts totalling 10 seconds whilst closing to 150 yards. After his first burst, he saw light blue smoke coming from the starboard side of the engine of the e/a which increased in volume and strikes all over the fuselage and tail plane. After the fourth or fifth burst, the e/a started to take evasive action consisting of gentle weaving turns. Strikes on the fuselage and tail plane were seen during two further bursts. Before the last burst, the e/a straightened out and flew low over the water and shortly after carried out a tight loop off the deck reaching approximately 700 feet and then dove into the sea without leaving any trace. At the top of the loop, the cockpit cover and what appeared to be armour plating came away from the e/a.

Green Section, 412 Squadron: L to R Barry Needham & Fg Off Lloyd 'Pip' Powell (+17 Jun 43) with Fg Off Hugh Maclean (Needham)

"Green 1 had closed in to 200-250 yards range on the other e/a when he opened fire from astern with a 1½ second burst seeing strikes all over the fuselage and tail plane. He fired several more short bursts totalling nine seconds from astern at the same range which he was not able to close. After these attacks, white smoke was seen coming from underneath the fuselage of this e/a.

"At this time the other e/a crossed over in front to the right about 300 yards away and pulled up over the vertical disappearing behind Green 1 who also carried out a climbing turn to 500-600 feet but could see no sign of the e/a. Green 1 then dived after the other e/a which was now ½ mile ahead but could not catch it. When last seen, it was flying south at sea-level five miles west of Le Havre issuing white smoke..."

Wenger was able to nurse his damaged aircraft back to Caen and on inspecting the engine, discovered a 20mm cannon shell in the oil tank. Barry Needham had managed to inflict damage on the fighter-bomber and in 2001 was sent the remains of the cannon shell by 'Poldi' Wenger's brother as proof!

As his Focke-Wulf 190 was damaged, much to his annoyance Wenger was not able to participate in an attack on Dartmouth the following day. The attack was yet again highly successful from a German viewpoint and both memorable and terrifying for Dennis Thyer who was a 14 year-old schoolboy at the time:

"It was a fine clear day, about 1000 hours and it was a Friday, I think. I did jobs for a fisherman who wanted me to row his dinghy to Dartmouth and fetch some diesel oil. Moored in the middle of the river opposite the Royal Dart Hotel was the Belfort, a converted cargo vessel which tended a fleet of a dozen or more MLs and MTBs. In the evening, many of these fast – well armed craft returned and moored alongside. At dawn, some left the harbour often with an outgoing convoy. Usually four or so craft remained alongside the mother ship. Further up the river two coal hulks were anchored...

"On arrival at Dartmouth, a large drum of diesel oil was lowered into the dinghy...I [had to row hard on the return] and the boat moved slowly with the current taking me a little up river. When about 20 yards abreast of the Belfort, I changed direction and headed parallel to her with the intention of turning across her bow to get around her. I was pulling hard against the current looking up river when I noticed three planes travelling over Noss from Hillhead direction. As these low-flying fighter-bombers passed over the shipyard, a bomb was dropped which caused a large explosion and initiated a smoke and dust cloud. Two of these planes, flying side by side, proceeded towards the Naval College whilst a third turned down river towards me. This aircraft, flying very low and with cannons firing, passed over the coal hulks and dropped a bomb which hit a small coaster tied alongside. By now, machine-guns were firing at the planes but some guns could not fire because the plane was flying so low and they feared hitting the houses on the opposite side of the river. There was a lot of noise which echoed and re-echoed within the valley. It was frightening.

"A couple of sailors on the mother ship were shouting and waving frantically at me to come to the side of the ship for protection. I could see the fighter flying towards the ship so I thought it wiser to stay in the open. In any case, I couldn't row fast enough to reach the ship in time. The plane passed, mast height, over the ship with its cannon blazing. The guns of the MLs and MTBs directly beneath were firing at it and the noise was deafening. Lewis guns, Oerlikon cannons, pom-poms and other guns all opened up. Something fell from the plane which looked like part of its landing gear but the plane flew on under intense fire towards the Castle and safety. I could clearly see the pilot, dressed in flying helmet and jacket, looking down towards Dartmouth as the aircraft flew over the ship. Two more planes then re-appeared from the Townstall direction, low-flying down the valley, over the market place and church before following the other plane towards the river mouth and away from the guns. One of these planes had dropped a bomb on the Naval College.

"The air raid siren started to sound as the planes were disappearing. When it stopped, there was a deathly silence. The air was saturated with smoke and the smell of cordite. I felt thankful that I was unharmed and recommenced rowing. I noticed that the small cargo vessel, the Fernwood, had sunk and the tops of its masts were sticking out of the water. The raid only lasted a minute or two but the happenings are as vivid now as they were then. I can still smell cordite when I recreate the picture in my mind."

One bomb fell on the Philip and Son shipbuilding yard. Philip and Son constructed vessels for both the Admiralty and the RAF including corvettes, minesweepers and minelayers and air-sea rescue and refuelling launches. The bomb fell on the machine shop, hitting a steel girder in the plating loft and exploded. The resulting damage was extensive and in the region of 20 of the workforce were killed and 40 injured. Nevertheless, despite the damage, the yard was partly working again two days later.

In addition to the shipbuilding yard, the coal hulk *Dagny,* collier *Fernwood* and a pontoon crane were sunk. Furthermore, ML155, HMS *Selkirk* and RFA *Berta* were all damaged. On land, two bombs were dropped on the Britannia Royal Naval College, one landing on 'B' Block, the other on the Quarter Deck. At the time of the attack, the cadets were on leave and a meeting was being held to discuss the evacuation of the college should it be attacked! The attendees had a practical demonstration of what to do and not to do and no one was hurt. Sadly, a member of the Women's Royal Naval Reserve was killed.

The following day, 10/*JG* 2 visited the area around Dartmouth again, attacking landing craft just outside the harbour, sinking Landing Barges 332 and 362 and damaging a tug. However, this would be the last attack in the west of England until the second week of October 1942 as the *Jabo's* focus now turned towards targets in Kent and Sussex.

It is believed that *Jabos,* presumably from 10/*JG* 26, attacked Bexhill and Hastings on the morning of 21 September and then Rye the following day;

Landing barges off Salcombe come under attack by 'Poldi' Wenger, 19 Sep 42 (Wenger)

these attacks resulted in minimal damage. However, the attack on Hastings two days later was more successful and had much greater repercussions.

As with a number of south coast towns, Hastings was being used as a holding unit for aircrew cadets prior to their departure overseas under the British Air Training scheme. Although no documentary evidence had been found, this must have been common knowledge to *Luftwaffe* intelligence officers, purely from the fact of the frequency that the hotels housing the trainee aircrew at such towns as Hastings, Eastbourne, Bournemouth and Torquay were attacked. On 24 September 1942, an early morning reconnaissance by 5/JG 26 reported shipping targets off Hastings. It is then known that two *Rotte* of *Jabos* attacked Seaford and Dymchurch early that afternoon and then a 'maximum strength' *Jabo* attack was apparently carried out against these ships at about 1700 hours Central European Time. However, at 1630 hours at least seven Focke-Wulf 190s, which had presumably broken away from the attack on the ships, streaked towards Hastings:

"It was about 1630 hours on a sunny afternoon when a group of about 30 of us cadets were returning to the Marine Court, Hastings after Physical Exercise on a playing field at the back of St Leonards when all hell broke loose. Number One FW 190 attacked at roof-top level and scored a direct hit on the dining room of the Marine Court. Number Two FW 190 attacked our unit and two large houses collapsed alongside us. There was no time to take cover. This was followed by cannon and machine-gun strafing. On the top of the Marine Court's flat roof was a lone Vickers machine-gun, manned I think by an Aussie named Hutchinson. He opened up but was obliged to fire downwards as the attacking aircraft were well below the height of the Marine Court complex. The net result was three cadets killed plus at least a dozen seriously wounded, although I believe that many of them recovered sufficiently to resume their flying training careers.

I was one of the fortunate ones and escaped with minor wounds to my head and backside. The bits of shrapnel from the cannon shells of the FW 190 were carefully removed and I went through to Canada only to be shot down in June 1944 but that is another story!† On reflection, I suppose that the casualty list could have been worse. On a lighter side and more personal note, my injuries compared with the rest were pretty superficial, mostly abrasions to the head. I was more concerned about my backside and being of a shy disposition, I did not report the matter to the busy medical staff. The next day, all was discovered and I got a well deserved roasting from Nursing Sister Moultrie when a neat pattern of cannon shell splinters were discovered in my seat!"

LAC Geoff Salisbury

"At about 1630 hours, after returning from some form of exercise or training, we had gone up to our quarters when there was a very big bang followed by machine-gun fire. We then saw a single-engined German aircraft speeding south at a very low altitude. It transpired that the aircraft had flown low over Hastings flying west, dropped their bombs, one of which hit a house in Warrior Square and the second one hit the eastern end of Marine Court. The aircraft then fired at a flight of our lads who were returning to Marine Court from the west of St Leonards and then beat a retreat over the sea.

"In the part of Marine Court where several of us occupied what would have been one of the flats, one of our number was having a bath (he had a red-hot date that evening!) when the bomb went off. The vibrations caused the enamel sides of the bath to crash to the floor and when he looked out of the window, all he could see was a cloud of white dust. He started shouting in a very concerned way (he had experienced bombing in London), saw the white dust and really thought he had 'bought it' and was in the clouds in heaven!

†Halifax serial MZ539 of 76 Squadron was shot down on the night of 28-29 June 1944. Sgt G E Salisbury and five crew evaded capture but the pilot was killed

Bembridge under attack, 26 Sep 42 (Wenger)

"By about 0500 hours the next morning, we had our breakfast, left our kit bags containing our flying clothing on our beds, marched in full kit to a goods yard to the west of St Leonards and boarded a train which took us to Harrogate in North Yorkshire..."
LAC W H Thomas

Whether by luck or judgement, the attack killed two trainees and 23 civilians, injured 27 trainees and 43 civilians and necessitated the move of the holding unit away from the threat of lightning raids.

Just four more 'tip and run' attacks are recorded as having took place before Summer rolled into Autumn, the worst one occurring at 0919 hours on 29 September 1942 when two *Jabos*, again believed to have come from 10/*JG* 26, successfully bombed the Betteshanger Colliery west of Deal in Kent, killing two and injuring at least 25.

The final three months of 1942 would now see a change in the tempo of 'tip and run' attacks but such raids would still remain a considerable headache to the British defences, forcing yet more means of effectively combating them.

6
New Tactics and Weapons

OCTOBER – DECEMBER 1942

October 1942 now saw a reduction in the number of 'tip and run' attacks with, for a change, Kent and Sussex receiving the majority. In order to ensure the success of attacks in this region, the fighter-bombers now had their own escorts but still the majority of aircraft lost during these months were due to anti-aircraft fire. With the raids now being undertaken by 10/*JG 26*, it must have been a relief to 10/*JG 2* not to lose a single *Jabo* in combat for nearly four months; the same cannot be said of 10/*JG 26*. Their first loss in combat in over a month occurred on 10 October 1942 when a *Schwarm* attacked gasworks west of Margate in Kent. The German records state that *Uffz* Werner Schammert was seen by his *Rottenführer* to turn right whilst he had turned left back out to sea. Schammert's fighter-bomber was then seen to climb and dive back towards land after which his *Rottenführer* saw a heavy barrage of *Flak* and despite flying up and down the coast for five minutes, no sign was seen of Schammert. The British report explains what happened:

> "This aircraft came in over Pegwell Bay at 150 feet and flew over Manston [airfield]. The pilot then flew a left-hand circuit over the Bay and came in for a second time over Manston at 500 feet. His bomb was aimed at dispersed aircraft but apparently fell short…
> "The pilot made a second left hand circuit to search for his Number One with whom he had lost touch during the previous runs. As he came over Manston, his aircraft was hit by AA fire and apparently set on fire slightly wounding the pilot. He pulled up to 1500 feet, baled out and his aircraft crashed into a house where it disintegrated…"

The Civil Defence records for Ramsgate describe the last moments of his aircraft:

> "People on their way to work saw a Focke-Wulf 190 descending in flames over the town. With a deafening report, the machine crashed into the rear of 27 Wellington Crescent and penetrated right through the building, the engine flying across Wellington Crescent and lodging in the railings surrounding the gardens. A fire broke out in the house which was wrecked but members of the National Fire Service braving exploding bullets quickly extinguished it. The pilot of the plane baled out as it was crashing and landed safely in an alleyway at the rear of Denmark Road."

Uffz *Werner Schammert, POW 10 Oct 42* (Schammert)

It would appear that Schammert's inexperience (he had only been with the *Jabostaffel* a few weeks) had got the better of him as the *Jabos* rarely carried out a second run because by then the defences were invariably ready.

It was about now that the RAF assigned a new weapon to counter the 'tip and run' raiders. The Hawker Typhoon had been introduced into service in early Summer 1942 and so far had proved to be a bit of a disappointment, even though its full potential had not yet been realised. In August 1942, the commanders of the three Typhoon squadrons complained that the Spitfire, not the Typhoon, was better used on offensive sweeps whilst the Typhoon's superior speed and fire power would be better used countering 'tip and run' Focke-Wulf 190s and therefore basing the three squadrons near the eastern, south-eastern and south-western coasts. This was accepted and by the end of September 1942, a total of five Typhoon squadrons were employed in this manner.

The tactics adopted by the Typhoon squadrons was another matter. It would appear that those developed by 609 Squadron of 15 patrols a day by two aircraft flying at low or even lower altitudes with a further two on 'cockpit readiness', were soon adopted by other squadrons. Standing patrols then positioned themselves two to six miles from the coast and waited. There was an additional hazard in that the Typhoon at some angles could look like its German opponent but this was partially solved by painting both the Typhoon noses white and black with white stripes under the wings. Still, success was hard to come by as a the Intelligence Officer of 609 Squadron wrote:

The remains of Schammert's FW 190 (After the Battle)

Enter the Typhoon-serial R7713/PR-Z 609 Squadron with L to R: Sgt Johnny Wiseman and Flt Sgt 'Babe' Haddon (both killed in action 14 Feb 43)

"…what with having to keep one eye on engine temperature, scan the air for enemy raiders, watch each gun position and Spitfire with suspicion and guard against crashing into cliffs or balloons, the whole enterprise seemed unprofitable. By the end of November [1942], with nothing to show for it, anti-aircraft fire had claimed one Typhoon, the weather two Typhoons and their pilots…"

Nevertheless, the first Typhoon success occurred on 17 October 1942. The loss report submitted by 10/JG 26 afterwards records what happened:

"After a Jabo attack on a block of flats in Hastings, moments after leaving the English coast at 1442 hours, they were attacked by two 'Tomahawk' fighters. Fw Niesel suddenly climbed to reach a layer of clouds at 300 metres. The Tomahawk flying behind Niesel followed while the second Tomahawk turned in and attacked him from the side. At 150 metres height, Fw Niesel turned left and dived; moments after that, he crashed into the sea at an acute angle. His Rottenführer did not see a parachute nor any wreckage on the sea after the attack."

486 Squadron had moved to the airfield at West Malling in Kent just a week before. Plt Off Gordon Thomas and Sgt Keith Taylor-Cannon had unsuccessfully tried to intercept a 'tip and run' attack on Rye on 14 October 1942 but three days later, Thomas, this time flying with Sgt Artie Sames, was more successful. Focke-Wulf 190s of 10/JG 26 had successfully attacked Hastings, hitting St Columbs Church, Warrior Gardens and Pevensey Road, killing two civilians and injuring another 16. It was when the German fighter-bombers were on the way back that the two 486 Squadron Typhoons pounced:

"At 1325 hours, when flying east to west at 500 feet about ½ mile inland, they observed two FW 190s flying roughly north-east over the sea at 20-30 feet and about 1½ miles ahead. Yellow 1 [Thomas] saw a bomb burst in the town [Hastings].

"The enemy aircraft then turned port due south and out to sea where they split up, one flying south-east at sea-level and the other continuing south at about 20-30 feet followed by Yellow Section flying at 345/350 at sea-level. Yellow 1 opened fire at long range with several short bursts of cannon fire and noticed splashes in the sea short of the e/a which immediately started to weave. Yellow Section closed to within 500 yards and the enemy aircraft began a spiral weave. Yellow 1 opened fire again with several more short bursts and observed strikes on the side of the fuselage. The e/a pulled up violently and then winged over to port and down to sea-level right across Yellow 2's [Sames] line of fire, then straightened out and climbed up slowly. Yellow 2 fired three short bursts at 200-250 yards striking the fuselage and engine. A jet of flames burst from the starboard side of the engine, the hood was jettisoned and parts of the aircraft fell away and it turned over and fell burning into the sea, disappearing immediately…"

Pilots of 486 Squadron, Dec 42: L to R: Fg Off Gordon Thomas, Flt Sgt Frank Murphy, Sgt Keith Taylor-Cannon, Sgt Artie Sames, Fg Off Spike Umbers & Plt Off Rupert Dall (via Thomas)

Despite this first success, it would be another two months before Typhoons were able to shoot down a second German fighter-bomber and in the meantime, the *Jabos* continued to prey on southern English coastal targets virtually unhindered and still meeting with considerable success.

The next *Jabo* success occurred on 21 October when four aircraft, presumably from 10/*JG* 2, attacked the small Devonshire town of Totnes. The attack was witnessed by 13 year-old schoolboy William Harvey:

> "*I was a pupil of Form IVa of the King Edward VI Grammar School at Totnes and for a fortnight during October 1942, Form IVa was required to assist in the potato harvest at the Dartington Hall Estate. This involved a line of about 30 boys drawn west to east down the steep field picking up the potatoes and bagging them as they were thrown to the ground by the digging machine.*
>
> "*Just before 1100 hours† on 21 October, I suddenly heard the sound of aircraft to our right and over the high hedge, I could see four aircraft approaching. The first noticeable detail seen was that the wings of the planes were clipped and in this split second, they were thought by myself and some of the others to be Mustangs but when we saw they were each carrying a bomb, there was a shout of 'Jerries!' and the whole band of potato pickers ran for the hedge.*

†The attack occurred at 1023 hours

10/JG 26 prepares for and takes off from Wizernes on another mission (Storsberg)

"On reaching the hedge, I was unable to see the aircraft but could hear explosions and machine-gun fire from behind the hedge which, of course, was from the direction of the town centre of Totnes. Suddenly, from behind the hedge at a height of no more that 100 feet came a Focke-Wulf 190. It flew as far as Dartington Hall, probably half a mile to the south of us, turned and came back over us towards Totnes town centre. The pilot's head was clearly visible as it passed overhead and I remember that the main colour of the aircraft appeared to be yellow. Following perhaps another half minute of machine-gun fire, I saw all four aircraft in line abreast heading east towards Paignton and disappearing into the distance.

During our midday meal break, I went to the town to ensure my family was safe and to see what damage had been done. Having made sure that my mother and brother were safe, I went into the town to see what had happened. I found that four bombs had been dropped. The first landed at the back door of a house in Priory Avenue, reducing the building to rubble. Miraculously, the two ladies in the kitchen at the time got away with cuts and bruises. The parish church was situated about 100 yards away from and above the bomb's impact – every window on the north side of the church was damaged. The second bomb hit the Penzance-bound platform at the railway station, killing an RAF officer† on the platform and demolishing the stationmaster's office and the roof of the footbridge. The third bomb exploded harmlessly in the garden of a house, narrowly missing a road bridge over the railway line. The fourth bomb landed in a field behind the creamery adjoining the railway station, only yards from a bridge which carried the railway over the River Dart."

Four days later, the *Jabos* struck again in Devon when four fighter-bombers attacked their favourite target of Torquay. LAC Jim Ferguson was serving on No. 1 Initial Training Wing and witnessed their arrival:

"I was billeted in the Sefton Hotel on the Esplanade and my room mate and I occupied a room with a sea view (no supplement!) on the second floor. We had just returned to the room after Church Parade and I saw three single-engined aircraft in close company coming in, low over the sea from the east. Reckoning myself to be good at aircraft recognition, I quickly identified them as RAF Typhoons. Wrong!

"In front of the Sefton, on the cliff top, was a sand-bagged anti-aircraft position, consisting of twin Lewis machine-guns and manned by a sergeant of the Durham Light Infantry. He got it right and began firing at these intruders, although I think that he would not have had the required range as the FW 190s (I had changed my tune) were a little to the south of us. There were sounds of exploding bombs so me and the other lad ran downstairs, out to the surface shelter at the side of the billet and on getting outside, I fell and got my 'best blue' covered in red Devon earth.

---

†Two civilians were killed in the attack and seven injured. Flt Lt Herbert Wood, a native of Totnes, was the RAF officer who was killed

"Later that morning, some of us were rounded up and told to do guard duty at the Palace Hotel down the road which had been hit. There was extensive damage to the building and numerous casualties…"

Following the outbreak of war, the Palace Hotel was selected to be an RAF officers' hospital. By the end of 1940, it was fully functional, treating in the region of 150 in-patients of all types. On Sunday 25 October 1942, the hospital was full with a total of 203 in-patients, one of whom was Fg Off Freddie Sowrey:

"I had joined 26 Squadron (Mustang Is) in March 1942. In August of that year, I developed an eye infection called Iritis where the iris sticks and can tear round the edges unless treated. With medical science at the time, this was a lengthy business and a spell at the RAF convalescent hospital at Torquay was thought to be a good way of putting people back into good shape.

"On Sunday 25 October 1942, I was going into Torquay for lunch but 1100 hours found me in the billiard room watching a very capable Polish player and standing by the large sash windows looking out to sea over the lawns and woodland in front of the Palace Hotel.

"Two aircraft appeared head-on, low, and I thought that they were Me 109s. When gun flashes appeared on the leading edges of the wings and strikes could be heard on the upper storeys, I decided that it would be safer to lie down under the window. There was a gigantic flash and I found myself head down under rubble, able to move only my left foot through approximately 15 degrees. After an unpleasant time with the weight increasing and other problems, my (barely) 20 years decided that there was little future in this so started shouting 'Get me out of here!' Ultimately, I heard a voice say 'There's one here' and digging started. A hole appeared and a wonderful British soldier found my hand which he held until my head was in the clear when a Woodbine or similar was stuck between my lips! I think that we were stretchered to the entrance hall and then to the local hospital for a few days before a hospital train was organised to take the survivors up to Loughborough…"

Fg Off Sowrey was one of the luckier ones. 14 RAF officers, the most senior being Gp Capt Humphrey Little, were killed as well as five staff, three of them female. Additionally, two members of the 10th Devon (Torbay) Battalion Home Guard were killed and a further 30 officers and 10 staff, all but one of the staff female, were injured. Just two bombs were dropped on the hospital – the first scored a direct hit on the south side of the east wing, wrecking two sections of the wing from roof to ground level. The second exploded 50 yards from the north-west corner of the west wing, landing on a main road, the blast from which extensively damaged the west wing. The majority of casualties resulted from the first bomb. The milk bar was one room that was destroyed and had the attack occurred just 24 hours later, it would have been packed with staff and patients exactly at the time of the attack; being a Sunday, luckily it was not open.

Two more 500 kg bombs were dropped on Babbacombe during the attack, the gas holder machine-gunned and three civilians injured; all four German aircraft returned to France unscathed.

The *Jabos* would carry out just one more attack in October 1942 which would yet again prove to be an embarrassment to the British. Adolf Hitler was becoming increasingly annoyed by Bomber Command's offensive and apparently ordered a full strength vengeance attack which was aimed against Canterbury. It was intended that this should be the biggest *Jaboangriff* to date and therefore 10/*JG* 2 and 10/*JG* 26 were to operate at full strength. The two *Jabostaffel* were further reinforced by eight or nine aircraft from *Hptm* Helmut-Felix Bolz's II/*JG* 2 as well as an unknown number from *Hptm* Willi Hachfeld's III/*ZG* 2. This latter unit formerly flew Messerschmitt 110s and had been withdrawn from the Mediterranean to Cognac in western France in September 1942. They then started to convert to the Focke-Wulf 190 and when combat ready, would return to North Africa in order to undertake anti-shipping operations.

Uffz *Heinz Ehrhardt on a training flight; Ehrhardt would later fly with 1/SKG 10* (Ehrhardt)

The German pilots were informed of the attack three days in advance and it was set for the evening of 31 October. III/*ZG* 2 and 10/*JG* 2 positioned at Merville and at 1740 hours Central European Time, took off and headed north. Records disagree as to the size of the total force – British records say that 30 aircraft attacked, some German records say 52, some say 58, including escorts, whilst another well respected historian states that the escort numbered 62 Focke-Wulf 190s, the *Jabos* totalling 68†.

†The number of bombs dropped would indicate that there were in the region of 30 *Jabos*

Nevertheless, the attack came as a total surprise to the British defences and to those on the ground in Canterbury:

"We lived approximately a mile from the city centre and immediately opposite the barracks. I was eight at the time and had gone on an errand that Saturday afternoon to the top of St Martin's Hill. I was riding my bike back along the pavement when, without any previous warning siren, a 'Tugboat' sounded (meaning attack imminent). I had just passed the gap between numbers 14 and 15 Littlebourne Road (I lived at 26) and almost immediately I saw a German plane flying towards me, parallel to the houses, and just above rooftop level, heading for the city. It was so low that I could see the pilot's face quite clearly.

"At the same time, I could see my Mother rushing down our front steps and running down the road towards me. We dashed into the Anderson Shelter in the garden of Number 22 and squeezed in with several other neighbours and children who had been at Number 23. Shortly afterwards, we heard an explosion. We children were over-excited and I remember the little girl who lived at Number 14 hoping it was her house that had 'caught it'. Her wish came true! We discovered afterwards that a bomb had gone through the roof of Number 14, through a wardrobe and out of the corner and down a bank. It then ploughed a furrow in the road, jumped the hedge and sped across the playing fields to explode in the dining room of the Barracks..."
Mrs Pam Jarman.

"I remember settling down to a snack and a cup of tea. One of our cats was asleep in the room with me. Suddenly there was an enormous explosion. I am not sure whether the air raid siren had sounded but I was inclined to disregard them, there being so many during that day.

"I rushed downstairs where we had a Morrison wire cage type of shelter in a room at the back of my Father's shop. As I was approaching the doors, there was another huge explosion and the door leading to the yard was blown off its hinges and crashed into me. I managed to make the extra few yards to the shelter but was in a very dazed state luckily with only a few bruises.

"The raid was over in a few minutes and although my father's shop was not damaged, our living accommodation upstairs was caught in the blast with some walls, ceilings and windows badly damaged. The cat that was with me in the room when the first explosion occurred was missing for several days – where he went to we never knew!"
Roy Arnold

The Canterbury City Police report for the attack makes more sombre reading:

"At 1709 hours, a sharp attack was made on the city by a formation of between 30 to 40 fighters and fighter-bombers. The planes came in from the direction of Dover – the fighter-bombers, consisting of about 12 machines [sic] flying at roof top level. The latter dropped between 20 and 25 HEs and all the planes carried

out an indiscriminate machine-gunning of the City and the area around.

"*Considerable damage was caused to private dwelling houses on this occasion. The Electricity Works suffered some damage from blast. Supply was not interrupted and later the undertaking switched over to the Grid system. One HE fell near a public service vehicle which was proceeding from Herne Bay to Canterbury and nine people were killed by glass and blast.*

"*On this occasion, the Local Danger Warning sounded about two minutes before the attack and the Public Air Raid Warning one minute after the Local Danger Warning. Therefore, although the raid was sudden, the public appreciate that the warning system was not at fault.*"

Pilots of 10/JG 26, early Oct 42. L to R: ?, Uffz Werner Schammert (POW 10 Oct 42), Fw Emil Boesch (+12 Mar 43), ?, Uffz Richard Wittmann, Ofw Karl-Heinz Knobeloch (+ 28 Oct 44), Uffz Erich Schwarz, Uffz Alfred Immervoll (+23 Jan 43) (Wittmann)

From a German viewpoint, the attack was yet another success. The German formation joined up over Calais and headed north at zero feet, maintaining complete radio silence. The fighter escort, made up from both *JG* 2 and *JG* 26, was instructed to remain close to the *Jabos* and only to climb when they had attacked the target. The formation approached the Kent coast at wave-top height in three waves, crossing near Deal, then hedgehopped towards the outskirts of Canterbury where they climbed, dropped in the region of 31 bombs which killed in the region of 30 people† and damaged countless buildings, and then streaked back for France.

†Canterbury Police records state that 29 civilians were killed, 53 detained in hospital and 42 slightly injured and not detained. Military casualties are uncertain

British defences claimed to have shot down 10 fighter-bombers and suspected a further aircraft had been destroyed when it hit a balloon cable. The actual losses were much less. *Uffz* Alfred Immervol's fighter-bomber lost

Uffz *Ernst Henning (+24 Sep 43)* and Fw *Alfred Hell,* 5/JG 2 (Hell)

part of its wing when it collided with a balloon cable but he landed safely whilst the only aircraft to be actually shot down during the attack was flown by *Fw* Alfred Hell of 5/*JG* 2, who was acting as one of the temporary *Jabos:*

> "*...We took off from an airfield in Belgium at 1800 hrs. Over land we formed three waves and turned in the direction of the coast. We were flying very low over the sea (wave-hopping). Some minutes later we reached the English coast and by hedge-hopping we approached Canterbury where we climbed and dropped the bombs.*
>
> "*I was in the third wave and was flying on the left side. Far left I could see a*

balloon barrage and in my aircraft I could feel the blast of the exploding bombs. After the bombs had been dropped we turned and flew back, at low level, shooting at several targets with our guns. During this return flight I suddenly felt a hard blow, saw smoke coming from the engine and the aircraft began to shake.

"At the same moment I pulled the joystick, gained some height, jettisoned the canopy and, after unfastening the seat belts, I jumped high over the aircraft's tail unit keeping a firm hold on the ripcord. I pulled the ripcord, the parachute opened at once and after swinging back and forth I hit the ground. When I came to again, I must have been dazed for some time, some British officers were standing in front of me and the road to captivity began."†

To add further embarrassment, during the dogfights that followed the attack, Fg Off Ronald Gibbs of 91 Squadron and Fg Off Geoff Galwey of 453 Squadron were shot down, Gibbs being killed. Claims were submitted by *Lt* Josef Wurmheller of 1/*JG* 2 for two Spitfires and one Spitfire each for *Ofw* Willi Stratmann of 2/*JG* 2, *Hptm* Helmut-Felix Bolz of *Stab* II/*JG* 2 and *Fw* Johann Edmann of 5/*JG* 26. Additionally, a Typhoon of 609 Squadron flown by Plt Off Roy Payne was probably shot down by Plt Off Donald Mercer of 122 Squadron. Payne thought he had been shot down by friendly anti-aircraft fire and baled out over Pegwell Bay whilst Mercer reported shooting down a Focke-Wulf 190 into Pegwell Bay at exactly the same time. Despite RAF fighters claiming six destroyed and four damaged, the only loss was *Lt* Paul Galland of 5/*JG* 26. Paul, the younger brother of Adolf Galland, was sadly killed.

One of the unlucky RAF pilots-Plt Off Roy Payne (right) with Plt Off Gilbert of 609 Squadron

One of the successful fighter pilots on 31 Oct 42, Lt Josef Wurmheller of 1/JG 2 (Morzinek)

†*Fw* Hell was flying a Focke-Wulf 190 A-2, *Wk Nr* 5250 coded black 2. He was hit light AA fire and after baling out, his aircraft crashed at Little Stonar near Sandwich at 1705 hours

10/JG 2 seen at Marseilles-Istres, 29 Nov 42 (Wenger)

As a vengeance attack, the attack on Canterbury was an unmitigated success with the British acknowledging that 70% of the total weight of bombs fell in the target area but at the same time failing to acknowledge their failure to intercept the raid†.

The attack of 31 October 1942 was the last 'tip and run' attack of any note for over a month as on 8 November 1942, American forces landed in north-western Africa and the Germans immediately moved fighter units, including both *Jabostaffeln*, to southern France as a precaution against any Allied invasion. 10/*JG* 2 was the first to depart, flying to Marseilles-Istres on 9 November with 10/*JG* 26 joining them five days later. 10/*JG* 26 was by now commanded by *Oblt* Kurt Müller who had joined the *Staffel* in October 1942 from *Jagdfliegerschule* 2. Twenty-five year-old Müller was an experienced fighter-pilot, having flown with 2/*JG* 1 and 8/*JG* 27 until January 1941 and was already the holder of the *Frontflugspange in Gold* for fighters. He took command on 4 November 1942 from *Oblt* Paul Keller, who moved to command 4/*JG* 26; 'Bombenkeller' was destined not to be with his new *Staffel* for long.

Both *Jabostaffeln* had a very quiet and no doubt relaxing time on France's Mediterranean coast especially as no operational flights were flown. For those who had been flying 'tip and run' missions for a number of months, the stress must have been starting to show. Indeed, some pilots

†AWA Report Number BC/G/11 p.2

had already been quietly replaced and a number had turned to drink as a way of coping. In a letter home, *Lt* Leopold Wenger, whose short holiday was not without incident, wrote:

> " *I have sat on the Mediterranean coast for some days and have tried to put right all parts of my body again. Indeed, I did not arrive by aeroplane but by railway because all that is left of my plane is a heap of wreckage. During a flight over the French hills on 17 November, my engine failed suddenly and I had to make an immediate force landing. The ground was mountainous and therefore not very promising. Nevertheless, I almost would have succeeded in carrying out a good belly landing if there had not been a two metre high stone wall around the narrow meadow. Since I had no alternative, I had to go through it, whether I liked it or not. In the course of the landing and because of the impact, I lost consciousness and luckily for me, my plane did not catch fire. However, I soon regained consciousness after the plane or should I say the part in which I was sitting had finally come to a standstill. To my great amazement, I saw the whole tail of my beautiful aircraft stuck in the ground 10 metres away on my right. Now I wanted to get out but I couldn't open the cockpit. I managed to blow off the cabin roof with the help of the built-in explosive charge and then climbed out. However, I could not step onto the wings as I normally did as they were simply not there. I gradually lost my energy but fortunately two Frenchmen came along, supported me and dragged me to a car. After questioning at the Gendarmerie in Givors, they took me to the nearest hospital…*"

Whilst the two normal *Jabostaffel* were away, one III/ZG 2 was still re-equipping and training at Cognac and it would appear that, in order to gain experience flying missions with the Focke-Wulf 190, some attacks were carried out by them. The only recorded attack undertaken by this unit alone occurred on 3 November 1942. Four fighter-bombers from 8/ZG 2 carried out what they described as a *Terrorangriff* against Newton Abbot in Devon. The four aircraft never made it as far as Newton Abbot, preferring to drop four 500 kg bombs on Teignmouth. They then split – two headed out to the south-west over the sea whilst a second *Rotte* turned towards Torquay, machine-gunning Maidencombe. However, as the four fighter-bombers joined up again and headed for France, they were intercepted by two Typhoons of 257 Squadron flown by Fg Off Geoffrey Ball and Plt Off Pete Scotchmer both of whom had been on cockpit readiness for just such and attack. Geoffrey Ball wrote in his combat report:

> "*I was leader of Blue Section on standby at Bolt Head and we were scrambled on a vector of 120 degrees. We actually flew on 140 degrees for three minutes and then turned onto 120 degrees for five minutes. My Number 2 heard the controller transmitting so we pulled up from sea-level to 1000 feet to hear the message 'Aircraft to starboard'. I weaved to starboard and to port and saw four FW 190s in wide line abreast at sea-level heading south three to four miles in front of me. I told my Number 2 '12 o'clock' and we dived in a right hand turn,*

Pilots of 257 Squadron – Fg Off Geoff Ball is at the front, 2nd from the left (via **Rayner**)

Plt Off Peter Scotchmer (via **Rayner**)

coming two miles behind them at sea-level. After a six minute chase at 360 IAS, I was in range of the outside left e/a which made gentle turns to port and starboard as if undecided as to what evasive action to take. At 300 yards I fired a four second burst from astern to 10 degrees deflection. After strikes and a flash on the starboard side of the cockpit and engine, I saw a column of smoke and pieces flying off the aircraft as it hit the sea. I pulled up to starboard after another e/a which I lost sight of through my windscreen being misted up. I started to chase the fourth e/a but thinking that the other two were behind me, I turned to see where they were and saw wreckage of my e/a on the water and a burning oil patch from the e/a shot down by my Number 2. As fourth e/a was a long way ahead and nearly over the French coast and third e/a was lost in cloud, I told my Number 2 to return to base independently…"

Both *Lt* Hermann Kenneweg and *Uffz* Johann Hannig were killed; III/ZG 2 never flew further attacks against the British mainland and moved to North Africa shortly afterwards.

Despite the *Jabos* being in the south of France, as an interim measure, German fighters were now instructed to carry out a series of *Störangriff* or *Tiefangriff*, harassing or nuisance attacks against anything and everything but using machine-guns and cannons, not bombs. The first such attack apparently took place on 29 November 1942 but resulted in the death of *Ofw* Heinrich Bierwith of 5/JG 26:

"On 29 November 1942, two FW 190s carried out a low-level cannon attack on the Ashford Running Shed where I was serving my engineering apprenticeship. A locomotive fireman, George Barnes, was killed by a cannon shell on the footplate of his engine. The two planes flew on across Romney Marsh and attacked a two-coach passenger train leaving Lydd station hauled by a D3 Class tank engine Number 2365. The leading FW 190 opened fire without any apparent effect. The second plane flew so low that it hit and ripped away the steam dome of the locomotive's boiler. The resulting explosion of high-pressure steam caused the aircraft to crash, disintegrating over a wide area. The pilot's body was found later in a drainage ditch. The loco's crew were unhurt except for some scalds sustained by the fireman.

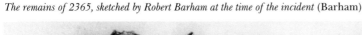

The remains of 2365, sketched by Robert Barham at the time of the incident (Barham)

"I was one of those despatched to recover the wrecked loco and was posted on its footplate to monitor any bits that might fall off! It was a very cold and frosty morning and the ride home was not a comfortable one. The locomotive was repaired and back in service six weeks later..."
Robert Barham

A *Störangriff* the following day was more unusual but also resulted in two more German deaths. The attack was carried out by two Focke-Wulf 190s of 4/*JG* 26, flown by *Lts* Wilhelm Cadenbach and Roland Prym. Roland Prym had joined 5/*JG* 2 in October 1941 before transferring to 4/*JG* 26 in March 1942 and it must have been nostalgic for him when his *Staffel* was temporarily moved to II/*JG* 2's airfield at Beaumont-Le-Roger a few days before the attack.

Lt *Roland Prym, 4*/JG *26* (Prym)

Shortly after midday, both aircraft took off and headed north. The exact route flown by the German fighters is not known. However, at 1225 hours a Boulton Paul Defiant of 2 Anti-Aircraft Cooperation Unit which was engaged on a target-towing exercise to the west of the Isle of Wight, was attacked by a Focke-Wulf 190, presumably flown by either Cadenbach or Prym (no other German claims were submitted at this time). The pilot, Fg Off Stephen Rowland, was wounded but the Canadian drogue operator, Sgt Robert Brookes, was fatally wounded. Just under 20 minutes later, two Focke-Wulf 190s were seen approaching Exeter airfield, opening fire on the main runway and runway extension, wounding six workmen. Oblivious to what was going on below him, Sqn Ldr Douglas Wilson DFC, who was flying Hurricane AE979 of the Royal Aircraft Establishment's Experimental Section, soon became the focus of German attentions:

"I was on my way to Haldon Racecourse where I was going to carry out an impact on a balloon cable ('my' balloon being tethered to a second to recover same after loss of its cable). I was just south-south-west of Exeter when I was shot up by two FW 190s in turn. At the time, I was almost directly above Exeter Airport at around 3,000 feet and never saw the 190s. The reason? My sliding

hood was solid metal (top half) and metal grid on the sides to prevent the chance of a whirling balloon cable from taking off my head! So I had very limited side view, nil back view but normal forward view. I remember the cannon shells coming up my backside, then a frightful bang as my aircraft's backside was hit.

*"So I jettisoned my hood and had a good look around. By this time the 190s had gone – whither I knew not. I was, too, somewhat preoccupied with my predicament. I was able, after a little while, to reduce speed but found that I could not maintain height. Even with the control column fully back, wheels and flaps down didn't help. I just continued to lose height. Being directly over the airfield, and by now too low to bale out (and remember thinking 'Not B***** likely'), I decided to attempt a landing and reckoned that the wheels would take the shock without too great a risk of doing damage to myself.*

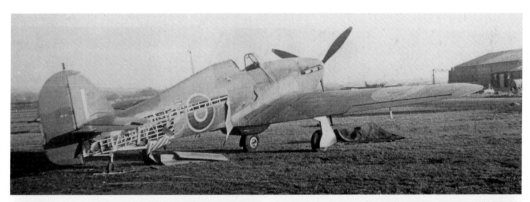

The damage inflicted to Douglas Wilson's Hurricane (Wilson)

"On coming into land on the runway, a sudden thought came to mind – if you close the throttle suddenly, the nose drops, conversely if you open it quickly, the nose rises. So, just before touching the ground, I opened the throttle and as the nose rose quickly, cut the engine. The result – one of the best three-point landings I had ever done!! Needless to say, I was delighted.

The Hurricane was so badly damaged in the attack that it had to be written off. However, the German pilots were not aware of this and what happened afterwards is revealed in two official sources. First is the Operations Report from HQ 3 Anti-Aircraft Group:

"[One] aircraft then climbed steeply to about 2,000 feet and made off down the Exe Estuary. It was neither seen nor heard by Light AA Exmouth. Troop Commander Light AA Teignmouth states that he saw an aircraft in the neighbourhood of Landstone Cliff which, while endeavouring to fly at wave top height along the coast, crashed into the sea almost certainly on account of either engine failure or misjudgement by the pilot. A convoy previously reported to have destroyed this aircraft was at least five miles off the coast whereas this aircraft went into the sea about 2,000 yards off the coast..."

The fate of the second Focke-Wulf 190 is related in a terse message from the Commander-in-Chief Plymouth to the Admiralty:

JG 26 Damage caused to a 91 Squadron Spitfire (either serial W3445 or BM517) during a Störangriff on Lympne, 11 Dec 42 (Nash)

"Following received from NOIC Dartmouth. Begins. Attack on HMT FINESSE and WILLIAM MANNELL. A. Nov 30th. B. 1247 [hours]. C. 080 [degrees] Berry Head 15 miles. D. NW. E. Low dive. F. One FW 190. Plane shot down by light armament of FINESSE. Pilot killed."

So far, these attacks had cost *JG* 26 dear but they continued for much of December 1942 with only one more loss occurring when, on 7 December, *Ogefr* Willi Muskatewitz of 1/*JG* 26 killed himself by flying into Oxendean Hill near Jevington in East Sussex. However, with the threat of invasion receding, it was decided to bring the two *Jabostaffeln* back from their enforced holidays. 10/*JG* 2 had returned to Caen on or about 12 December 1942 and probably flew their first *Jaboangriff* on 14 December when two of them each dropped a 500 kg bomb on military targets north-west of Lulworth in Dorset. This is the first time during the month that German records mention Focke-Wulf 190s dropping bombs as opposed to purely machine-gunning. On returning from this attack, the two fighter-bombers met head on with two Westland Whirlwinds of 263 Squadron which had been on patrol north of Barfleur. Fg Offs Max Cotton and John Coyne claimed to have damaged one of the German aircraft but their optimism was better than their aim!

Two days later, 10/*JG* 2 carried out another 'tip and run' attack, this time dropping four bombs on the centre of Stoke Fleming in Devon. 10/*JG* 26 had apparently returned from Istres on 11 December and its first recorded attack was on the afternoon of 19 December; it was destined to be a mission from which its new *Staffel Kapitän* would not to return.

*Armourers in front of Wk Nr 081, Blue 3 of 10/*JG* 2 (Wenger)*

The target that afternoon was housing eight kilometres north of Deal. The German pilots reported hitting the target with all four 500 kg bombs after which a fire-ball and large plume of smoke were seen. There was only one casualty, apparently to *Flak* – the aircraft flown by *Oblt* Kurt Müller. However, Fg Off Raymond 'Cheval' Lallemand of 609 Squadron claimed a Focke-Wulf 190 destroyed in the right area at the right time:

"Yellow Section was on standing patrol off North Foreland-Dungeness and was three miles south of Ramsgate flying north at 1,000 feet (owing to haze) when Controller reported bandits north of Dover flying north. Two FW 190s were then sighted at 150/200 feet in line abreast going south-east from Deal. Yellow 1 selected starboard e/a and opened fire at 800 yards in an attempt to slow it down but saw no results. He closed to about 500 yards and fired another short burst allowing slight deflection as e/a was turning and weaving. He closed still more and fired a third time. He was aiming for a fourth burst when e/a began a climbing turn and Fg Off Lallemand saw flames pouring from the cockpit as e/a was in a vertical bank. E/a then seemed to slide towards the water and almost inverted as it hit the sea..."

Fg Off 'Cheval' Lallemand

Lallemand's wingman Flt Sgt *'Babe'* Haddon damaged another Focke-Wulf 190 and then Lallemand, just as he was about to land, saw an aircraft *'diving towards the sea near Ramsgate, evidently hit by the guns'*. As Müller's was the only German aircraft lost, Lallemand's report is fairly conclusive as are the vivid memories of Frank Standen, a crew member of High Speed Launch 127 which was based at Ramsgate:

"I have referred to my Skipper's diary in which he recorded the various 'pick ups' we made and the entry for 19 December 1942 is as follows:
Position 060° Deal Coast Guard one mile. Type: German fighter-bomber (bombed Sandwich). Personnel: Lt Muellins [sic] (dead) multiple injuries.

"We were on standby in harbour when a raid was taking place over Sandwich. We could see air activity in the Deal area and decided that we should put to sea in case we were needed. As we headed towards Deal, we spotted an aircraft circling and realised it was marking something in the water. This turned out to be a parachute still floating and we picked up the shrouds and recovered a body of a Luftwaffe pilot who was well and truly dead.

"We approached the floating parachute slowly, this being on our port bow with no body visible. I was 'up forrard' and fished about with a boathook to locate the shrouds which were well below the surface of the water and were running under the bow to the starboard side. We worked the 'chute around the bow to the starboard side and commenced to draw the shrouds on board. As we did, a body appeared from beneath the water and seemed to be without a flying helmet as I could see the back of the head with hair and indeed ears. We worked the body to the starboard crash nets that were aft of our wheelhouse and yelled to the Skipper that the pilot was dead and that we were not sure what nationality he was. As he was being circled by one of our aircraft, we assumed that he was one of ours. We retrieved the canopy and placed that on the deck aft of our mast and then about four of us managed to get the remains aboard.

"Oblt Muller [sic] had been hit by a couple of 20mm shells which left very little of his body to recover. We bundled the remains in some balloon fabric which we always carried for such unfortunate retrievals and despite this, when we returned to Ramsgate, the Naval medical officer insisted on opening it up before he pronounced poor Oblt Muller dead."

The remains of Kurt Müller are hauled aboard HSL 127 (Standen)

With yet another *Staffel Kapitän* lost, *Oblt* Paul Keller, who had in the meantime been awarded the *Deutsches Kreuz in Gold*, was recalled from 4/*JG* 26 to take command of the *Jabostaffel*; his time as *Staffel Kapitän* would last a little over three more months.

For the remaining days of December 1942, a mixture of *Störangriff*, *Tiefangriff* and *Jaboangriff* were carried out. The only days that bombs were recorded as being dropped by fighter-bombers were 22, 29 and 30 December. The raid on 29 December was unusual as it appears to have been carried out by a *Rotte* from 8/*JG* 2, led by the *Staffel Kapitän Oblt* Bruno Stolle. Their target was Eastbourne and despite not being seasoned *Jabo* pilots, their attack had the inevitable results as the police at Eastbourne recorded:

> "...at 1456 hours, two enemy aircraft dropped bombs on the Borough. The machines are believed to have been FW 190s and two 500 kg bombs were dropped.

Paul Keller returns to take command of 10/JG 26 (Storsberg)

Oblt Bruno Stolle, 8/JG 2 (Stolle)

> "The planes made a run over the Town from a west to east direction, machine-gunning as they dived – the first bomb landing in the allotments adjacent to the Gildredge Hospital. This bomb ricocheted over Longland Road, striking a chimne- stack, over Dillingbrough Road, passing through Number 67 Victoria

Drive and exploding in Number 62 Victoria Drive opposite. After having struck the ground it travelled an approximate distance of 200 yards before it exploded.

"The other bomb exploded in the grounds of Court House, Moat Croft Road, burying itself fairly deep in the soft ground before it exploded…"

Two civilians, one aged 77, the other 85, were killed an at least 33 more were wounded. Two houses were destroyed, three extensively damaged and countless more suffered varying degrees of damage. If this was not bad enough, after dropping his bomb, Bruno Stolle bounced a pair of Spitfires from 91 Squadron on patrol off Beachy Head and the Spitfire flown by recently married and recently commissioned Plt Off Irvin Downer was shot down and its pilot killed.

The year for both *Jabostaffeln* finished on 30 December, with six aircraft from 10/*JG* 2 briefed to attack Newton Abbot in Devon in the morning and four from 10/*JG* 26 briefed to attack Bexhill in the mid-afternoon. Both formations failed to attack their intended targets. Instead, 10/*JG* 26 attacked Camber, south-west of Dungeness, whilst 10/*JG* 2 dropped their bombs on Exeter, as was witnessed by Michael Payne:

"It was a weekday during the school Xmas holiday because I was cycling across the river to pass a message to a teacher for my father (a deputy head) who was organising the start of the new term.

Stolle's victim on 29 Dec 42-Plt Off (seen here as Flt Sgt) Irwin Downer (Nash)

"I was on the main bridge and saw a FW 190 come low up the river, right overhead, and an explosion near the industrial site near the Basin (coasters came up the canal with coal, timber, petrol, cement, etc). The other aircraft were over the city, flashing over the view between buildings so quickly that I thought it was a 109 – but not so. Later, I heard about (and saw) a house demolished by a bomb about a mile down-river, a sort of 1800s villa only about a quarter of a mile from the extensive barracks later occupied by Americans. I also learned later that the explosion I saw was a bomb that had bounced out of the gasworks area (beside the Basin)..."

Six 500 kg bombs landed in widely separated districts of the City, numerous buildings were damaged and destroyed, seven civilians killed and an unknown number injured. Yet again, the 'tip and run' attackers had successfully bombed their target (albeit they could have made a mistake by flying up the River Exe instead of the Teign), wreaked death and destruction and yet again got away unscathed.

So ended the first year of 'tip and run attacks. The Home Office, amongst other political and military organisations, was quick to analyse the successes and failure of these attacks over the preceding nine months. In an end of year report, produced by the Key Points Intelligence Directorate:

"It is clear that attacks were directed against gas and electricity undertakings, railways, trains and in some cases a terror raid was made on residential and shopping areas. Gas works and electricity undertakings in exposed coastal sites provide in themselves a good target and it may well be that the enemy were encouraged to develop these attacks in view of the repeated warnings of the Government for the necessity of limiting both industrial and domestic fuel. The undertakings at Brighton suffered severely in the several attacks made on them and as a result of the attack on the St Ives undertaking in August, domestic supplies were held up for about two months..."

Analysis carried out by the War Office on 'tip and run' attacks up to the end of 1942 was even more blunt. Bearing in mind that the maximum number of fighter-bombers available to the *Luftwaffe* at this time was in the region of twenty-eight, 40% of all daylight attacks in 1942 were carried out by *Jabos*, with low-level attacks being preponderant in the latter half of the year. Four out of every five fighter-bombers attacked recognisable military targets, average efficiency on each attack was 71% and German losses had been light.

From a British viewpoint, the small number of German fighter-bombers was creating far more work for the Observer Corps, RAF and anti-aircraft defences than they should have. In addition to an expansion of the Observer Corps satellite posts and increased fighter defences using new (and untried) tactics, the increase in anti-aircraft defences was dramatic. The numbers of light anti-aircraft guns assigned to combat 'tip and run' attacks rose from 43 in March 1942 to 543 in November 1942. Searchlight battery personnel were withdrawn from their primary duties and trained to man twin machine-guns whilst the RAF Regiment anti-aircraft guns and personnel and 400 Royal Navy rocket projectors which fired wire obstacles into the paths of enemy aircraft were also assigned to the battle†. Despite all of this:

> *"the increase in gun strength was not accompanied by any corresponding rise in the success rate…The first big weakness lay in the early warning arrangements which failed to record raid approach or did so too late. Out of forty-four attacks in August 1942, only eight were preceded by radar warning…"* ††

These downbeat reports appeared to hold out little hope and the future for southern Britain which, despite new tactics and weapons, still appeared bleak.

1943 would bring mixed fortunes for both the British and the *Luftwaffe* and neither side could have envisaged that the campaign would only continue for just over another five months.

†Routledge, N W (1994) p.403
††Ibid

7
Worse to Come

JANUARY – FEBRUARY 1943

The result of 10/JG 26's attack on Bexhill, 2 Jan 43 (Saunders)

There would be a two-day respite for both the attackers and defenders before the 'tip and run' attacks began again on 2 January 1943. The first raid took place around breakfast time when 10/*JG* 26 attacked Bexhill, the four pilots reporting good hits on housing. Just after midday, it was 10/*JG* 2's turn when eight of them attacked Kingsbridge in Devon, reporting hitting the town centre. On the way back, the German pilots spotted two Spitfires off Start Point and in a brief dogfight, felt certain they had shot one down as it was seen to have been hit by cannon fire. As 310 Squadron's Operations Record Book states, this was almost the case:

Kingsbridge under attack-1237 hrs, 2 Jan 43 (Wenger)

"At 1150 hours, Yellow Section was ordered to carry out an anti-Rhubarb patrol Torquay to Start Point, being relieved by White Section, pilots Plt Off Ladislav Zadrobilek (Spitfire AR610) and Plt Off Karel Zouhar (Spitfire AB467). This Section, when near Torquay, saw rockets being fired at 1220 hours from the direction of Dartmouth and then observed bombs bursting in Kingsbridge. Zouhar then saw two FW 190s quite close ahead at sea-level and gave chase, firing a short burst when some three to four miles over the sea but did not observe results as at this moment, Zadrobilek called on his radio that he

was wounded and Zouhar broke off to give him protection. It would appear that Zadrobilek was engaged by two or three more FW 190s and had received a cannon shell which broke his left arm, his aircraft being badly shot up (Category 'B') by cannon and machine-gun bullets. Despite his serious wounds, Zadrobilek returned to Exeter and made a perfect landing at 1255 hours but was too seriously wounded to be interrogated."

Ladislav Zadrobilek (Popelka)

Karel Zouhar (Popleka)

It is clear that by now, many of the *Jabo* attacks were starting to be directed against non-military targets. Back in May 1942, a *Jabo* pilot from 10/JG 26, the first to be captured, made mention that some of the targets attacked were *'cows, cyclists, motor-buses and railway engines'* leading the interrogator to deduce that there was a lack of a defined bombing policy. However, another 10/JG 26 pilot captured in January 1943 admitted that pilots:

"...have been given no specific objectives but have been told quite frankly to attack anything and everything liable to terrorise the British public. Trains, motor buses, gatherings of people, herds of cattle and sheep etc have been mentioned specifically at the briefing as likely targets..."

However, it appeared that the rank and file of the *Wehrmacht* were not in agreement as to such indiscriminate raids. For example, the *Kriegsmarine* wrote in October 1942 that the attack on Canterbury on 31 October 1942 was a reprisal raid ordered personally by Adolf Hitler and that the *Kriegsmarine* regretted every bomb that was not dropped on shipyards and ships. Nevertheless, such indiscriminate attacks did occur and the legality of whether such towns as Kingsbridge were legitimate targets is debateable but they were still a drain on military resources and a continued source of irritation, worry and, for many, even terror. Southern Britain would continue to experience these apparently indiscriminate raids over the next five months.

The following day, the two *Jabostaffeln* attacked again, one to the east, one to the west, so keeping the British defences guessing where they would occur. 10/*JG* 26 attacked Folkestone, not at low level but, for some unknown reason, from an altitude of 4800 metres. However, 10/*JG* 2's attack was more traditional, as witnessed by two teenage boys from the Isle of Wight. Ken Phillips, then just short of his 18th birthday, remembers it vividly:

"We, Steve Peddar and myself, were walking towards Shanklin along a rutted grassy lane. To our right was a field in which was stationed a searchlight unit. Its defensive Lewis gun was just over a thorn hedge that marked the boundary of the field with the lane. Over to our left was the so-called County Ground and the main Shanklin-Sandown road across which, in full view, was Winchester House of the Girls Friendly Society.

"We were surprised to see the local 'Raid Imminent' red maroons fired into the sky over Shanklin to be followed only a second or two later by a gaggle of FW 190s racing above the rooftops of Shanklin. Youthful excitement was quickly dispelled by some consternation on our part as one FW 190 banked sharply to its right and headed straight down the lane towards us, as I recall it now, 30 feet (or less!) off the ground, all guns firing. I do not suggest that the pilot was the slightest bit interested in shooting two boys in a lane – I doubt very much he even saw us. However, the searchlight unit, if he saw that, would have been a legitimate target.

"Banked at a steep angle, the FW 190 continued its turn and headed over Winchester House, still firing its guns, and off out to sea. All over, all quiet. Total time of raid perhaps 20 or 30 seconds, not more.

"We both agree now, after a lapse of almost 60 years, that the soldier manning the Lewis gun was using some very nasty language in his futile attempts to fire the thing. With an enemy aircraft literally only yards away from him, it is doubtful such an opportunity would be presented again throughout the rest of his career! Other memories are of bits of Winchester House flying in all directions and the high plumes of smoke and dust over Shanklin created by the exploding bombs."

Amazingly, photographic evidence of the attack on Winchester House exists. The pilot of the lone Focke-Wulf 190 was *Lt* Leopold Wenger who, like the previous day, had managed to photograph part of his attack,

Winchester House being strafed by 'Poldi' Wenger, 3 Jan 43 (Wenger)

probably having been attracted to Winchester House by the searchlight unit and unaware that it was a hospital. All he noted afterwards was that they had raided Shanklin, they had hit the town centre, that they had experienced much *Flak* and had spotted two Spitfires on their return.

On 4 January 1943, just one attack was carried out when 10/*JG* 26 singled out Winchelsea in Sussex, the specific nature of the target again not being stated in German records. However, the records do mention that the Focke-Wulf 190 flown by *Fw* Herbert Müller was hit by light anti-aircraft fire and then flew into high-tension cables and that the other pilots saw the aircraft hit the ground and burst into flames, Müller being killed instantly.

It would then appear that, probably due to weather, no more raids were carried out for the next four days until 10/*JG* 2 returned, yet again, to Torquay. Eight fighter-bombers approached the town from the south-east, line astern and, as usual, at zero feet. They crossed the coast at Babbacombe where two aircraft peeled away and turned further north. The first bombs dropped were aimed at the Palace Hotel, one hitting the central block, the other just missing, and five more aircraft dropped their bombs in the town itself; the final aircraft was forced to drop its bomb in the sea due to a technical problem. The Germans reported hitting 'a housing block', presumably the hotel, and spotted two Spitfires. The two Spitfires were flown by WOs Jaroslav Sala and Antonin Skach of 310 Squadron who were unable to intercept the fleeing German aircraft. Luckily, this time there were no casualties at the Palace Hotel but as the damage was so severe and as this was the second time the hotel had been successfully attacked, the decision was made to close the Hospital and it was relocated at Cleveleys Hydro in Blackpool, far away from 'tip and run' raids.

For the next 12 days, just six attacks were carried out. 9 January saw a raid on Fairlight in Sussex by 10/JG 26 – the target should have been Hastings but on the run into the target, the three fighter-bombers flew over a patrol boat and fearing that the defences would be waiting, headed for Fairlight where they dropped their bombs on housing. 10 year-old Jim McKendry, who at that time lived in the village of Pett, remembers the attack:

"On Saturday 9 January 1943, whilst having breakfast, we were visited by fighter-bombers. The bombs landed at the top of the village. There was a gardener who was sitting in a greenhouse cleaning the shoes of his elderly

WO Jaroslav Sala (Popelka)

WO Antonin Skach (Popelka)

employers. When he went to put the shoes at their back door, he found that their bungalow had received a direct hit. The roof of the White Hart public house across the road was severely damaged and a Crusader tank breasting the hill was turned in the direction from whence it had come. There wasn't a pane of glass broken in the greenhouse – the noise and blast had gone away from it."

Again, it appears that there was no military reason why such villages as Pett were being targeted, even if the German pilots had spotted the tank, there was no mention of it being attacked. However, each target always had something to do with the war effort in some way or another and the demoralising effect of such attacks would have had the desired effect. A good example of this is Teignmouth in Devon which was singled out by 10/JG 2 on 10 January 1943; it is best related by Joyce Garside who was just 18 at the time:

"Teignmouth is an attractive and well-known coastal town. It had a shipbuilding yard and was a major source of employment in the town. In peacetime, pleasure boats, yachts and cruisers were built, in wartime, it built air-sea rescue pinnaces, motor torpedo boats and other small military craft. The yard was also used by the Americans as a repair base. All of this must have made it to the eyes and ears of German intelligence which caused Teignmouth to suffer more than its fair share of air attacks.

"The worst attack prior to 10 January 1943 had been on 13 August 1942 when eight high explosive bombs killed 14, injured 42 and destroyed 16 houses. Early in the afternoon, five locations in the town were bombed and two hotels were demolished. The Germans did not concentrate on the shipyard and the railway line, the latter being particularly vulnerable at Teignmouth. Planes flew low over the town, raking civilians with gunfire – the pilots could clearly be seen in their cockpits. In all, 88 residents were killed, 228 wounded and about 300 houses totally destroyed.

"During the attack, I was with my sister who lived about a mile and a half from Teignmouth on the coast. We could hear the bombs – it was frightening. We grabbed my small nephew and dived for cover under a bed for protection. My younger brother ran all the way from the town to break the news that our friends from school days with which we had spent the previous Sunday had all been killed – the wife, her husband, her brother and two year old son. Her father was found dead next day, floating beside a ship in the river.

"I remember as if it was yesterday and the horror of the aftermath. We knew many of the people lost. One bomb ricocheted through a bathroom front window (the bathroom was occupied), on through a side window, dropped its fins half-way up the street and then exploded right at the top. It was so frightening…"

German records describe the attack on Teignmouth as a *Störangriff* – a nuisance to Teignmouth. It is believed that it was led by 10/JG 2's new *Staffel Kapitän*, *Hptm* Heinz Schumann, Fritz Schröter having been given command of III/ZG 2 taking over from its *Gruppen Kommandeur*, *Hptm* Wilhelm 'Bomben-Willi' Hachfeld who was killed in an accident on 2 December 1942. Schumann was a very experienced fighter pilot, having flown in Spain with *J*88 and then 4/*JG* 52 and *Stab* I/*JG* 51. By mid-1941, he had destroyed 21 enemy aircraft in the air and countless more on the ground before being posted to be a flying instructor; he must have relished the chance to be back on operations.

Seven fighter-bombers approached the town from the south-east, following the coast. They were flying in four abreast with three abreast following and after having dropped two bombs on boats in the harbour, which were also machine-gunned, they turned over the town, dropping five bombs, four of which landed close to the railway line and blocking it. The German pilots admit that *Flak* was heavy and had probably damaged one fighter-bomber and shot down another and that just two Spitfires were seen but did not attack. Even *Lt* Leopold Wenger, who was flying and whose aircraft was damaged, wrote:

> "…at about lunchtime, we attacked the town of Teignmouth on the south coast with heavy bombs. The effect was enormous but unfortunately, a good comrade of mine did not return. We only hope he was taken prisoner…"

The German pilots had still not correctly identified the Hawker Typhoon. Admittedly, 12 Spitfires of 310 Squadron were airborne from Exeter at the time on a practice sweep and when they were at 1,000 feet, they were informed that German aircraft were near Exmouth and immediately vectored to intercept. Hurtling down to 300 feet, dropping their long-range tanks as they crossed the coast they flew to 30 miles south of Start Point but saw nothing. However, it was two Typhoons that met with luck as well as almost shooting down an unsuspecting 310 Squadron Spitfire.

266 Squadron had been carrying out what was termed as 'anti-Rhubarb patrols' from just after midday. The first two pairs saw and reported nothing, except that one of the Typhoons on each patrol had suffered a minor technical problem. The third pair that day, Fg Off John Small and Plt Off Sam Blackwell, had taken off at 1415 hours; John Small's combat report makes exciting reading:

> "…we had crossed the coast, west of Exmouth and flew roughly 210 degrees some five to seven miles offshore, turned before reaching Start Point and returned on same line until just short of Exmouth when about turned and after flying for two minutes sighted eight aircraft low on the water, my height being about 300 feet, heading for what I thought was Torquay. Immediately reported e/a to Controller and my Number 2 after opening throttle fully and increasing revs also fully. E/a were flying fairly close line abreast. One section nearest coast being slightly apart from main formation. I closed quite quickly on e/a being just about 250 yards behind aircraft I had decided to attack, it being the innermost one of the outer section. As they reached the coast, I saw bomb strikes in the water and one burst on houses on the waterfront. Flak was quite intense and all over the place, heavy bursts were behind and to port. I gave one fairly long burst crossing waterfront and over town, bead being on fields behind the

Fg Off John Small of 266 Squadron is believed to be back row, far left (via Thomas)

Fg Off Sam Blackwell is seen at the back; the other pilots are L to R: Plt Off Borland, Plt Off Thompson and Plt Off MacNamara (via Thomas)

town. E/a turned to starboard, gave another burst throttling back as range was fast decreasing as e/a was crossing coast gave final burst at about 100 yards range, saw flashes on aircraft and one very bright flash indeed from about the cockpit. E/a nosed down, still turning to starboard, I kept firing and it struck the sea some 30 to 50 yards ahead and 300 to 500 yards off-shore. I had no time to evade cascade of water and debris that came up and felt a decided jar. On pulling out I saw an aircraft to port at about 600 feet. I gave chase, saw splash of water and thought it had jettisoned bomb. Caught this aircraft some 10 miles off-shore and was about to fire when I recognised it to be a Spitfire which had jettisoned long range tanks…"

The unlucky German pilot was 22 year-old *Fw* Joachim von Bitter whose plane hit the sea 500 yards off the cliffs known locally as the 'Parson and Clerk'. Von Bitter had been with the *Jabostaffel* since the end of March 1942 and had been awarded the *Eiserne Kreuz* I just two days before his death. His body was washed ashore at Dawlish Warren three days later and buried at Exeter with full military honours.

As John Small was breaking away from almost shooting down a Czech Spitfire and its pilot, Sam Blackwell was gaining on three more fighter-bombers:

Fw *Joachim Von Bitter* (Weyl)

Von Bitter's grave at Exeter. During the war, his dented cigarette case and signet ring were returned to his family via the Red Cross (Weyl)

> *"...I chased these and closed to within what I estimated to be 500 yards of one. I gave short continuous bursts and saw strikes on both fuselage and wings. One cannon jammed which made accurate shooting difficult. Visibility out to sea was not good and I gave up the chase having spent all my ammunition."*

It is probable that Blackwell damaged either the Focke Wulf 190 flown by Lt Kurt Eckleben or Lt Leopold Wenger, the latter's aircraft being damaged in the starboard wing root by a 20mm cannon shell.

A bemused 'Poldi' Wenger (centre) after his return to Théville on 10 Jan 43. By the rudder is the new Staffel Kapitän, Hptm *Heinz Schumann; 3rd from left almost facing camera is* Uffz Kurt Bressler *(Wenger)*

The possible reason for Wenger's bemusement is the hole in the starboard wing of his fighter-bomber; Heinz Schumann looks on (Wenger)

The only attacks of note over the next 10 days took place on 15 January. At 1357 hours, four aircraft from 10/JG 2 were spotted approaching Eastbourne from the west; the Chief Constable's report began by stating what then happened:

> *"...four enemy aircraft, each carrying a bomb of large calibre, approached the town from a westerly direction. One bomb demolished several small dwellings at Green Street, another fell amongst similar property at Duke Street, an area which has already suffered considerably from air attacks; a third fell at the rear of the Imperial Hotel, Devonshire Place and the last amongst fairly large four-storey houses at Wilmington Terrace. Whilst there were a number of casualties at all four incidents, the one at Wilmington Terrace proved to be the most serious, four persons losing their lives in one building..."*

Again, the four German aircraft returned to France unscathed; the same could not be said of Eastbourne as seven civilians lost their lives and 38 suffered varying degrees of injury. Three hours later, it was 10/JG 26's turn but the attack was not as straightforward as it seemed, according to an account of the attack given by one of the pilots, *Lt Hermann Hoch*:

"...Not more than one operational flight was normally made on any one day. An exception to this rule was on Friday January 15 when four pilots were sent off to attack Rye. They were sighted and fired upon by a patrol vessel lying some three miles off Rye and were then attacked by coastal AA. The aircraft therefore attacked and, as they believed, sunk the patrol vessel and then returned to base. They incurred the wrath of Jafü 2 for not having attacked their primary target and to their disgust were immediately sent out again. This time one of the pilots, Lt Erwin Busch, was unable to retract one wheel of his undercarriage so the formation flew to Merville where they jettisoned their bombs, after which they landed for the second time at St Omer. Jafü 2 was angrier and the order was given to take off for a third time. They were given a close escort of four fighters and this time crossed the coast east of Dungeness to attack Tenterden. One of the escorting fighters was shot down by AA..."

Although the two aborted attacks cannot be confirmed, German records stated that houses in Tenterden were bombed and that a Focke-Wulf 190 from the escort flown by *Uffz* Herbert Bremer of 3/*JG* 26 was hit by *Flak* and plunged into the Channel off Rye, killing the pilot.

On 17 January, two fighter-bombers from 10/*JG* 2, one flown by *Lt* Leopold Wenger, attacked Ventnor on the Isle of Wight but this was a minor attack compared to what would occur just three days later. On the morning of 18 January, *Hptm* Heinz Schumann led about 10 aircraft from his *Staffel* to St Omer to join *Oblt* Paul Keller's 10/*JG* 26. This move was apparently in preparation for a reprisal attack on a major British town for the Bomber Command attacks against Berlin on the nights of 16 and 17 January 1943. However, weather now intervened and it was also assessed that St Omer was not suitable for a massed take off of fully laden fighter-bombers, so early that afternoon, both *Staffeln* took off and flew low-level to Abbeville/Drucat. Again, the weather intervened and the attack postponed for that day and the day afterwards without the German pilots knowing what was being planned.

At 0848 hours on 20 January 1943, a *Rotte* of Focke-Wulf 190s from 8/*JG* 26 led by *Lt* Hans Kümmerling, took off on a weather reconnaissance between Dungeness and Eastbourne. At 0910 hours, they reported spotting two small ships headed west and that the weather was 8-10/10ths cloud at 1,000 metres off Brighton with showers but that visibility was 30-50 kms. Their mission complete, they turned for home and as they did, two Typhoons pounced. Fg Off Raymond 'Cheval' Lallemand and Fg Off Peter of 609 Squadron Raw were on a defensive standing patrol when 'Totter' rockets were spotted coming from Dymchurch. It was thought that these two German aircraft were about to carry out yet another 'tip and run' attack and Lallemand, who had shot down 10/*JG* 26's *Staffel Kapitän* exactly a month before, was hopeful of repeating that success:

"...Two FW 190s were then seen to starboard and below flying east inshore of a convoy. Fg Off Lallemand had begun to dive on them when both e/a began a climbing turn towards him. Leaving the second to Fg Off Raw, he attacked the leader at close range allowing half a ring deflection on his first short burst.

Pilots of 10/JG 26 early 1943. L to R: Lt *Otto-August Backhaus (+ 9 Apr 43),* Uffz *Alfred Immervoll (?) (+23 Jan 43),*
Fw *Emil Boesch (+12 Mar 43),* Lt *Siegfried Storsberg, ?,* Ofw *Karl-Heinz Knobeloch (+ 28 Oct 44),* Uffz *Joachim Koch
(+29 Mar 43),* Uffz *Herbert Büttner (?)(5 Feb 43), ?* (Storsberg)

The only 10/JG 26 pilots identified are Emil Boesch (front left) and in the background, Uffz *Alfred Immervoll and* Uffz
Richard Wittmann (Storsberg)

Seeing no results, he increased his deflection on his second and third bursts, finding himself able to out turn e/a. On the second burst, he saw strikes on starboard wing. One the third, he saw strikes on port wing and flames emerging from region of e/a's cockpit. He then saw blue smoke either side of his own cockpit and thinking he was being attacked by e/a's Number 2, he pulled in a climbing turn, weaving but seeing nothing. The e/a he attacked was reported to have gone into the sea by other sources.

"Fg Off Raw pursued the second e/a towards France but lost sight of it owing to oil on his windscreen. A moment later he saw it heading towards Dover and getting fired at by a convoy..."

It wasn't a good start to the day. Hans Kümmerling was killed but his *Rottenflieger* managed to return to France and submit his report. It was decided that following the results of another weather reconnaissance flight by a Messerschmitt 110, probably from 1/123, in the area from Calais to the Thames Estuary and onwards to Great Yarmouth, the attack they had all been waiting for would at last be carried out.

The tactics were involved but effective. At 1150 hours, two Focke-Wulf 190s from 10/JG 2 would take off first to carry out a diversionary *Jabo* attack against Ventnor on the Isle of Wight. Then 10 minutes later, 10 Messerschmitt 109s of *Einsatz Staffel (Jabo)/Jagdgruppe Süd* together with a number of experienced pilots from *Jagdgruppe Ost*, which had flown up from their base at Saintes in south-western France, would take off with a close escort of eight Focke Wulf 190s to carry out a diversionary attack against Tunbridge Wells. At the same time, 28 *Jabos* would take off, together with another close escort of eight Focke-Wulf 190s. These *Jabos*, which were carrying a mix of predominantly SC500 and a few SC250 kg bombs, had been briefed to attack London, flying in at low-level in close formation and to carry out a *Terrorangriff*, bombing anything that they saw. In order to further draw the RAF fighters away, 29 Focke-Wulf 190s and 10 of the new Messerschmitt 109 Gs would carry out a diversionary sweep to the east of the Thames Estuary and would then escort the *Jabos* home. *Uffz* Heinz Budde of 6/JG 26 had cause to remember this day for a number of reasons:

Uffz Heinz Budde, 6/JG 26 (Budde)

"...6 Staffel had received the Bf 109 G in late December 1942. It was intended that because of our pressurized cockpits we would be the High Altitude Staffel, flying at 12,000 metres above the other Staffel of our Gruppe. However, our planes were not ready and despite having flown 48 operational flights with the FW 190, this was only my third flight in the Bf 109 G..."

Despite the different take off times and objectives, all the German aircraft succeeded in getting airborne on time although a number suffered technical problems. From the main attack, *Lt* Hermann Hoch of 10/*JG* 26 jettisoned his bomb in the sea and another two pilots dropped their bombs on Eastbourne. From the main diversionary attack, one Messerschmitt 109 aborted and the remaining *Jabos* reported having bombed Wadhurst because enemy fighters were spotted high above Tunbridge Wells. However, reports of this attack are, from the German viewpoint, confused. 30 German fighters, reported as being mainly Messerschmitt 109s, crossed the coast at zero feet near Eastbourne at 1234 hours, penetrated just 15 miles inland before turning west, re-crossing the coast near Brighton. Although the German pilots made no mention, at 1240 hours, they flew over the East Sussex town of Lewes from the north, dropping six 250 kg bombs and machine-gunning the town. Two civilians were killed, 45 injured (11 of them seriously) and 30 properties were damaged beyond repair.

Meanwhile, further north-east, much worse was about to happen. The Observer Corps reported that at 1222 hours, in the region of 34 Focke-Wulf 190s had crossed the coast at zero feet between North Foreland and Beachy Head, thus fanning out over a wide area of Kent and East Sussex. At 1230 hours, 28 *Jabos* of which 20 carried SC 500 bombs and five carried SC 250 bombs (three having been forced to jettison their bombs earlier) were over south-east London flying at heights of 60 to 100 feet. The balloon barrage in that area of London had just been brought down for maintenance during that lunch hour and most of the inhabitants of that part of London were going to or at lunch; they were unaware of an attack until the first bombs exploded and only then did the sirens sound, by which time it was too late as nine year-old schoolboy Eric Brady was about to find out:

> "*At my school in Sandhurst Road, Catford, it was lunchtime and dozens of children were running about the playground, many excited about going that afternoon to a performance of Shakespeare's Midsummer Night's Dream. Many more children were in the school dining room on the ground floor of the three-storey school, most of us eating sandwiches we'd brought in.*
>
> "*My older sister Kitty, at 14 years-old, was talking to the headmistress on the deserted hall on the first floor. They caught the faint sound of a distant air raid warning. 'Tell the teacher in charge to get the children in the dining room to the shelter' she said quickly. She knew we could get there in two minutes – many drills had ensured that.*
>
> "*Kitty ran down the stairs to warn us and as she came into the room, the sudden roar of low-flying aero engines burst on us as two FW 190s arrived. 'Get under the tables!' screamed the teacher – it was too late for the shelters. Kitty dashed towards me and as she did so, a bomb hit and exploded, bringing that end of the school down upon her and the rest of us. She was caught unprotected and killed, we think, instantly. I had only been able to get halfway into the crowded space under the table and the whole of my left side was exposed. A block of masonry hit my head and pinned down my left arm above*

my head. Another smashed my ankle. All around, injured, terrified children were crying and screaming.

"Immediately after dropping their bombs, the FW 190s began machine-gunning the streets and houses. A mother with her year-old baby walking down the road by the school dived for the only cover – a hedge. Both were killed by the same machine-gun burst. Passers-by and people from nearby houses ran across immediately to start rescue work. A soldier on leave pulled frantically at rubble to get to his daughter. A vicar grabbed a rope and organised a group to pull away big lumps of masonry. The nearby church of St Andrews became a mortuary and first aid station.

"As the first bodies were being brought out, my mother and three year-old brother arrived. On its bombing run, a FW 190 had flown very low over our house. As she heard the bomb explode, she knew it was the school that had been hit. The bomb exploded at about 1230 hours – I was pulled out about 1900 hours – the rescue work went on after dark.

"My family was the only one that had a name on both lists pinned up in the reception area of the local hospital – the 'Dead' and the 'Injured and Detained'. My parents were told of the list of my injuries – left ankle, multiple fractures; left arm, brachial plexus injury resulting in paralysis that was likely to be total; left elbow, dislocated; spinal injury; head, concussion (possible brain damage); severe general bruising. Final assessment: possible death, in any case permanent and severe disablement. In the event, although disabled, I have been able to lead a normal life but still cannot remember any detail of my life prior to 20 January 1943."

With impunity, the fighter-bombers dropped their bombs and strafed buildings before heading south. A gasholder was set alight, the Royal Naval College at Greenwich was hit as was the Deptford West Power Station and Surrey Commercial Docks. To add insult to injury, the Germans also shot down 10 barrage balloons, the barrage being hurriedly winched back up during the attack. The loss of life was high and the effect on morale considerable. At Sandhurst School, 38 children and six teachers were killed whilst at least a further 26 civilians were killed and countless more injured in Sydenham, Brockley, Catford, Deptford and Downham and many buildings and vehicles were destroyed and damaged.

The *Jabos* now managed to make it to the southern outskirts of London, still having not been intercepted. Their approach over Croydon was witnessed by 12 year-old Ken Hopper:

"I was in Ashburton Park, Croydon – there were lots of children in the Park at the time on lunch break. There had been no warning when we heard the noise of many low aircraft approaching from the east from the Beckenham direction. There is a Fire Station in Long Lane with a 50-60 foot practice tower and I saw six or seven FW 190s skimming across the roof tops and swerving to miss this tower. They were certainly below the top of the tower. They were firing the guns into the Park amongst the children and we dived to the ground and I saw the

earth churning up across the Park. We ran into the shelters that were on the edge of the Park nearby to Woodside Station. I don't think that anyone was hit, at least I never heard so. I think that there must have been more aircraft than I saw as the ones I saw could not have fired into the Park from their angle of flight. I believe that the sirens sounded some time after the event."

However, it was about now that the only *Jabo* loss over the mainland on that day occurred. The attack on London had not been a success for *Lt* Hermann Hoch of 10/*JG* 26. Originally a member of I/*JG* 26, he had been injured in an accident on 21 August 1942 and had only recently joined the *Jabostaffel* – this was only his fourth *Jaboeinsatz*. One of the last to take off, he had struggled to catch up with the formation which he then lost sight of in mist. However, he decided to press on but dropped his bomb in the Channel in order to catch up. Crossing the coast near Eastbourne, his aircraft was fired at and shortly afterwards, his engine began to vibrate. It is then believed that he then met up with the German diversionary attack and machine-gunned a train near Tunbridge Wells before his Focke-Wulf 190 was damaged again either by an unknown aircraft or more likely by light anti-aircraft fire from an airfield. Now losing fuel, he realised that he would not make it back across the Channel so decided to crash-land. Near Capel in Surrey, he spotted a ploughed field but on the final approach, hit some trees which ripped the

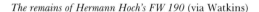

The remains of Hermann Hoch's FW 190 (via Watkins)

engine from its mountings. The remains of the aircraft then ended in a thicket and Hoch, amazed to find he was uninjured, placed his parachute, papers and maps in the cockpit and prepared an explosive charge which, two minutes later, destroyed what was left of the fighter-bomber.

Meanwhile, as the *Jabos* turned for home, the RAF was at last getting to grips with the German escort even if the first casualty was probably British. Flt Lt Richard Easby and Plt Off Barry Fey of 91 Squadron were airborne at the time of the attack and were warned of Bandits near Deal at 14,000 feet. Climbing into the sun, they became separated and Barry Fey then felt his Spitfire go out of control. He had been bounced by *Hptm* Klaus Mietusch, *Staffel Kapitän* of 7/JG 26 whose 'kill' was witnessed by Frank Standen on High Speed Launch 127:

> "There were two Spits, we called them 'Gert and Daisy' and on this day as they passed overhead, a flight of German fighters arrived and immediately the Spits climbed to intercept. Suddenly one of the Spits was hit but the Germans turned towards the French coast. We saw the damaged Spit pull up and the pilot 'hit the silk' as we watched. We were once again the stand-by boat in harbour and actually had some aircrew on board who were liasing with us to learn something about ASR. Our Skipper, who had also seen the action, came running down the quay and we had already started the engines and were ready to cast off. He came down the ladder and jumped aboard as we moved off.
>
> "We left harbour and headed towards the falling parachute which was only a couple of miles off Ramsgate. By the time that the pilot hit the 'drink' and his Mae West had bounced him up from the water, we were alongside and hauled him aboard.
>
> "The Skipper's diary noted: 'Date Jan 20th 1943. Position 149 degs 2 miles. Type: Spitfire. Personnel: Plt Off Fey (Hawkinge). Followed parachute after dogfight over Ramsgate'.
>
> "Plt Off Fey was uninjured and in high spirits and said he saw the launch leaving Ramsgate Harbour and thought to himself 'That's for me!' The liaison aircrew aboard were most impressed and I hope it helped their morale!"

It was not long before other combats were taking place and the most dramatic ones involved the Messerschmitt 109 Gs of 6/JG 26. At 1118 hours, two Typhoons of 609 Squadron had lifted off from Manston, flown by Belgians Flt Lt Jean de Selys Longchamps and Flt Sgt André Blanco. After 30 minutes on standing patrol, they reported seeing condensation trails from between eight and 12 aircraft at 20,000 feet near Deal. Being short of fuel, Jean De Selys radioed back to Manston and another two Typhoons, flown by Belgian Fg Off Jean Creteur and Fg Off Johnny Baldwin, were scrambled at 1229 hours, exactly a minute before the first bombs exploded on London, and headed out to sea at full boost.

Jean Creteur had joined 609 Squadron in May 1942 but Johnny Baldwin was very much the 'new boy', having joined the Squadron on 17 November

1942 direct from 59 Operational Training Unit. The Belgian had yet to shoot down any German aircraft whilst Baldwin had only succeeded in damaging a Focke Wulf 190 on 15 December 1942. However, for the 24 year-old RAF pilot, his score was destined to rise dramatically in 20 minutes time.

Fg Off Johnny Baldwin (via Thomas)

Climbing to 14,000 feet, nothing was seen by the two pilots but Jean de Selys radioed to them to climb to 20,000 feet and on reaching this altitude, they spotted eight Messerschmitt 109s to the east of Manston. Still flying at full boost, the two Typhoons hurtled towards the unsuspecting German fighters and at 1244 hours, they pounced, causing the Germans to scatter in all directions.

The German pilots were totally unaware of the approaching RAF fighters. Due to their pressurised cockpits, they were flying at 20,000 feet whilst the other un-pressurised German fighters were 4,000 feet below them. The diversionary formation had been instructed to fly up and down the coast in an attempt to draw the RAF fighters away from the fighter-bomber attack. 6/JG 26 were approaching Ramsgate from the east, then turned south, flew to the South Foreland about two miles off the coast and then turned back towards Ramsgate. It was then that *Uffz* Heinz Budde noticed that he was getting low on fuel and at the same time spotted what he thought were two German aircraft approaching from astern:

Fg Off Jean Creteur

"I saw behind us aircraft which looked like FW 190s – they even had their noses painted yellow like FW 190s. Only when Uffz Heinz Marquardt was shot down did I realise that they were Typhoons!"

Uffz *Heinz Marquardt* (Marquardt)

Jean Creteur immediately suffered a jam to one of his cannon and in trying to follow one of the fleeing German fighters, got his Typhoon into a spin. By the time he had recovered, he had lost so much altitude that he was unable to rejoin the dogfight. Meanwhile, Johnny Baldwin had latched on to a Messerschmitt flown by Heinz Marquardt and opened fire from 100 yards. A withering burst of fire hit Marquardt's fighter in the tail which immediately began to go out of control. Marquardt struggled to get out and did so at 8,000 feet, landing in the Channel three miles east of Ramsgate at 1250 hours.

What happened next cannot be ascertained for certain. Heinz Budde had managed to get behind Baldwin and open fire, puncturing the Typhoon's fuel tank, a tyre and damaging the flaps before overshooting and heading into cloud. It was then that Budde spotted a pair of Messerschmitts, one flown by his temporary *Staffel Kapitän*, *Lt* Kurt-Erich Wenzel, and his wingman *Lt* Hans Mayer. Heinz Budde continues:

6/JG 26, Aug 42. L to R: Uffz Heinz Budde (POW 20 Jan 43), Uffz Heinz Marquardt (POW 20 Jan 43), Uffz Gerhard Vogt (+14 Jan 45), Oblt Theo Lindemann (St Kap), Lt Helmut Hoppe (+1 Dec 43), Lt Rudolf Leuchel (+25 Feb 44), Lt Kurt-Erich Wenzel (+20 Jan 43), Uffz Wilhelm Mayer (+4 Jan 45) (Budde)

"I saw Heinz Marquardt jump out of his plane and I then followed one of the Typhoons about 500-600 metres behind him but had to break off because I was short of fuel. I met two fighters from my Staffel – Lt Wenzel and Lt Meyer. Lt Wenzel then collided with my fighter from underneath, it lost both wings and I jumped out. Afterwards when I was in hospital, John Baldwin told me that he had shot at Wenzel and he saw him hit my plane. Baldwin circled around me when I was hanging in mid-air. Suddenly he disappeared just before I hit the water. He later apologised for doing this and told me that he had lost fuel because I had hit him in the fuel tank."

Johnny Baldwin's combat appears to get the sequence of combats mixed up but what is in fact his second combat confirms what happened:

"...[they] then attacked three e/a which had detached themselves and headed for Dover, showing smoke from boost...Fg Off Baldwin fired at the other two in quick succession from about 100 yards astern. The first shed its cockpit hood, then thick black smoke, the other disintegrated completely, pieces flying all over the sky. As it exploded, the starboard wing of the first, about 50 yards from it, broke off at the root. He fired again at this one and it spiralled down out of control...He searched below cloud but only saw a parachute at about 8,000 feet which he circled and fixed. Pilot floated some minutes, then appeared to sink..."

Wenzel's aircraft simply disintegrated and plunged into the Channel taking the 21 year-old German pilot with it. Furthermore, wreckage from Wenzel's Messerschmitt also hit Hans Mayer's fighter – he was injured in an eye and his fighter badly damaged but he was able to limp back to Abbeville where he told of the fates that had befallen three of his *Staffel*.

Heinz Marquardt was quickly picked up by an RAF air-sea rescue launch and landed at Ramsgate. However, Heinz Budde was not so lucky. He was forced to spend two days in his dinghy before he was picked up, close to death from exposure, 15 miles east of North Foreland. He was rushed to Ramsgate Hospital and was later transferred to Lingfield Military Hospital where he made a full, if slow, recovery. It was whilst he was there that he was visited by Johnny Baldwin. The two chatted for a while and worked out for certain that Johnny had shot down Heinz. Heinz was also pleased to find out the reason why Baldwin had circled him as he drifted down on his parachute. Baldwin was worried that the German had damaged his Typhoon (which indeed he had) and he was cautiously seeing if the flying controls were affected. Heinz Budde then presented Baldwin with a clasp knife (which went with the lifejacket that the RAF pilot had liberated from Heinz Marquardt) and both hoped to meet again after the War.

The skirmishes between the RAF and the *Luftwaffe* continued well into the afternoon, with Flt Lt Joe Atkinson of 609 Squadron claiming the last 'kill' connected with the lunchtime missions at 1435 hrs when he shot down *Fw* Alfred Barthel of 5/JG 26 who was engaged on an air-sea rescue sweep. One more related loss would occur early the next morning. Whilst on another air-sea rescue mission for missing pilots, the Focke-Wulf 190 flown by *Uffz* Wolfgang Taufmann of 4/JG 26 was shot down by Fg Off Peter Nankivell of 609 Squadron. Taufmann, who had celebrated his 21st birthday the day before, was killed.

The *Luftwaffe* lost 11 fighters on 20 January 1943, including one Focke Wulf 190 *Jabo* from the London attack and two Messerschmitt 109 *Jabos* from the diversionary attack; a further four fighters suffered varying degrees of damage. In human terms, seven pilots were killed or missing, three prisoners of war and three wounded. Fighter Command fared better – just two Spitfires were shot down – Plt Off Barry Fey of 91 Squadron who was slightly wounded whilst Norwegian Lt Peder Mollestad of 332 Squadron followed the German aircraft back to France only to be shot down and killed by the same pilot who had shot down Barry Fey – *Hptm* Klaus Mietusch. Sadly there was one more RAF casualty. Alerted by the successful diversionary attack by 10/*JG* 2 on Ventnor, two Typhoons of 486 Squadron intercepted a Mustang of 400 Squadron flown by Fg Off James Ferris off the Isle of Wight. The leading pilot identified the Mustang as 'friendly' but, due to a radio failure, his wingman did not hear the order to break off the attack and sadly, James Ferris was killed when his aircraft was shot down into the sea 10 miles south of St Catherines Point.

So ended the first 'tip and run' attack aimed against Britain's capital city. So serious were the after effects of the raid that, for the first time, the problem of *Jabo* attacks was debated in the House of Commons. A petition was signed by local residents complaining about the inability to prevent the raid and questions were asked as to why the defences were down and what was being done to combat these lightning attacks. In a particularly evasive reply, the Secretary of State for Air, Sir Archibald Sinclair, said that the balloons were down for maintenance and that '...*the best deterrence to such attacks as that on 20th of January is the infliction of heavy casualties on the attackers...*'† which was precisely what did not happen. A further question, asking whether the Secretary of State for Air was satisfied that everything was being done to combat *Jabo* raids, resulted in a similar response: '...*the tactical measures best suited for defending this and other areas which are subject to varying forms of attack are under constant review...*'.††

All of this still did not alter the fact that Britain's capital city had been bombed in broad daylight by a force which penetrated nearly 100 miles at high speed and low-level into enemy territory and still managed to drop its bombs onto recognised targets with good effect and then returned virtually unscathed.

There was a three day break before the *Jabos* returned again. At 0925 hours on 23 January, four aircraft from 10/*JG* 26 took off to attack Hailsham, claiming just 25 minutes later to have successfully dropped four 500 kg bombs on the town before heading southwards, machine-gunning and setting on fire what they stated was an electricity power station. What actually occurred was they had dropped their bombs on Polegate, killing three and wounding six, and then machine-gunned the Old Town district of Eastbourne. The attack on the Old Town was experienced by Eileen Steel:

"The attacks on Eastbourne were rather frightening because one did not hear the aircraft in advance as one did with heavy bombers and they appeared unexpectedly. The general air raid siren was usually too late in sounding but in Eastbourne we had a special siren which we called the 'Cuckoo' because of its two tone sound. When we heard that we knew that an attack was imminent and quickly took cover, if possible.

†Parliamentary Debates Commons 1942 – 43 Vol. 386 p.477
††Ibid

"On this day, I was home on leave from Kenley and walking with a friend along a parade of shops in what we call the 'Old Town' which is adjacent to the Downs. Then without warning there was a burst of machine-gun fire and the German aircraft flew very low from under the cover of the Downs and just above the rooftops; of course we both dived for cover. Being in uniform, I thought they were firing at me because I could not see what else could be the target as this area was purely residential. Some time later I discovered that there had been a gun emplacement on top of one of the shops..."

The four fighter-bombers now continued south towards Beachy Head, not knowing they were heading straight towards a machine-gun post manned by soldiers of Princess Patricia's Canadian Light Infantry. One of the gunners was Private Carl Darrock:

"We were stationed at Rottingdean but were sent to Beachy Head on a daily basis. This day, four German planes came in to bomb Eastbourne [sic], one of them being slightly behind the others. After they had bombed going in and shot it up, they came out again, one of the planes again slightly behind. When he saw the other two being fired at, he dipped down under a 25 foot cliff on the water's edge and headed straight for us. We, Private Jack Andros and myself, opened up with our Bren guns. I feel we killed the pilot as the plane veered and dived into the water. When the authorities came to investigate, all that was left was a patch of oil on the water. About six days later, a body was washed onto the beach.
"We received a bit of money and a three day pass to London for what we did!"

German records confirm that *Uffz* Alfred Immervoll had turned to starboard and everyone else to port when they came under fire. His fighter-bomber plunged into deep water 400 yards offshore from Cow Gap, Beachy Head. Five days later, sections of a German aircraft, including part of a bomb rack, were washed ashore near to where the crash had occurred and two days after that, a body, later identified as Immervoll, drifted ashore.

Believed to be Uffz *Alfred Immervoll, killed in action 23 Jan 43* (Storsberg)

Attacks for the remainder of January 1943 were, apart from one, quite uneventful for the German pilots – Sandbanks, Bournemouth by 10/*JG* 2 on 25 January and Ramsgate on 26 January, Bexhill and Hastings on 28 January and Margate on 30 January all by 10/*JG* 26. However, there was one more raid which afterwards and even today points an accusing finger at *Jabo* attacks against clearly non-military targets. Eight fighter-bombers from

10/*JG* 2 had taken off at 1515 hours to attack Kingsbridge in Devon. However, due to the weather, they decided to attack Loddiswell, north west of Kingsbridge, noting that they destroyed houses in the village, including a church, before machine-gunning the village and heading out to sea. They actually attacked Aveton Gifford, another small village between Loddiswell and Kingsbridge and the Observer Corps report submitted at the time was quite precise as to what exactly the Germans did:

"There was no likely target within a two mile radius of Aveton Gifford. There is no apparent reason why the raiders dropped their bombs on this village...

"...The church at Aveton Gifford is just visible from ROC Post H2 and Observer on duty heard planes and saw church hit by bomb. A few seconds after, seven e/as were seen flying only about 20 feet over the brow of a hill towards Golf Pavilion 200 yards north-east of Post spraying this and Post with cannon and machine-gun fire. Pavilion and fairway between it and Post pitted with shell and bullet holes. Post was not actually hit...

"...An eye witness (attached to Naval College, Dartmouth) was in his back garden at the north-eastern end of the village (Aveton Gifford) and saw bomb No.5 hit Church. ...From the evidence available, it would seem that there were altogether eight raiders but as they were flying so low and using the valleys for cover, it was impossible for them to be observed in full number..."

Seven bombs were dropped, one scoring a direct hit on the church, another on the Rectory. Two more fell in the marshes to the west of the village, causing considerable damage and plastering everything with mud and, curiously, dead eels, many of which dangled from the telephone wires. Another bomb fell to the east of the village, damaging a terrace of cottages so badly that they had to be demolished whilst the remaining two fell in fields, exploding harmlessly. Of the 110 houses in the village, only five were undamaged. 20 villagers were injured, three seriously, and one, five year-old Sonia Weeks, killed. Her death made quite an impact on a number of people, especially Alan Edgcombe:

"...I was stopped by the Police and asked where I was going. I told them I lived in the village and was going home. 'What work do you do?' they asked. I told them I worked as a builder. 'You go up to the Rectory,' they said 'there's people trapped in there and they need all the help they can get'. So I joined the chain of men passing rubble out from the collapsed building so that the people could be released.

"At last they got Sonia Weeks out. She was quite dead. They passed her down the line. It was a very moving and upsetting experience for me, a boy approaching 16 years of age, to hold this lifeless five year-old for a few moments until then next man in the line took her. Then her mother and grandmother were brought out as well as the Rector's wife, all of them very shaken and filthy, but at least they were alive."

Aveton Gifford Church (via Irwin)

Although the villagers were not to know it, retribution was swift. Fg Off Clive Bell and Sgt Noel Borland of 266 Squadron had been scrambled, being initially told that there were 'Rats' at Torquay and then at Brixham. Shortly afterwards, he was told to head for Dartmouth where he spotted 12 Spitfires circling aimlessly. Bell, not seeing or being told anything, began circling himself, allowing his wingman to catch up as he had experienced starting problems. Obviously frustrated, he asked for a vector and was told to head for Start Point – his combat report now takes up the story of what unfolded:

"I immediately straightened out on the best vector for Start Point, I was within sight of the coast and thus probably better able to judge the correct vector for Start Point than Operations. While approximately half way there, I sighted an FW 190 at 2 o'clock about 1,500 yards from me, I immediately 'Tally Ho'd' over the R/T, gave chase and slowly closed the range to what I imagine must have been about 500 yards as my first burst fell in the water about 15 yards behind the e/a. My next burst appeared to be very slightly in front. The e/a being so low that it actually flew through the spray sent up by the cannon shells. I think I probably first hit it then. The next burst hit it fair and square and bits

Fg Off 'Monty' Bell of 266 Squadron (sitting 1st left) (via Thomas)

flew off it and smoke poured from it. The e/a then pulled up very suddenly and steeply, I gave it one short final burst after which it plunged into the sea. I then pulled up in a climbing turn to the left to avoid the shower of spray and bits which came up after the e/a had hit the water. There was a column of smoke left over the place where the e/a hit the water…"

Clive Bell had shot down a very experienced *Jabo* pilot. *Fw* Karl Blase had been with 10/*JG* 2 since the start of May 1942. He had been one of the two pilots who carried out the audacious attack on Yeovil on 5 August 1942 and was one of the few pilots from the *Staffel* who had been credited with shooting down an RAF fighter†. He had been recommended for the *Deutsches Kreuz in Gold* which he never received – his body was never found but the award was made posthumously on 16 March 1943.

†Blase was credited with a Spitfire east of the Isle of Wight some time in July or August 1942 but as it was unconfirmed, no record has been found

Probably as a result of the weather, evidence can be found of just 12 attacks carried out by both *Jabostaffeln* in February 1943 and even these 12 attacks had the desired effect – the defences were generally helpless to prevent them and public annoyance was increasing. The attack on Eastbourne on 7 February was a good example:

"…four FW 190 fighter-bombers dropped four 500 kg SD type bombs from a south-westerly direction at practically zero feet, gaining height to cross the coastline, east of the Beachy Head Lighthouse. They then dispersed, flew over the Downs, dived to about 150 feet over the town, released their bombs, fired their cannon and machine-guns and passed out to sea, approximately over the fishing station, turning south-west.

"Ground defences did not open fire until the raiders were crossing the coastline on their outward journey. The Regional Alarm sounded at Police Headquarters immediately prior to the fall of bombs but was somewhat belated in another parts of the town. The National Alarm was later sounded throughout the Town with the exception of Police Headquarters.

"British fighters were in the air immediately before and after the fall of bombs but apparently no interception took place. This, of course, was the subject of public comment."

The attack was yet again witnessed by Basil Wootton:

"Being one of those warm sunny February Sundays, my friends and I decided after lunch that we would all cycle up and over to Friston airfield. The east to west route would follow the A259 through Eastbourne, up over the Downs. Part of the journey was over a long steep hill requiring any cyclist to walk, pushing their bikes. Nearing the brow, there are a couple of bends in the road.

"We were just approaching the second bend when, out of sight from the direction of the sun, there was an increasingly loud sound of an aircraft diving, seemingly towards us; we were trying to look up towards the sea to see what was coming – it wasn't the sound of a Merlin! Coming out of the sun's glare against the clear blue sky, the German markings could be seen beneath an FW 190 almost now at our level and about 100 yards to the south of us. Also, what appeared to be a spare fuel tank seemed to have been released from the wing although it wouldn't have carried one for such a short flight across the Channel. We temporarily lost sight of this as the plane flattened its dive to a level beneath us when, in a flash of a second, we could see from above the pilot in his cockpit and the clear markings on top of the wings, racing away eastwards over the town. What it released could now be seen flying away, seemingly horizontally across the town. It was a bomb which seemed never to land until, in total silence, it stopped with a flash and a vertical spray of smoke, debris and, like minutes later, a very booming double bang and its echoes. The two copper-topped towers where the explosion took place identified the spot as the then Eastbourne Technical School and Public Library.

"By then, the FW 190 was well out to sea and probably back in France

when the air raid warning sirens could be heard, closely followed by a barrage demonstration by the Bofors guns lining the south side of Prince's Road; we didn't bother with Friston that day!"

Yet again, 15 lost their lives and 57 were injured to one degree or another.

Despite the lack of missions, the *Jabostaffeln* were still suffering losses. It was clear that at last, the Typhoon was starting to prove itself at low-level, even if the Germans were still slow to recognise and appreciate their new foe. The first loss of the month was from 10/*JG* 26 on 5 February 1943. This time, the standing patrol from 609 Squadron was able to prevent the attack as Fg Off Peter Nankivell's combat report proves:

"...four aircraft were sighted in two sections line astern, flying parallel, at zero feet, four miles to the south and slightly ahead.

"The Typhoons turned towards them and within half a minute, all four turned south and jettisoned their bombs. As a result of the turn, one of the four was left 500 yards behind and within four or five minutes, Blue 1 (Fg Off Nankivell) had caught up near enough to identify him as a FW 190. His first attack from 400 yards dead astern fell slightly behind, a longer burst from about 300 yards produced a large flash near the cockpit. After some evasive corkscrew action by e/a (climbing and diving turns between 0 and 200 feet) and further short bursts from Blue 1, e/a began a slow climbing turn to port, shedding pieces and dropping undercarriage. At 1,200 feet, e/a rolled onto its back, pilot baled out and aircraft crashed into the sea halfway between Hastings and Fecamp."

Believed to be Uffz Herbert Büttner, killed in action 5 Feb 43 (Storsberg)

The German pilots had been briefed to attack Hailsham and were approaching the coast when the Typhoons attacked:

"Schwarm was attacked by two Curtiss P-40s. Uffz Herbert Büttner was behind and a P-40 was able to fire two bursts whereupon Büttner put his plane into a steep climb and baled out. The initiated air seas rescue operation had to be aborted because 10 Spitfires and six small British vessels were at the scene."

The *Luftwaffe* had successfully fought the P-40 many times before, especially in North Africa, so why they now thought that the P-40 was able to hold its own against what was clearly a far superior fighter is puzzling. Sadly, Herbert Büttner did not survive whilst Peter Nankivell was shot down and killed just two days later. Of note is although the air sea rescue mission failed to find the *Jabo* pilot, *Uffz* Heinz Gomann of 5/*JG* 26, one of the German pilots participating in the mission, successfully bounced two of the Spitfires sent to intercept them, shooting down and killing the successful Commanding Officer of 611 Squadron, Sqn Ldr Hugo Armstrong DFC.

The Typhoon would at last be recognised as the RAF fighter which was causing the *Jabos* so much trouble. After having so many missions cancelled

Lt *Leopold Wenger's Blue 12, 24 Feb 43; he flew this aircraft in the attack on Exmouth, 26 Feb 43* (Wenger)

due to bad weather, eventually on 26 February 1943, eight fighter-bombers from 10/*JG* 2 attacked Exmouth in Devon, targeting the gas holder and housing. *Lt* Leopold Wenger was one of the eight pilots:

" *In February 1943, we could not fly very much because the weather was still bad. We could not go into action again until 26 February. We attacked the town of Exmouth at noon. It was a very hard mission – very rarely have I*

Photographs taken by Wenger during the attack on Exmouth; the last one shows steam from the train he attacked (Wenger)

encountered Flak firing so accurately. Still, we taught the town a good lesson. In addition, I shot at a gasholder and set it on fire and harassed a moving train. Again, I was able to take some quite good photos. Unfortunately, we had losses in the aerial battle which followed the attack…"

It is believed that this was the attack witnessed by 16 year-old Ken Rendall:

"Exmouth was hit by fighter-bombers carrying bombs and firing cannons. I was a boy messenger for the General Post Office (GPO). When the sirens went, all the GPO staff went to the basement except three of us messenger boys who immediately went to the rooftop! There we saw three fighter-bombers attacking our local gasometer, each in line astern. All three aircraft fired their cannons at the gasometer which did not blow up but just caught fire and rapidly the stored gas was burnt up. The enemy aircraft then peeled off and beat a hasty retreat across the Channel to France..."

German records state that on the return flight, the *Jabos* were attacked by what they describe as two Spitfires and 4 Royal Typhoons and the aircraft flown by *Fw* Hermann Rohne and *Uffz* Kurt Bressler were seen to crash into the sea. Yet again, the victorious Typhoons came from 266 Squadron, and in yet another exciting high-speed low-level chase, Sqn Ldr Charles Green and Sgt Richard Thompson claimed the Squadron's fourth and fifth *Jabos;* this is what Richard Thompson wrote:

Sqn Ldr Charles Green, CO of 266 Squadron (via Thomas)

"I was Yellow 2 on anti-Rhubarb patrol taking off from Exeter at 1200 hours. At about 1215 hours, Control called up and said Bandits were bombing Exmouth when we were off Dartmouth. We proceeded full throttle towards Exmouth until we were within about 10 miles when Yellow 1 altered course to starboard until we were flying approximately south-east. We continued in this direction at full throttle, overtaking a Spitfire which had previously seen the e/a and told us that e/a were straight ahead. Shortly after passing the Spitfire, I saw four to six e/a flying very low over the water. Soon after, Yellow 1 opened fire and damaged one aircraft and then broke off and attacked another which I saw explode and hit the water. I followed the one that Yellow 1 had damaged which had one leg of its undercarriage hanging down. I opened fire at 200 yards and closed in to about 20 yards but owing to my guns firing unevenly, I had great difficulty in keeping my aircraft steady. The e/a took mild evasive action and I closed in and pulled just over the top of it, probably very close to him because he hit the water at the same time and bits of his aircraft broke my spinner in half and did other minor damage. The broken spinner caused the engine to run very roughly and I thought that I had engine trouble so I climbed steadily until we reached the coast. Landed at Exeter 1245 hours."

The weather in the first two months of 1943 had limited the number of 'tip and run' attacks but it appeared that the British defences were at last exacting a limited toll against the attackers – Typhoons had accounted for five fighter-bombers in these two months, light anti-aircraft fire a further three. However, all eight aircraft were shot down after dropping their bombs on the designated target and these losses did not deter the *Luftwaffe* or affect the potency of the attacks.

From March 1943 onwards, a greater number of raids would now be flown, especially when the weather improved. Like the attack on London on 20 January 1943, a number of these were by much larger formations of 20 or so fighter-bombers, a fact which would be noted by the Observer Corps:

"...many minor attacks were made [in March 1943] by aircraft in small formations with occasional more ambitious attacks by formations of between 12 and 30 fighter-bombers with or without an escort or rear cover. In January [20th], 12 [sic] fighter-bombers bombed the crowded areas round Poplar and Bermondsey from low altitude with considerable morale effect. This was followed by several other similar attacks on Eastbourne, Hastings, London and Ashford..."†

If the attack on London on 20 January 1943 had "considerable morale effect", similar raids in March 1943 would have an even greater adverse effect on morale for British civilians.

However, although both protagonists did not know it, Britain only had to suffer another three months of 'tip and run' misery.

†*Royal Observer Corps Narrative 1943* p.101

8
Changes

MARCH – APRIL 1943

March 1943 might have promised much but it started badly for 10/*JG* 2. It is assumed that the intended target for a 'tip and run' attack was Bognor Regis but only one aircraft was reported to have participated, this being flown by *Uffz* Ernst Läpple. Läpple was older than other pilots in his *Staffel*, being almost 27, as well as being a qualified technical engineer. It is assumed that he might have been carrying out some form of technical evaluation on this day but had the misfortune of being intercepted by the now ever present Typhoon standing patrol. However, he almost unwittingly brought down one of his attackers as the report filed by 486 Squadron shows:

"Black Section [Black 1 – Sgt Murray Jorgensen and Black 2 Flt Sgt Wallace Tyerman] was flying in line astern, No.2 slightly to starboard, north-east for Selsey Bill which was about 10 miles away when they were given vectors which brought them to a point four or five miles south of Bognor where they saw a single aircraft dead ahead, about 600 yards away and flying so low that its slip stream left a wake.

"Our Section, ASI 310 at 700 feet, closed easily and recognised a FW 190 carrying a bomb or bombs under the fuselage. By this time the aircraft was getting near to Bognor and, without taking deliberate aim, Black 1 fired two very short bursts without seeing strikes, with the object of diverting the e/a away from Bognor. In this he was successful, for the Hun turned to port, at the same time jettisoning a bomb which burst on hitting the sea and threw up a large column of water right in front of Black 1 who pulled up sharply in an attempt to avoid it. Unfortunately, quite a lot of water entered the intake causing his engine to cut. After informing his No.2, he flew to Selsey Bill and when near Siddlesham, the engine stopped. Sgt Jorgensen made an excellent forced landing in a field and was unhurt...†

"When his Leader pulled away, Flt Sgt Tyerman closed to 50 yards and opened fire with two one-second bursts from astern 15 degrees to starboard. The port leg fell and vivid orange flashes were seen all along the trailing edge, fuselage and wing root. The e/a slid along the surface of the sea and disintegrated in a burst of flame followed by a column of black smoke which rose to 1,500 feet."

†Typhoon serial R8706 coded SA – U was damaged Cat 'B' in the force-landing

486 Squadron, Tangmere, 1943. Flt Sgt Wallace Tyermann is back row far left; Murray Jorgensen is front row far left. The pilots are back row L to R: Tyerman, Powell, Fail, Wilson, Sqn Ldr Desmond Scott, Saward, Froggatt, Danzey. Front L to R: Jorgensen, Thomas, Swinton, McCarthy (via Thomas)

486 Squadron might have succeeded in preventing this attack but the British defence would not be so lucky for the remainder of the month.

It was about now that changes began to occur to the *Jabostaffeln* which both affected the numbers and designations of the *Luftwaffe's* fighter-bomber units on the Western Front. The first change had already affected 10/*JG* 26 – on 17 February 1943, it had been re-designated 10/*JG* 54 and remained at St Omer-Wizernes when the remainder of the *Geschwader* moved temporarily to the Eastern Front, exchanging with *JG* 54.

The other changes were more substantial and permanent. First of all, the numbers of fighter-bombers participating in 'tip and run' attacks increased dramatically. The first such raid took place on 7 March 1943 when in the region of 18 aircraft from both *Jabostaffeln* attacked Eastbourne just after midday, killing 14 civilians and seven servicemen. Michael Ockenden, who was just five at the time, clearly remembers the event despite his age:

> "*On that Sunday, I was due to go to my grandparents for lunch. They lived next door to me and my uncle was home on leave – he had not had any leave at Christmas so my grandmother had made a special lunch, including Christmas pudding.*
>
> "*I was playing with a clockwork train and my father was with me. Suddenly, the spring broke and my father started to take the train apart to find out what could be done. As a result of this, I was late going round to my*

Oblt *Siegfried Storsberg of 10/JG 26 next to his Flak damaged Black 1, Wizernes, 1943* (Storsberg)

grandparents and so my grandmother came to fetch me because lunch would be spoilt. Suddenly, we heard the 'Cuckoo' alert and we all went to the foot of the stairs. I remember an explosion and all the ceilings coming down. My father threw himself on top of me and there was a great cloud of dust.

"We then went back up the stairs and out onto our flat roof. I remember my grandmother saying 'I must find Dad'. Then we saw my uncle coming up the outside stairs next door – he was completely grey from the dust and there was a wound to his head. I stayed with my mother and grandmother; my father and uncle went over to look for my grandfather. He was lying at the bottom of the outside stairs and was severely injured. They put him on a door and carried him to the end of the lane to wait for the ambulance. The ambulance did not come so some Canadian soldiers took him to hospital (still on the door) but he died later that afternoon.

"My grandmother always used to say that we both owed our lives to that broken spring..."

Amongst the normal 10/*JG* 2 and 10/*JG* 54 pilots flying on this mission were a number from a new fighter-bomber unit who were there to gain combat experience. In December 1942, it had been decided to form a dedicated fighter-bomber *Geschwader-Schnellkampfgeschwader* 10 (*SKG* 10). The first *Gruppe* to be declared operational was *Hptm* Fritz Schröter's III/*SKG* 10 (formerly III/*ZG* 2) which continued to operate in North Africa. I and II *Gruppen* were also formed, albeit on paper, at the end of December 1942 and appear to have been physically formed in February 1943. I *Gruppe* was commanded by *Ritterkreuz*-holder and former *Stuka* pilot *Maj* Heinrich Brücker and was based at St André whilst II *Gruppe,* under the command of another *Ritterkreuz*-holder, *Oblt* Helmut Viedebannt, a former *Zerstörer* pilot, was formed at Caen-Carpiquet. Leadership of the *Geschwader* was given to another experienced *Zerstörer* pilot and *Ritterkreuz*-holder, *Maj* Günther Tonne. At least two II/*SKG* 10 pilots, *Lt* Fritz Setzer and *Maj* Walter Grommes took part in the Eastbourne attack, attached to 10/*JG* 2, and on the following day it is believed that 7/*SKG* 10 carried out its first 'tip and run' attack when a trawler was bombed north of the Eddystone Lighthouse.

SKG 10 was at the same time also undertaking night flying practice with the intention of both I and II/*SKG* 10 flying at night. It would appear that I/*SKG* 10 flew very few daylight 'tip and run' raids, seeming to spend much of its time training purely for nocturnal attacks, whilst II/*SKG* 10 flew some daylight missions as well as training for nocturnal attacks. However, according to *Lt* Fritz Setzer of 5/*SKG* 10 these nocturnal missions were clearly not a good idea:

"...it was absurd. The aircraft were not equipped and the pilots not experienced for night missions. There was no experience in night and instrument flying and we did not have a navigation system. All the 'training' consisted of was a few night landings before a mission..."

Oblt *Helmut Viedebannt*, Gr Kdr II/SKG *10, 25 March 43*

Hptm *Graf von Sponeck* & Maj *Tonne*

Maj *Günther Tonne*, Gesch Kdre *SKG* 10, *25 Mar 43*

The reason for the visit – The award of the Eiserne Kreuz *to two pilots. L to R:* Hptm *Hans Curt Graf von Sponeck,* St Kap *5/SKG 10,* Maj *Tonne,* Hptm *Karl-Friedrich Böttger Gr Ia II/SKG 10,* Lt *Fritz Setzer, 5/SKG 10*

The Staffel Kapitän *pours the champagne; in the background, a brand new* Jabo

The next major attack took place against Hastings in the afternoon of 11 March with II/*SKG* 10 as well as the other two *Jabostaffeln* participating. An official British analysis of the attack details what happened:

> *"It is believed that 26 aircraft attacked Hastings on this occasion. The e/a crossed the coast at Fairlight, three miles east of Hastings, in three formations and flew north to Guestling where one bomb was dropped. They then turned west and south, flying across the town from the north-east in line abreast. Throughout the flight overland, they were at less than 150 feet. Three e/a hit by AA were seen to crash in the sea. Apart from six bombs which may have been aimed at the railway, the attack was directed indiscriminately against the town. There was no serious damage."*

The report appears dismissive of the attack which was far more effective than it leads one to believe. 25 bombs were dropped in Hastings, killing 38, seriously wounding 39 and wounding 51 as well as destroying 40 houses and blocking the railway line. The fighter-bombers had appeared without warning from the north flying at rooftop height – the Silverhill district was badly hit and the Royal East Sussex and Buchanan Hospitals suffered blast

Worthing under attack by 10/JG 2, 9 Mar 43. Despite the attempts of 486 and 610 Squadrons, the attackers returned to France unscathed (Wenger)

damage but no patients were injured. This attack was probably the one witnessed by teenager Don Spear:

> *"I was walking along the seafront from Hastings to St Leonards. I heard the roar of an aircraft behind me and turned and faced a FW 190 flying down the middle of the road at rooftop height. His target appeared to be a large block of flats, Marine Court, which at the time was part occupied by the RAF.*

"As the FW 190 was almost above me, the pilot released his bomb and he started to bank left. The bomb flew through the air, hit the road and bounced over the railings into the sea, sending up a he column of water. I then looked at the FW 190 which was now flying very close to the water. I also observed at least two more FW 190s further out – within a few minutes, they were out of sight."

Again, *Lt* Leopold Wenger, who was participating in the attack, managed to take a photograph which clearly shows the Marine Court at St Leonards.

Hastings, 11 Mar 43. The church in the foreground is Christ Church, London Road, St Leonards; in the distance is Marine Court (Wenger)

The official report was also over optimistic as to German losses. Headquarters 11 Group wrote that:

"...standing patrols were immediately detailed to the raid but the attack was so sharp that the enemy were passing out to sea six minutes after they were sighted..."†

†HQ No 11 Group Operations Record Book, March 1943, p.7

A Focke-Wulf 190 A-5 of 6/*SKG* 10 was damaged by *Flak* but almost managed to make it back to Belgium, eventually crashing into the sea three kilometres east of the airfield at Coxyde. Its pilot, *Fw* Kurt Barabass was killed, the first *SKG* 10 pilot to be killed in operations over the United Kingdom.

There would be no respite from the raids as before breakfast the following day, the *Jabos* attacked again with another reprisal for Bomber Command's repeated pounding of German cities. With 10/*JG* 2 and elements of II/ *SKG* 10 now operating temporarily from Coxyde, the attack was aimed against Ilford and Barking to the east of London. Similar to the 20 January attack, the *Jabos* had a substantial escort, a fact mentioned in the official British report:

> "*A low-level attack was made early in the morning on Ilford and Barking. There was haze on the low ground and the attack was probably planned to surprise our defences. 24 FW 190s operated over Essex where numerous machine-gun incidents were reported. 16 e/a reached London and dropped HE bombs. No Key Points were affected. About 20 enemy fighters patrolled the Thames Estuary and a further 20 flew off the Belgian and French coasts as rear cover. 70 RAF fighters were up and they destroyed six e/a. Balloons were ordered up from 1,500 feet to 5,000 feet just as the bombs were being dropped. Two e/a penetrated the barrage area but all the bombs dropped outside.*"

Thames barges under attack in the River Crouch, 12 Mar 43 (Wenger)

The German pilots noted afterwards that there were many balloons over the target area and that they were intercepted by Spitfires. Despite '70 RAF fighters' being airborne, any interceptions took place after the fighter-bombers had struck and even then, only 122 and 331 Squadron, both based at Hornchurch in Essex, managed to intercept in any numbers, as shown by the 122 Squadron diary entry for the attack:

> *"Weather fine. Brilliant sunlight with much ground haze early. A really 'operational' day which was taken advantage of to the full.*
>
> *"The Squadron came to readiness at dawn. An hour later at 0730 hours, 'A' Flight was scrambled, followed three minutes later by 'B' Flight, to intercept 12 e/a reported coming in from the north-east at 5,000 feet. When our boys were airborne and climbing, they saw FW 190s at zero feet bombing and machine-gunning the Romford-Ilford areas. They turned and went down but were too late. The interception became a chase at roof top height as far as four-five miles out from Southend but our aircraft were unable to catch up. Plt Off W Edwards and Sgt F E Livesey both fired from long range but only Plt Off Edwards saw strikes on the e/a. He claims an FW 190 damaged. All aircraft had returned to base by 0835 hours."*

331 Squadron were a little luckier, if not optimistic, with Focke-Wulf 190s being claimed as destroyed by Sgt Fredrik Eitzen, 2/Lt Bjørn Bjørnstad and Lt Helge Sognnes. 2/Lt Rolf Engelsen and 2/Lt Erik Fossum shared another and Capt Leif Lundsten destroyed two more. German losses were much less than the Norwegian pilots thought – the escorts suffered no losses whilst *Ofw* Herbert Korth of 10/*JG* 2 was killed when his fighter-bomber crashed near Coxyde and another aircraft landed with 15% combat damage; *Fw* Emil Bösch of 10/*JG* 54 was last seen 10-20 kilometres north of Dunkirk and although two air-sea rescue missions were flown, no trace of him was ever found.

Fw *Emil Bösch, 10/*JG* 54, killed in action 12 Mar 43* (Storsberg)

Only minor damage was inflicted on the London suburbs but it still resulted in the deaths of 31 and a further 43 being injured. Furthermore, the residents of Ilford were vociferous in the failure of the defences in preventing the attack, the sirens again being sounded only after the attack had started and the time it took for the fire and rescue services to respond to numerous incidents. 'Tip and run' attacks were still proving to be a serious embarrassment to the military, who had again failed to thwart a daylight attack on the Nation's capital, and a severe irritation to the civilian population.

Retribution, albeit small and not witnessed by the civilian population, came on 13 March 1943. At lunchtime on 12 March, II/*SKG* 10 attacked Salcombe without incident but when they tried a repeat performance the day afterwards, the RAF's most successful 'tip and run' killers struck. Fg Off John Deall and Sgt David Eadie of 266 Squadron were already airborne on an anti-Rhubarb patrol when they were ordered towards Start Point to intercept enemy aircraft in the Salcombe area. They quickly spotted five aircraft flying fast and low and headed east. John Deall shot down one and damaged another which was then finished off by his wingman. Although the pilot of the second victim baled out, both *Fw* Hermann Schorn and *Uffz* Erwin Ziegler were killed.

Attacks for the next 11 days resorted to using the usual number of fighter-bombers, the first of which was against Frinton and Walton on the Naze by 10/*JG* 2 on the afternoon of 14 March 1943. The only change to the *modus operandi* occurred on 23 March when 20 *Jabos* raided Bournemouth. The same evening, the only loss of the 11 days occurred. During an attack in poor weather in the Dartmouth area, five aircraft from

Flt Lt Johnny Deall, 266 Squadron (via Thomas)

Flt Sgt 'Scottie' Eadie (via Thomas)

II/*SKG* 10 came under fire from light automatic weapons which broke up the formation. The aircraft flown by *Oblt* Oswald Laumann, the *Gruppen Adjutant* of II/*SKG* 10, was seen to be hit and smoke began to pour from its engine. The Focke-Wulf 190 then skimmed low over the village and crashed in open farmland on the outskirts of

Strete, killing the pilot who was apparently on his first operational flight. The aircraft broke up into three main sections, the engine cart-wheeling onwards to end up on a tennis court. The fuselage, though destroyed, still bore the markings of a black triangle ahead of the cross and a green 'H' after it. This, together with the identity disc of the dead pilot, was of great interest to the RAF:

> *"All the effects of the pilot who was shot down were destroyed with the exception of two coins – one German and one Polish – and his identity disc. The latter is of a series only once previously encountered on a pilot of 2/Schlachtgeschwader 2 shot down in southern Tunisia on March 7th.*
> *"The aircraft markings of* ▲+H *is also unhelpful as an indication of unit.*

Clearly visible on the FW 190 in the background is the ▲+G*. In the foreground are* Hptm *Graf von Sponeck,* Maj *Tonne,* Hptm *Böttger,* Lt *Setzer and an unidentified* Ofw

A makers plate recovered from Oblt *Laumann's FW 190*
(Parnell)

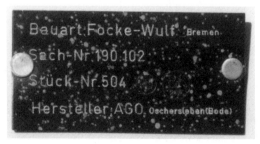

At the time of the Battle of Britain, the combination of a triangle and a letter was known to be the markings of II/LG 1 [sic] but it is over two years since an aircraft of that unit has been shot down over this country."

It would be another three weeks before the identity and existence of *SKG* 10 would be confirmed by British intelligence.

After well over a week of inactivity due to poor weather, it was decided to fly another mass *Jaboangriff*. The chosen target this time was Ashford in Kent, a major railway junction. Again, both of the experienced *Jabostaffeln* participated with *Oblt* Paul Keller leading the first wave. That evening, *Lt* Leopold Wenger wrote of the attack:

"After some days of unfavourable weather, it was 24 March before we could fly a major attack against Ashford, the important railway junction north-west of Folkestone. During this attack, I was able to observe the effects of the exploding bombs very well – all the bombs were direct hits. I was in the second Kette and received heavy Flak. Close to me a plane exploded in the air. Whilst diving, a light Flak gun opened fire at me, ripped open the engine cowling and

Bombenkeller *and a mechanic, Wizernes* (Storsberg)

a hole in the wing. My Rottenflieger was quickly at hand and able to knock out the gun. Then a gasholder exploded and all sorts of debris flew through the air – when we turned back there was just one big cloud of smoke over the town.. Today, the Kapitän is with the Luftflotte Chef to receive the Ritterkreuz; he will be pleased when he hears about our attack†…"

The identity of the 'exploding plane' was revealed in the loss report submitted afterwards by 10/*JG* 54:

"On 24 March 1943, Oblt Keller led a formation of Jabos to attack Ashford. After the bombs had been dropped and whilst flying a wide climbing turn to starboard, Oblt Keller received a direct hit. His aircraft exploded in a huge bright red flame. Therefore it can be assumed that his bomb had also exploded. The propeller, which was flying away by itself, was the only part of his plane which could be seen after the explosion."

The official British report is graphic as to the attack's effectiveness and suggests another reason as to how *Bombenkeller* was killed:

"…this attack was heavier and more successful than the enemy's previous efforts. The enemy aircraft flew across Ashford at low level from south-east to north-west. Two of the five bombs aimed at the railway works did considerable damage whilst three bombs which fell to the north of the works damaged rolling stock. The remaining enemy aircraft appear to have made an indiscriminate attack on the town. One enemy aircraft made a cannon attack from roof top height on a petrol lorry standing in the yard of an agricultural works and the lorry exploded. The bomb carried by this aircraft was hit by light anti-aircraft fire and the enemy aircraft blew up. Extensive damage was caused to the works as a result of the double explosion…"††

The attack on Ashford was devastating, resulting in the county of Kent's greatest number of civilian casualties as a result of an air attack for the whole of the war – 51 killed, 76 badly wounded and 78 suffering lesser wounds. Memories are particularly vivid:

"I was in Ashford hospital for a hernia operation – in those days, they didn't send you out the next day as they do now. You were in for three weeks with 10 days in bed.

"The warning went just before the raid started and all patients who could went to the shelter. Several others and myself were still confined to bed. The raid was carried out by FW 190 fighter-bombers, flying very low, presumably the main target was the railway works. There was a lot of anti-aircraft fire when suddenly there was a loud explosion – one of the FW 190s had been hit and exploded over

---

†*Hptm* Heinz Schumann was notified of the award of the *Ritterkreuz* on 19 March 1943
††AWA Report No BC/18 May 1943 p.7

Ashford under attack, 24 Mar 43; the attacking FW 190s are visible in the second photo (Wenger)

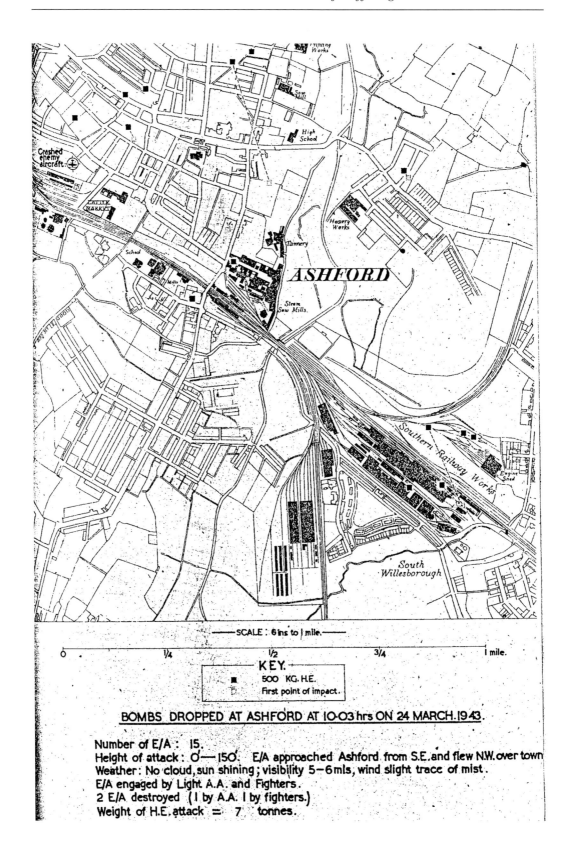

SCALE : 6 ins to 1 mile.

0   ¼   ½   ¾   1 mile

KEY.

■   500 KG. H.E.

▣   First point of impact.

BOMBS DROPPED AT ASHFORD AT 10·03 hrs ON 24 MARCH.1943.

Number of E/A : 15.
Height of attack : 0—150'. E/A approached Ashford from S.E. and flew N.W. over town
Weather : No cloud, sun shining ; visibility 5—6 mls, wind slight trace of mist.
E/A engaged by Light A.A. and Fighters.
2 E/A destroyed (1 by A.A. 1 by fighters.)
Weight of H.E. attack = 7 tonnes.

Stanhay's Agricultural Engineers in Godinton Road, about a quarter of a mile from the hospital, killing and wounding quite a number. Seconds after, a lump of ceiling crashed down between my bed and the old gentleman in the next bed. On inspection afterwards, they found a lump of the FW 190's engine had come through the roof and lodged in the cross beam between our beds.

"After what seemed quite a long time, the casualties started to be brought in the ward which was soon full. Camp beds were put in the middle and down the corridor with three men ending up in the Women's Ward! Some of the casualties were very serious, in fact some didn't make it.

"I was 12 and a half when this happened and those days there were no trauma clinics or counselling. You just had to get on with it."

Jim Poynton

"I can remember vividly the raid. At the time, I was a young telegram boy and had just come on duty and collected a number of telegrams for delivery, one of which was for an address in Kent Avenue. I was cycling along the High Street and can remember the window of Gutteridges the Chemists oscillating violently – it was restrained by large rubber suckers and wires. A quick glance over my shoulder revealed a Focke-Wulf 190 skimming the top of the Town Hall. At this point, I jumped off my bike and stood with my back against the wall of the Castle Inn. The slates were cascading off the roof and crashing into the road in front of me…"

Peter Wall

"At the time, I was working at 'Crumps' in the High Street. Haywards Garage was hit (one killed) and a bomb fell on Waghorn's Slaughter House, just behind the High Street in St John's Road. We were asked to help, being butchers and only a few yards away. Tom Weeks, an old journeyman butcher went and we carried the injured and dazed sheep out on an old door to where Tom had to put them down. I remember how heavy they were and how awkward it was clambering over the rubble…"

George Hooker

"Each day I cycled the six miles from my home in Bethersden to arrive at Stanhay's Motor Garage at the lower end of Bank Street by 0730 hours. The morning [of 24 March 1943] progressed normally until at approximately 1030 hours, the 'danger' hooter in the garage sounded (preceding the air raid siren as it quite often did) and we ran across the road to take cover in the basement beneath the Corn Exchange. As I ran down the steps an explosion helped me to the bottom – this was the FW 190 exploding over the Agricultural Works.

"The raid was over in seconds and we emerged from our shelter. At that time I was a Police Messenger and I cycled to the Police Station, eventually finding the front garden of the house where the body of a German pilot lay. Later I was told that a friend with whom I travelled to work at times was missing in the ruins of Drayswards Garage in New Street and when the building was demolished some time later, his body was found.

"It was said at the time that Lewis gunners on the railway bridge in Godinton Road had destroyed the 190 but as the raiders had come across from the Newtown Road direction, it is more likely that other gunners were responsible..."
  Bill Jarvis

A number of buildings were hit. At the Beaver Road Primary School, quick thinking by teachers ensured that in the region of 300 children between the ages of eight and 11 were safe in their shelters when a bomb scored a direct hit on their school. Two classrooms were obliterated – only minutes before, they had been full with about 80 pupils. However, the worst devastation was in and around the railway. Bob Barham was a Supernumerary Fitter at the Locomotive Works and had heard the 'Immediate Danger' sirens:

"As I ran out through the doors towards the air raid shelters, all Hell broke loose. Green and yellow streaks flashing by on all sides – Christ! Tracer shells! Stuttering roar of aircraft cannon, aircraft engines – loud, getting louder. Bloody Hell! Five of them, head on, very low – big radial engines, FW 190s, big black bomb dropping from the belly of one. It all happened in seconds, yet in slow motion as I flung myself to the ground. Heavy explosions, the ground kicks me in the stomach, engine noise deafening as the FW 190s sweep over at roof top height. They're gone and I get up and race for the nearest shelter because I can hear more of the sods coming. There is a great clattering of feet as many others join me, surging down the shelter steps.

"More machine-gunning, a crescendo of noise as the second wave sweeps over. Another lot of bombs and sand trickles down from the shelter roof. Ack-ack firing back now. The rattle of light machine-guns and the slower bark of a Bofors. In the background, the belated mournful wail of the public air raid warnings siren started. Yet a third wave comes in – their bombs further away...

"...As I emerged from the shelter, I was shocked to see a great pall of dense black smoke rising above the Shed roof – God, that one must have been bloody close! It was closer than I thought. People were running. I joined them and later wished I hadn't... A 500 kg bomb had hit 'E' Class Loco No.1515 on the right hand side of the boiler just below the steam dome. It had torn open a riveted seam, entered the boiler and twisted the fire tubes to resemble the rifling in a gun barrel before bursting through the tube plate into the firebox striking the foundation ring below the fire door which unfortunately for the poor Fireman still on the footplate, was open. The bomb then turned through 180 degrees to emerge some 20 yards in front of the engine where its delayed-action fuse caused it to detonate a few seconds later, leaving a crater 40 feet across and 15 feet deep. The blast caught the 55 ton loco, pushing it over sideways to lean drunkenly against the Coal Stage with its side framing ripped vertically upwards.

"The Driver apparently not seriously hurt, was lying near the edge of the crater and urged those who came to help him see to his Fireman first as he was trapped on the footplate. His Fireman was indeed trapped under nearly two

tons of coal. The boiler, with several hundred gallons of steam and water under pressure, had literally exploded, all of the water converting instantly into steam at nearly twice the temperature of boiling water…"

Bob's memories of the terrible injuries suffered by the poor Fireman are still vivid today; he continues:

"When we reached him, he was conscious and screaming in his agony. As he was being stretchered away, his cries of 'God, dear God, please let me die' haunted my dreams for many weeks. Mercifully, heavily sedated with morphine, he succumbed to his injuries some three hours later. By the time our First-Aiders returned to the Driver, he too had died. Although having no outward signs of injury, the blast had caused fatal damage to his lungs. After roll call another person was found to be missing – a labourer and near neighbour of ours. His body was found some hours later, buried under ashes in the Disposal Pit, another victim of blast-damaged lungs.

"Not surprisingly, everything not in the immediate vicinity had been blotted from one's mind. Now, with time to think more clearly, the full impact of what had happened began to dawn. I realised with horror that one third of the 600 foot long Loco Works Erecting Shop had virtually gone. Only the girders and stanchions supporting the overhead cranes remained over a 200 foot length…"

Casualties could have been worse at the Railway Works – the 'Immediate Danger' warning was sufficient to ensure that all but eight of the 2,000-strong workforce were under cover. As Bob concludes:

"Just how many lives were saved that day by the two men who gave the 'Immediate Danger' warning will never be known but for them in their post on top of the Railway Works bath house, the casualty list would have certainly been very much longer. They must have been very, very alert."

A great number of casualties occurred in and around Godinton Road as a result of *Bombenkeller's* aircraft exploding. The main part of his aircraft fell in allotment gardens and his body was thrown from the wreckage, landing in the recreation field at Barrow Hill. He was one of many to die in that area of Ashford that day as Don Flisher remembers:

"When I was 14 in late 1941 and left school, I declined my Dad's invitation to start an apprenticeship in the railway works as it seemed to me that Jerry was forever slipping in and slinging a few bombs into the works. So instead, I found myself a job in town in a small agricultural repair works called Stanhays in Godinton Road, just a low single-storey batch of about five small workshops and stores…

"…On this day, the FW 190s came in very, very low and there was no warning time…by this time, the guns were firing (them and us) and all the 100 or so employees were running through the works, heading for the shelter. I was working just outside the small canteen and had just popped in for the

10 am break when all of this started. The shelter was only a few feet away but to reach it, I would have had to go back though the workshop and out a side door and run about 20 yards to reach the shelter. While trying to make up my mind as to the best thing to do, all Hell broke loose as the FW 190s strafed the works. By this time I was alongside a wall on the floor and this saved my life as there was then an almighty explosion close by and all the roof and some of the walls disappeared…"

Like Bob Barham, what Don then saw is too terrible to describe, and even after 60 years, Don still remembers what he saw, what had happened and how many of his workmates had died. However, he continues:

"We didn't know at that time that there was a plane involved but a little later, one of the chaps came into the place and said 'We must have got one of the ********; they have just found a body outside and it is not one of ours as it has got flying boots'. Fourteen workmates died there, also the baker in a little two-man bakery alongside the works and of course the German pilot… After getting over my injuries, I thought if it's got my name on it, I'll get it anyway so what the Hell and I started my apprenticeship in the boiler works of the Railway Works in 1944."

The attack had been devastating and even those who experienced it will acknowledge that the Germans appear to have been aiming at the Railway Works which they did hit, putting it out of action for three weeks. However, the majority of casualties and devastation resulted from what nowadays is called 'co-lateral damage'.

People in Ashford who were alive at the time still think that the Germans lost more aircraft to RAF fighters on the way back; the truth is entirely the opposite. Two Spitfires of 91 Squadron were patrolling exactly where the *Jabos* were transiting, headed for France. As they tried to intercept, they were bounced by 5/*JG* 26 who were covering the *Jabo's* retreat – Fg Off Raymond De Hasse, who was on his first operational flight, was shot down and killed by *Uffz* Peter Crump whilst Fg Off Jim Anstie was wounded and his Spitfire badly damaged by *Fw* Wilhelm Freuwörth; Jim Anstie recalls:

"I can only add that I was hit in the header tank which immediately threw out a load of glycol so there was no alternative but to go through the gate and headed for the coast. Shortly after this, the old 'Rolls'† finally gave up the ghost, still streaming smoke. There was the alternative of a field with anti-invasion tripods or a wood. The wood was a definite 'No' so the field it was. I had to sideslip to see ahead so was not able to pick a clear spot. The left wing hit a tripod, spun me sharply and we finally came to rest minus both wings and the Rolls but miraculously no fire. In spite of locking the harness, my forehead hit

---

†Rolls Royce Merlin engine. Jim Anstie managed to crash-land at 400 yards short of the runway at Lympne at 1026 hours

91 Squadron, April 1943. Jim Anstie is 2nd from the left and has just returned following his wounds. The pilots are L to R: Turner, Anstie, Mitchell (+ 16 Jun 43), Todd, Benson, Hoornaert, Telfer, Matthew, Ingram, Sqn Ldr Harries, Kynaston (+ 15 Aug 44), Pannell, Mart, Huntley, Down, Johnson, Easby, Naismith, Bond (+ 19 Sep 43) (Anstie)

the windscreen but I only needed a couple of stitches in sickbay. After a couple of days in Canterbury Hospital, a week's leave followed…"

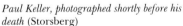
Paul Keller, photographed shortly before his death (Storsberg)

Sqn Ldr Ray Harries and Plt Off Albert 'Shag' O'Shaughnessy claim to have intercepted the retreating German aircraft, shooting down one and damaging another but the *Luftwaffe* just suffered the one loss – Paul Keller.

Just two more 'tip and run' attacks took place in March 1943 but the results were nowhere near as devastating as the one on 24 March. The first was carried out by 10/*JG* 54, now commanded by the very experienced *Lt* Erwin Busch, against Brighton in the late morning of 29 March 1943. The raid was witnessed by John Stoner:

"Early in 1943, I found my first full-time job as a junior clerk in the office of estate agents Dutton, Briant and Watts. One of my duties was to cycle to various streets in Brighton to collect rent owing on properties for which we were responsible (can you imagine a 15 year-old being allowed to do it today!)

"On Monday 29 March 1943 I was being shown round by one of the partners, Mr Draycott. We had got to Edward Street and met a lady who agreed to come back to her house in Grosvenor Street. She paid us her money and told us that next door had done a "Moonlight Move" so we could not collect from there. We carried on our way, had been gone about 10 minutes when there was an incredible noise and a Focke-Wulf 190 hurtled over just above the roof tops. I can see it today with the black crosses on the side and the pilot under the canopy. We dropped our cycles in the middle of the road, Mr Draycott dived into a front door one side of the street and I found one on the other side – it was as well that people didn't lock their doors in those days!

"When things had quietened down, we made our way back to where we could see a cloud of smoke and dust and found that poor old Grosvenor Street was a scene of devastation – the house that we had called at was a pile of rubble. The most poignant moment was when with a slithering sound, an eiderdown fell from the roof almost to where we were standing. I remember thinking 'Good Lord – somebody slept under that last night'. As there was nothing we could do, we made our way back to the office, only to find that there had been two other bombs not very far away, one in Gloucester Place, the other on the school clinic near to the fruit and vegetable market, both badly damaged and with casualties to be dug out. Sadly, we later learned that the lady we met in Edward Street had been killed."

Frank Conybeer also has vivid memories of the attack:

"I was training at a Royal Navy radio school which had taken over the St Dunstan's Home at Kemp Town. Such raids were not uncommon. Often the enemy planes arrived before the air raid sirens could be sounded and the first indication of a raid was when the Bofors guns positioned at intervals along the seafront opened up.

"On this day, three other ratings and myself were walking from the radio school towards our civilian billets for lunch break. We were walking towards College Road and were about 50 yards away when half a dozen Focke-Wulfs shot across in front of us at roof top height. We could clearly see the markings as well as the pilots. A detachment of Canadian soldiers was billeted in a large four-storey building in College Road and I vividly remember seeing one of them standing on the top landing of an iron fire escape on the side of the building and firing a Bren gun at the planes as they flew past almost level with him.

"Almost simultaneously, there were several heavy explosions and we threw ourselves to the ground against a wall. Then, conscious that our naval uniforms made a conspicuous and inviting target for machine-gun fire, we ran across the road to take shelter in the nearest shop. It turned out to be a wine shop and, had it been hit, we would have probably been cut to ribbons by glass from the bottles surrounding us.

"One of the bombs demolished a couple of houses near the general hospital and, with other Navy personnel, I spent the rest of the day as part of a human chain removing the rubble brick by brick in a careful search for people buried in the wreckage. A number of bodies were recovered and I saw one woman

Bomb damage at Brighton, 29 Mar 43 (Burgess)

brought out, plastered from head to toe in thick grey dust and deeply shocked but otherwise unhurt."

Yet again, mayhem and devastation was brought to another south coast town, resulting in the deaths of 18 civilians, the youngest of whom was four months old. However, by luck, two RAF fighters were in the right place at the right time to intercept. Fg Off Francois Venesoen and Sgt Edward Sutton of 610 Squadron were engaged in cine-gun practice and training but due to the thickening cloud, Francois Venesoen decided to lose height and broke cloud cover over Brighton. The 610 Squadron Operations Record Book relates what happened next:

"Green 1 (Venesoen) saw four aircraft flying over Brighton and four explosions in the streets of the town. He identified them as FW 190s and Fg Off Venesoen told Ops that there were 'Rat's about and dived immediately in pursuit and once again informed Ops where the Huns were. Green 1 caught up with the Bandits as they went out and shot at the third one leaving the town at 600 yards. He swerved violently and went in another direction whilst Green 1 concentrated on Number Four who was much nearer to him. He closed up with this FW 190 from 600 yards to about 200 yards and saw the hood fly off and black smoke coming from the engine. The e/a turned over and dived into the sea 500 yards from the coast…"

The report filed by 10/*JG* 54 afterwards leave no doubt as to Venesoen being the successful pilot:

> "*During a Jabo attack on the town of Brighton, the first Schwarm, flying in a right hand turn, was attacked by two Spitfires which came from behind and were flying about 200 metres higher. They attacked the fourth aircraft (Uffz Joachim Koch). After a short burst of fire, both enemy aircraft climbed again and turned away. Uffz Koch's aircraft crashed into the sea about 100-200 metres south of the coast. A bale out was not observed.*"

Uffz *Joachim Koch, +29 Mar 43* (Storsberg)

Koch's resting place in Brighton – his body was washed ashore nearly a month later (Hall)

Francois Venesoen's initial attack also had the desired result as another *Jabo* ditched on the return flight, its uninjured and therefore unknown pilot being quickly rescued. However, a Typhoon of 1 Squadron flown by Fg Off Cyril Bolster which had been scrambled to intercept the retreating German fighter-bombers was bounced and shot down by the *Jabo's* rear cover, the successful pilot being *Ofw* Willi Stratmann of 2/*JG* 2.

The final attack of the month occurred before breakfast the following day when eight Focke-Wulf 190s of II/*SKG* 10 dropped bombs in the Salcombe area as well Bolt Head airfield, dropping at least three bombs on the airfield, one of which failed to explode, and damaging a few buildings.

April 1943 would see yet more changes to 10/*JG* 2 and 10/*JG* 54. *Hptm* Heinz Schumann was on holiday with his family in his home town of Leipzig and wrote to *Lt* 'Poldi' Wenger indicating that something was in the offing:

> "...*you are leading the whole bunch now, subject to the Reichsmarschall authorising the whole plan which Peltz suggested to him... As Maj Grommes has probably informed you, you should be given a Staffel. Although you are still a bit young for this, I have nevertheless nominated you and I think that you will run the show in great style...*

> "*I have done this in the interest of the Staffel because I did not want to put another new man in charge of them. However, because of the formation of a new unit, the Staffel is depleted. It will be your and Nippa's task to show the young blood what is what. That could be done with Radlewski, Eschenhorn, Pfeiler and perhaps with Basil (I still do not know what to make of him).*

> "*By the way, I feel bloody good on holiday and am enjoying my family. However, Poldi, I have to make a few requests. Send me a coupon for a uniform jacket as quickly as possible. Second, some cigarettes, third onions and some other food. Things are damned meagre here!*"

Heinz Schumann had been given command of the newly formed IV/*SKG* 10 – 13 *Staffel* would be formed from 10/*JG* 2 and would be commanded by 'Poldi' Wenger, 14 *Staffel* would be formed from 10/*JG* 54 and would be commanded by *Lt* Erwin Busch and 15 *Staffel* would be formed from the remainder of the original *Jabostaffeln* and would be commanded by 10/*JG* 2's *Lt* Erhard Nippa. Reference to a change being made by *Oberst* Dietrich Peltz, *Inspekteurs der Kampfflieger*, later *Angriffsführer England*, probably refers to the commitment of I and II/*SKG* 10 from the middle of April 1943, leaving IV/*SKG* 10 and occasionally II/*SKG* 10 to continue with 'tip and run' attacks. Furthermore, the creation of three *Staffeln* from two would have needed an influx of additional 'young blood' to IV *Gruppe*, as Heinz Schumann called them. The diary of one pilot posted in at this time, *Uffz* Friedrich-Karl Schmidt, shows that he arrived on 15/*SKG* 10 at Caen on 10 May 1943, flying with his *Staffel Kapitän* the following day, and that his *Gruppe* was then officially 'inaugurated' on 15 May 43. The result of all of these changes was that April 1943 was very quiet from a 'tip and run' viewpoint – Leopold Wenger only flew three attacks during the month and those were in the first week. The reduction in these raids was noted by the British but the reason why was never commented upon.

The first attack of the month was by Leopold Wenger and two other pilots against Ventnor on 1 April 1943. Wenger reported good hits in the town, setting a vehicle on fire with the only defensive fire coming from light *Flak*.

Dietrich Peltz (left) seen here as an Oblt and St Kap of 1/StG 76, 1939 (Grahl)

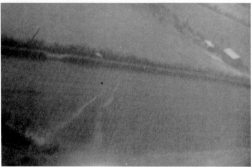

Ventnor under attack by 10/JG 2, 1 Apr 43. Clearly visible in the 1st photo are the radar masts above the town whilst the last photo shows a vehicle being strafed (Wenger)

197 Squadron had arrived at Tangmere on 28 March 1943 and two Typhoons were scrambled to intercept the German trio, the two pilots hopful of catching their first 'tip and run' raiders but the attack was too fast for them. The next daylight raid of April 1943 was against Eastbourne two days later and was carried out by between 12 and 16 fighter-bombers from 10/*JG* 2 and 10/*JG* 54. Again, Leopold Wenger took part and reported afterwards:

> *"Yesterday, 3 April, we had to fire on some of the Flak positions to put them out of action before we could attack Eastbourne. In the course of the attack, I was hit by Flak three times in the wings and fuselage. No doubt these will have been the last shots which that gun fired because my cannons did a good job. Our bombs were very effective and shortly after the attack, the whole town was enveloped in smoke and dust. Unfortunately, one of our planes was so badly hit that it crashed in the sea before reaching the [French] coast…"*

The *modus operandi* for the Germans was exactly the same as previous attacks on Eastbourne – they approached the coast at zero to 500 feet just before lunch time, climbing to make landfall at Beachy Head, then turning over the Downs to attack Eastbourne from the north. Widespread damage and destruction was caused throughout the town resulting in the deaths of 26 civilians (20 of them female) and 66 (again, 36 of them female) suffering

Eastbourne under attack, 3 Apr 43 (Wenger)

varying degrees of injuries. There were a number of military casualties, one of whom, presumed to be Ordinary Telegraphist Thomas Martin, saved the life of a baby; the baby's mother, Barbara Goacher, wrote the following on 13 April 1943:

> "...I was in the shop of Messrs Dale and Kerley with my baby Ian, aged four months... I left my baby in the perambulator on the ground floor and went up the stairs leading to the first floor, intending to get some baby rompers. A man's voice shouted 'Take cover!' and I ran downstairs where I had left the baby but found the perambulator empty. The sound of exploding bombs and anti-aircraft fire could be heard. I was pushed into the basement of the shop and shouted out 'My God, where's my baby!' and a sailor replied 'I have got somebody's baby' and I then saw that he had my baby underneath him. He was laying on the floor and it was apparent that he was shielding the baby with his body. The sailor got up and I saw that he was injured, bleeding profusely from the head. My baby was covered with blood but was only slightly bruised. I thanked the sailor very much for his action and he muttered something about 'one of his own' which I took to mean that he had a child. He tried to get out and I told him to take it easy as he was obviously seriously hurt. He did not say any more but flopped onto the floor in a collapsed state...
>
> "...I left the shop with my baby and did not see the sailor again. I can only assume that the sailor had taken the baby from the perambulator but as to whether he received his injuries inside or outside the shop I cannot say. I found that the perambulator had been blown by blast about 10 yards from where I had left it and was damaged. Whoever took my baby from the perambulator undoubtedly saved him from serious injury at the very least..."

Despite 'Poldi' Wenger's claim that they had neutralised the anti-aircraft defences, the British gunners put up a spirited defence but did not claim to have shot anything down. However, they did claim a victim as the 10/*JG* 54 loss report for the day indicated:

> "During the attack on Eastbourne on 3 April 1943, Uffz Fritz Ebert probably received a Flak hit in the engine. On the return flight, about 25-30 kms off Dieppe, he put the aircraft into a steep climb and baled out. Before that, he had reported on the radio that the engine was breaking down. This was immediately reported to Jafü 3 together with the request for those planes circling over the area to take a bearing. It was observed that Ebert was able to get out of his parachute harness and to inflate his life jacket and dinghy, also that he was about to climb into the dinghy. Further observation could not be made because our aircraft were attacked from above by British aircraft.
>
> After that, the Staffel flew air sea rescue missions for about eight hours over this area but Ebert could not be found any more. The Dieppe-based sea rescue vessel was also unsuccessful. It has to be assumed that Ebert was rescued by the British or that he had died in the Channel."

Sadly, the latter assumption was correct – 21 year-old Fritz Ebert's body was never found.

The penultimate attack of April 1943 took place on the 7th, was again led by 'Poldi' Wenger and is recorded as being the first carried out by 13/*SKG* 10. The target was Newport on the Isle of Wight which was attacked spectacularly before most of the town's inhabitants were awake, as schoolboy Rodney Charlesworth recalls:

Believed to be Uffz Fritz Ebert, lost 3 Apr 43
(Storsberg)

"I have, perhaps understandably, never forgotten being woken up that bright morning around 7 o'clock by a thunderous racket. My bed faced the window of my small bedroom and as my eyes opened, I saw a full frontal view of a FW 190 apparently heading straight for me. Behind it a mass of red and grey cloud billowed skywards from the joinery works a quarter of a mile down the road. As the FW passed over my roof, I heard its guns open up – the bullets hit a taller building across the road. My instant reaction had been to turn on my face in the bed – instinctive even if futile. My parents had dived under the Morrison shelter in the living room, only to dive out again and up the stairs to check on my state of health…"

Another eye-witness was nine year-old Peter Montgomery:

"…Six FW 190s attacked the saw mill, hitting it twice; the other four bombs fell on Dr Stratton's house, a grocery store and two groups of residential houses. My friend Ken Boon was awakened by the sound of aero engines and automatic gunfire followed by a loud pop ' like a balloon bursting' – a 500 kg bomb exploding in his grandparent's garden. He had the sensation of flying through the air and landed upside down. In that instant, he realised that he was buried. His mother was on the stairs when the bomb struck and saw that the rear of her house was now a pile of rubble, out of which protruded her son's legs. She began to dig him out with her bare hands…

"The seventh 190 attacked the railway bridge, its bomb overshot, passed through a local cinema and blew a shop to pieces. The eighth German pilot skip bombed the dairy. As I ran down the stairs, this bomb had skidded off a nearby

coal dump and was in full flight for its target. As I reached the foot of the stairs, the bomb plunged into the mill at the far end of the dairy. There was a noise like a huge door slamming and the stairs heaved. With a great crash, hundreds of window panes all broke at once. Fifteen feet from my face, the glass front door panels were sucked into the street. Still on my feet and still running, I dashed into the living room and flung myself face down onto the floor of our only shelter – a reinforced cupboard under the stairs. My mother, holding my small sister, piled in on top of me. The hideous noise then stopped, as though someone had flicked a switch. The raiders had gone, streaking low along the Bowcombe valley on their way to the coast, shooting at a herd of cows on the way, killing and fatally wounding a number of them…”

The attack cost the lives of 16 with nearly 217 suffering various injuries. Damage and destruction to buildings were considerable. However, for the Germans, the attack was not as easy at it appeared to those on the receiving end as Leopold Wenger later wrote:

“Each time during the recent attacks, things got heated. Yesterday morning, we attacked the capital of the Isle of Wight – Newport. Despite very heavy anti-aircraft fire, we dropped all bombs with direct hits. Unfortunately, again two of us were killed in the course of this attack. During the return flight, we had a running battle with British fighters (Typhoons). We came home bathed in sweat. The sorties are no longer easy – quite the reverse but the British are feeling our retaliation attacks, as they themselves report …”

Uffz Günter Eschenhorn and *Uffz* Rudolf Radlewski, two of the newer pilots who, just seven days before had been singled out for praise by *Hptm* Heinz Schumann, were killed, one shot down by *Flak*, the other by a Typhoon of 257 Squadron flown by Fg Off Peter Steib:

“I was leading a section of two aircraft (myself and Sgt Jack Mumford) on a standard anti-Rhubarb patrol between Portland Bill and the Needles and at low level. I was told by Control that enemy aircraft were attacking the Isle of Wight and were being intercepted by Typhoons of 486 Squadron from Tangmere. The Isle of Wight was inside their area of defensive responsibility. However, I elected to have a look-see and as we approached the southern point of the Isle of Wight, I saw four to six Me 109s [sic] crossing at low-level, heading for France. I turned in behind them and picked the rear-most aircraft to close on dead astern. I overhauled it quite easily at full throttle and when at fairly close range (150 yards) I gave it a very short burst of cannon fire which produced strikes and pieces started to come off the e/a, which I pulled up to avoid. Turning back and rolling over, I saw a white circle of foam where the Me 109 had gone into the sea.

“As I had then been airborne some time and with insufficient fuel to give further chase and return to Warmwell, I returned to my parent airfield and claimed one Me 109 destroyed which was confirmed by the ‘Y’ service. My

Fg Off Peter Steib (centre) photographed with his mechanics Geddes and Camp, 7 Apr 43 (via Rayner)

> *airborne time was 45 minutes and 36 rounds were fired from each cannon. I cannot believed now that it was a FW 190 not an Me 109 that I shot down – I always thought my aircraft identification was jolly good!"*

What would turn out to be the final 'tip and run' for over a month was against Folkestone at teatime on 9 April 1943 and was not without incident for both sides. Described by the *Luftwaffe* as a *Störangriff*, four fighter-bombers from 10/JG 54 dropped four 500 kg bombs on Folkestone, killing three, injuring 20 and damaging 286 houses. However, on the way back, one of the fighter-bombers started experiencing problems:

> *"After a Jabo attack on the town of Folkestone, the aircraft of Uffz Karl Heck showed a trail of black smoke which became thicker. About 20 kms north west of Cap Gris Nez, Heck climbed and jettisoned the canopy. The trail of smoke changed to white and Heck ditched successfully, the plane sinking at once. Heck was drifting in the water, his life jacket inflated. A Rotte stayed*

over this spot until they were forced away by enemy fighters. Several Rotte and Schwärme were unable to find Heck. All air sea rescue operations carried out until dusk came to nothing."

The *Luftwaffe* sent a patrol boat out from Calais, escorted by aircraft from *Stab* 6/*JG* 26, 8/*JG* 26 and 10/*JG* 54. The RAF, aware of what was going on mid-Channel, sent a mixture of fighters to catch the Germans – Spitfires from 611 Squadron and Typhoons from 1 and 609 Squadrons. One of the Spitfire pilots was Plt Off Harold Walmsley:

"On 9 April 1943, a section of aircraft led by Fg Off Gordon Lindsay (a great personal friend of mine) was patrolling at low-level off Dungeness. I believe that there was cloud cover and the visibility was poor. Sqn Ldr 'Bolz' Barthold was flying with us as a supernumerary to gain operational experience having returned recently from India.

"We were informed by Operational Control that there was 'trade' for us mid-Channel and given a southerly vector towards the French coast between Boulogne and the French Coast as I recall. About 10 miles off the French coast, whilst flying low-level, we arrived suddenly amongst an estimated eight FW 190s orbiting a German pilot in a dinghy and with a German ASR launch approaching. The element of surprise gave us the initial advantage (remember the visibility was quite poor) and I remember a FW 190 crashing in the sea quite close to the dinghy and wondering what the pilot therein thought about the situation!

"As was invariably the case in a dogfight, the situation became rapidly confused. We were all mixed up and wheeling around on the deck and, still outnumbered and expecting German reinforcements, disengaged as best we could to return home relatively intact. I believe that another Squadron had been scrambled in the meantime to take over but with what result, I know not."

A series of combats ensued. At 1900 hours, Sqn Ldr Barthold claimed a Focke-Wulf 190 destroyed three miles south west of Ambleteuse and Fg Off Lindsay another mid-Channel. Forty-five minutes later, Sgt R W Hornall of 1 Squadron intercepted five Focke-Wulf 190s shooting one down one mile east of Cap Gris Nez, the pilot of this one also baling out. 6/*JG* 26 reported the loss of *Ofw* Kurt Kruska north west of Boulogne and 8/*JG* 26 lost *Lt* Eugen Spieler 15 kilometres west of Boulogne. Although *Fw* Walter Grünlinger of Stab III/*JG* 26 claimed a Typhoon, no RAF fighters were lost.

However, there was one more German loss and one more RAF claim. 10/*JG* 54's final loss report before it became 14/*SKG* 10 records what happened:

"During the air sea rescue operation looking for a pilot who had ditched in the Channel, this Rotte was attacked by enemy fighters several times. The last attack was carried out from behind by two enemy aircraft. Our aircraft lost sight of each other in the haze 20 kms north of Cap Gris Nez and Lt Otto-August Backhaus has been missing since then."

Ofw *Kurt Kruska (far left) with, L to R:* Lt *Rolf Leuschel (+ 25 Feb 44),* Lt *Walter Matoni,* Lt *Helmut Hoppe (+1 Dec 43),* Ofw *Adolf Glunz and* Uffz *Heinz Marquardt (POW 20 Jan 43)* (Budde)

Lt *Otto-August Backhaus (left) in front of a 10/JG 54* Jabo (Storsberg)

Happier times-the last 10/JG 54 casualty, Otto-August Backhaus, with his Staffel Kapitän, Lt *Erwin Busch* (Storsberg)

Flt Lt Erik Haabjoern

Only Flt Lt Erik Haabjoern of 609 Squadron reported attacking two Focke-Wulf 190s from astern which then split up in the mist:

"I was flying as Red 1 with Sqn Ldr Lee as Red 2 in search of e/a patrolling ASR craft approximately 10 miles off Gris Nez. We were flying for about 15 minutes up and down the Channel unable to locate these when we came across two FW 190s flying in fairly close formation approaching us head-on at 200 feet. I warned Red 2 and at the same time turned sharply after them. They broke away and we took one each.

"Mine twice tried to get away by going right down and keeping on a straight north-east course which made it difficult for me to see him in the mist. Both times, out-of-range shots hitting the water all around him made him start weaving and this enabled me to catch him up quicker. After four to five short deflection bursts, the 190 began taking heavy evasive action but not really trying to out turn me, he pulled straight up to 2,000-3,000 feet and turned on his back where I got in a final burst at 250 yards. He jettisoned his hood and baled out, aircraft crashing 500 yards away from parachute..."

It was not an auspicious finish for the last day of action for 10/*JG* 54. It, like 10/*JG* 2, began to reform as one of the *Staffeln* of IV/*SKG* 10 and after a period of training its new pilots, would fly just three more 'tip and run' attacks.

In all, there would be just 16 more 'tip and run' raids between 7 May and 6 June 1943 but these attacks would involve much greater numbers of fighter-bombers and would pose an even greater, if short lived, threat to southern Britain.

9
The Final Throes

MAY – JUNE 1943

The dramatic reduction in 'tip and run' activity did not go unnoticed by the British and although no obvious reason could be given for it, the British still saw raids such as the one on the 3 April 1943 as wholly successful and that '...*it is clear from the results achieved in the 'tip and run' raids on coastal targets that our defences can be improved...*'†. Furthermore, a similar report analysing nocturnal bombing did not connect the reduction in daylight attacks with a commencement of fighter-bombers attacking by night, stating:

> *"The fighter-bomber appeared for the first time as a night bomber on the 16th/17th of April and it is presumably the new fast bomber†† which has been mentioned recently in German broadcast claims...They have operated mostly in the London and Home counties..."†††*

By the middle of April 1943, *Luftflotte* 3 had nearly 120 fighter-bombers available to attack Britain. The British were unaware of this massive force and if the *Luftwaffe* had utilised them in a similar tactical manner to the 'tip and run' raids of the previous 13 months, the British defences would have had considerable difficulty in countering them. Crucially, the *Luftwaffe* High Command, probably due to incomplete intelligence, now persisted in the belief that daylight *Jabo* missions had not achieved the desired effect and therefore the vast majority of *SKG* 10 would continue to be trained for nocturnal attacks, to the incredulity of many of their experienced pilots.

The first such raid on the night of 16/17 April 1943 was very much a farce from the *Luftwaffe's* point of view. During the day, 2/*SKG* 10 had already lost *Oblt* Franz Schwaiger in an accident and another pilot from I *Gruppe* had been forced to bale out when his Focke-Wulf 190 developed technical problems. Then the highly experienced *Staffel Führer* of 3/*SKG* 10, *Oblt* Fritz Trenn, collided with two other Focke-Wulf 190s from I *Gruppe* taking off

---

†AWA Report No BC/20 p.2
††Reference to the new unit, *SKG* 10, which was thought to be using a newer and faster FW 190 which was in fact not the case
†††AWA Report No BC/19 p.1

Loading up a FW 190 for night operations (Eberspächer)

from Poix, writing off three *Jabos* and killing himself in the process†. Two more aircraft were damaged in take-off accident for the mission and then during the attack itself, four pilots became disorientated. The *Staffel Kapitän* of 2/*SKG* 10, *Oblt* Hans Klahn died when his fighter-bomber crashed near Staplehurst in Kent and then three pilots from II/*SKG* 10 landed in quick succession at the RAF fighter airfield of West Malling near Maidstone in Kent. *Fw* Fritz Bechtold of 7 *Staffel* was the first, presenting the RAF with an immaculate Focke-Wulf 190 A-4. Then *Ofw* Otto Schulz from the same *Staffel* crashed into the undershoot, injuring himself badly††. Finally, *Lt* Fritz Setzer of 5/*SKG* 10, who had been critical of the wisdom of flying single-seat fighter-bombers at night, was forced to land his aircraft which had been damaged by *Flak*. On taxying in, a burst of machine-gun fire from an over-zealous gunner in an armoured car helped the already smouldering Focke-Wulf to burst into flames. There was one final casualty that night – *Fw* Werner Anrascheck of II/*SKG* 10 who failed to return from this mission.

Despite the disastrous start to these nocturnal attacks, the *Luftwaffe* persisted, meeting with better fortune on the nights that followed. Nevertheless, these raids were a just pin prick to the British and despite the initial concerns of the RAF as to being unable to shoot down the fighter-bombers, exactly a month after they started, Mosquito night fighters began to inflict heavy casualties on I/*SKG* 10.

On 7 May 1943, daylight raids recommenced when II/*SKG* 10, again operating from Coxyde in Belgium, attacked new targets – Great Yarmouth and Lowestoft in East Anglia at 0715 hours. Both missions were carried out simultaneously by 20 and 12 fighter-bombers respectively in an attempt to split the fighter defences and to try and catch the ground defences unaware. Both aims were achieved and the fact that Great Yarmouth and a nearby radar station were under attack was not evident to the British until the first bomb exploded. The Germans would have also got away unscathed but *Oblt* Willi Freudenreich of 7/*SKG* 10 collided with a telegraph pole at Newport in Norfolk and his fighter-bomber cartwheeled into the sea, killing him instantly.

A similar attack by II/*SKG* 10 four days later was equally successful and only by luck was the RAF able to intercept, as Fg Off Ron Smith of 613 Squadron remembers:

> "613 *Squadron was an Army Cooperation Squadron supposedly for fighter reconnaissance for the 9th Armoured Brigade. However, from April 1943 until July 1944, the operational role for our Mustangs was shipping recces off the Dutch coast. We were then based at Wellingore, a grass airfield satellite to Digby in Lincolnshire and using Coltishall in Norfolk as an advanced base for briefing and debriefing purposes.*

†Fritz Trenn had been awarded the *Deutsches Kreuz in Gold* and the *Ehrenpokal* whilst flying *Stukas* with III/*StG* 77. He was posthumously promoted to *Hptm* and awarded the *Ritterkreuz* on 25 May 43
††Otto Schulz was apparently so badly injured that he was repatriated in June 1944. However, he was reported to have been killed in a flying accident on 3 November 1944 whilst flying with 8/*JG* 6

Fw *Otto Bechtold's* Jabo *parked in front of the control tower at West Malling* (via Hall)

Lt *Fritz Setzer of 5/SKG 10,*
POW 17 April 43 (Setzer)

Fg Off Ron Smith in front of his Mustang (Smith)

Fg Off Bill Boddington (Smith)

Fg Off Henry Sackville; he was killed in action 4 days after
the 11 May 43 combat (Smith)

"On 11 May 1943, after an early start from Wellingore to Coltishall, four of us were briefed for a shipping recce, heading for Ijmuiden where Red Section, self and Fg Off Johnny Townsend would fly north to Texel and Blue Section, Fg Off Bill Boddington and Fg Off Henry Sackville, south to the Hook. In the event, we never got there.

"Our course from Coltishall took us over the coast several miles south of Great Yarmouth. While still inland flying at 1,500 feet, we saw smoke rising from Great Yarmouth away to our right and a number of fighter aircraft peeling off in front of us at sea-level. We put our noses down to fly low-level over the sea and gave chase. The dive enabled us to get within long range but not to gain more ground. It was apparent that the FW 190s had the legs of us and after opening fire, Townsend got a strike resulting in his target plunging into the sea. Strikes were claimed with no apparent result and the FW 190s pulled away. Two of our aircraft now had engine problems – the Mustang was an excellent aircraft to fly but the Allison engine never enjoyed the throttle being pushed through the gate for that bit of extra power. However, we all made safe landings at Coltishall…"

613 Squadron's report of the combat further amplifies what happened:

"By the time the coast was crossed, all the Bandits were heading east about half a mile in front. The initial dive of the leading Mustangs brought them to within about 400 yards of the Bandits which were clearly identified by all the pilots as being 10 to 12 FW 190s flying in loose formation line abreast about 30 feet off the water. After two or three minutes chasing, Fg Off Townsend, who was at 45 inches of boost and 2950 revs with an IAS of approximately 350 mph, closed to 250 yards and fired a three second burst at the nearest e/a which was more or less in the rear centre of the formation. Strikes were not observed but

Mustang AP248 of 613 Squadron; Fg Off John Townsend was flying this aircraft when he shot down the Jabo (Smith)

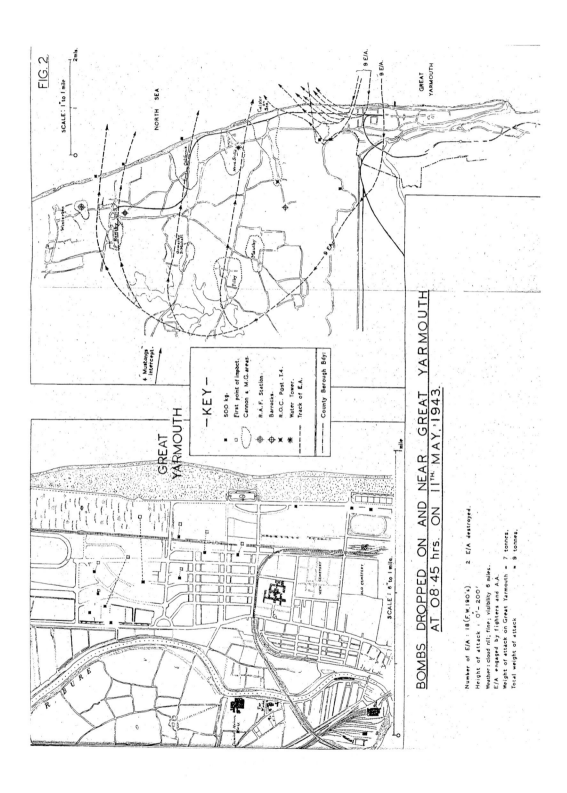

FIG. 2

BOMBS DROPPED ON AND NEAR GREAT YARMOUTH
AT 08·45 hrs. ON 11TH MAY, 1943.

— KEY —

■ 500 kg.
□ First point of impact.
⌖ Cannon & M.G. areas.
⊕ R.A.F. Station.
⊗ Barracks.
✳ R.O.C. Post. T.4.
Water Tower.
Track of E.A.
----- County Borough Bdy.

Number of E/A : 18 (F.W.190's).   2 E/A destroyed.
Height of attack : O'– 200'
Weather : cloud nil; fine; visibility 6 miles.
E/A engaged by fighters and A.A.
Weight of attack on Great Yarmouth = 7 tonnes.
Total weight of attack = 9 tonnes.

a cloud of black smoke streamed from the starboard side of the engine. Fg Off Townsend then closed and fired a slight deflection burst at the e/a which was turning gently to port. More smoke followed. Finally, Fg Off Townsend closed to 100 yards and gave one more burst of about three seconds whilst closing to 25 yards. E/a then slowed up so quickly that Fg Off Townsend overshot. He pulled to starboard and as he passed, the e/a hit the water and disintegrated..."

Despite anti-aircraft guns claiming one more aircraft and the other Mustang pilots claiming to have damaged other fighter-bombers, the only German casualty was *Lt* Joachim-Peter Giermann of 5/*SKG* 10. Again, the British defences had failed to prevent this attack which resulted in 49 deaths, 24 of them ATS girls whose billet on the seafront at Great Yarmouth took a direct hit.†

The following day, II/*SKG* 10, escorted by II/*JG* 1, were back again – this time 13 of them attacked Lowestoft and shipping off the coast early in the morning. One of the bombs dropped on the town bounced 150 yards, eventually exploding, killing five and severing the Observer Corps 'Imminent Danger' link. This was crucial as nearly 12 hours later, Lowestoft was attacked again and because the link had been severed, no warning was given to the town and its inhabitants. In the region of 25 fighter-bombers approached the coast, attacking the harbour and the north of the town, destroying 51 houses, seriously damaging 90 and damaging another 225. Thirty-two people were killed, 23 seriously injured and 28 suffered minor injuries. Three fighter-bombers also attacked Kessingland, a few miles south of Lowestoft, destroying three more houses and killing one – the village blacksmith. All of the fighter-bombers returned without any losses or damage. The official British report on the attack made stark reading:

"...the first warning received by anti-aircraft sites was the noise of falling bombs; the official warning was given two minutes after the first bomb had dropped. In addition to 21 bombs on land, several bombs were dropped in the sea near the harbour. Nine anti-aircraft sites were attacked with cannon and machine-gun fire and the gas works, electricity mains and a hospital were damaged..."†

Still persisting in attacking East Anglia, three days later and as the sun was setting, approximately 26 fighter-bombers were again heading for Lowestoft. However, in the three days since the last attack, barrage balloons had been positioned over the town so the Germans headed south, dropping bombs on Southwold and Felixstowe before heading back for the Continent. Although the bombing was scattered, it still killed 10 and injured 28 with 26 houses being destroyed at Southwold. Only a handful of RAF day fighters which were airborne at the time managed to intercept. Sgt Richard Hough of 195 Squadron claimed to have destroyed a Messerschmitt 109 off Southwold, his Typhoon being badly damaged in the combat. It is possible

†AWA Report BC/20 p.4

Pilots of 195 Squadron; Sgt Richard Hough is middle row, 2nd from right (Nentwich)

Plt Off Tadeusz Tarnowicz
(via Matusiak)

Plt Off Werner Kirchner (via Matusiak)

that the *Jabos* were escorted by *JG* 1 but no Messerschmitt 109s were lost by that unit on that day nor were any claims submitted. The only claims submitted for Focke-Wulf 190s were by 317 Squadron – Plt Off Tadeusz Tarnowicz claimed to have damaged one and Plt Off Werner Kirchner to have probably destroyed another as his combat report shows:

> *"I was leading White Section and while on standing patrol at 3,000 feet 15 miles east of Orfordness, I was vectored 240 degrees by the Debden Polish controller to intercept Bandits. After one or two minutes, I saw several Naval vessels ahead firing tracer (single red stream) at two aircraft which I recognised as two FW 190s flying towards us at sea level half a mile ahead. I turned tightly on reciprocal to attack No.1 enemy aircraft ordering my No.2 to attack No.2 enemy aircraft. My manoeuvre brought me close on the tail of the enemy aircraft and I fired a long burst of cannon and machine-gun from astern and slightly above. Aim was too high. Enemy aircraft turned sharp right and I followed closing to 150 yards firing a very long burst with cannon and machine-gun from 30 degrees right quarter hitting the enemy aircraft all the time. He relapsed now into a gentle right circle and side-slip towards the sea surface with plenty of black smoke coming from the fuselage. Although flying very low it was difficult to see*

the surface of the water and I had to pull up, catching a last glimpse of the enemy aircraft still side slipping towards the sea. After two or three seconds having gained a little height, I flattened out to look for the enemy aircraft but saw no sign of it at all, even though it had been flying just ahead of me…"

It is difficult to confirm who was responsible for shooting down *Fw* Hans Burkhard of *Stab/SKG 10* as he was reported to have been shot down by *Flak* 10 kilometres east of Southwold whilst *Fw* Bernhard Maasen of 7/*SKG* 10 was injured when he crashed at Maassluis, west of Rotterdam.

For the next few days, things were quieter in respect of 'tip and run' attacks. Interestingly, II/*SKG* 10 had another novel mission on 17 May 1943 with seven aircraft dropping 250 kg bombs on a formation of B-17s of the 1st Bombardment Wing attacking Lorient. This was not the first time that *SKG* 10 had tried this – on 16 April 1943, eight Focke-Wulf 190s of 6/*SKG* 10 had tried a similar tactic against B-17s also attacking Lorient. During the 16 April mission, the bombs, which were designed to explode on proximity, not contact, were seen to explode 100 metres above the American formation with unknown results. On the 17 May mission, the results were not recorded but *Fw* Karl Arndt was killed after combat, crashing at Ste Ave near Vannes.

After this brief interlude, on 23 May 1943, the *Jabos* were back with 20 aircraft from II/*SKG* 10 attacking Hastings whilst simultaneously, 26 aircraft from IV/*SKG* 10, this *Gruppe* undertaking its first mission since being redesignated, attacked Bournemouth. The British defences were all but overwhelmed by the two well coordinated attacks, even if the attack on Hastings was not a total surprise. This attack was witnessed by Les Clark:

"I had arranged with my mate who was also in the RAF to be on leave together. I had arrived home on 18 May and he on 22 May. Sunday 23 May was a nice day – right for May. In the morning, he came over to my house, my mother had just taken our photo in the back garden and we were talking when we heard aircraft. Keith Whimhurst and I looked at each other and said 'Jerry!!' and as we said it, we heard the sound of machine-gun fire followed by the thump of exploding bombs. My mother and our dog made a dash for the cellar. Keith and I dashed upstairs to my bedroom at the back of the house and as we looked out of the window, we saw five or six FW 190s skimming over the East Hill and Front. They had come in low from the east and dropped their first bombs on the Old Town about three quarters of a mile from us then flew out over the sea.

Keith Whimhurst and Les Clark; seconds after this photograph was taken, the Jabos attacked (Mrs P Clark)

"Columns of smoke had started to rise and in the midst of it, 'Moaning Minnie'† started wailing. Keith and I started off for the Old Town and when we got to Reeves Antique shop on the corner of the High Street and Courthouse Street, we saw that the Antique shop had suffered a direct hit and we could not get by as the road was taped off. A little further on, the Swan Hotel had suffered a direct hit – the smoke and dust was still rising, the rescue, First Aid, National Fire Service and Police were there so we went home.

"The Albany Hotel on the Front was demolished by a bomb which had first hit the coping of the Queen's Hotel – its bars were full of people at that time of the day – and exploded in the Albany. Canadian soldiers were killed as were some RAF personnel billeted in the Albany who were filing into lunch. 25 HE bombs were dropped and there was much machine-gunning. Five public houses and two hotels were amongst the buildings which received direct hits and many people were buried in the ruins. The Tower Hotel was hit by a bomb which penetrated to the cellar but did not explode.

"Rescue work went on throughout the rest of the day and night and following day. 25 people were killed, 30 seriously injured and 50 slightly."

The official report on the attack was descriptive if not slightly optimistic:

"Enemy aircraft approached from the south-east in brilliant sunshine across the line of flight. Overland, the e/a split up into groups, dropping 15 bombs on Hastings, one on Bexhill. Both towns were also attacked with machine-gun and cannon fire. Good warning was received by AA sites which destroyed two e/a. A third was destroyed by fighters. Several bomb craters along the Front were in the vicinity of gun positions which may have been the targets. The two piers at Hastings are prominent landmarks and there are a number of conspicuous buildings which probably make the town easy to locate."

II/*SKG* 10 lost two fighter-bombers in the attack. *Fw* Adam Fischer of 6 *Staffel* was a victim of *Flak* whilst *Ofw* Herbert Dobroch of 5 *Staffel*, who had just celebrated his 35th birthday, had the bad luck to be intercepted by a pair of Typhoons of 1 Squadron:

"Flt Sgt Ramsey was leader of Red Section which scrambled at 1258 hours to intercept e/a approaching the English Coast SW of Rye. Biggin Control ordered aircraft to fly at 2,000 feet on a vector of 230. Red 1 held this course until Control reported e/a were south of Rye at sea-level and with a view of getting between the enemy and his base, he altered course to 210 and dived to 0 feet. Crossing the coast just east of Rye, he saw clouds of smoke from bombs over Hastings and what appeared to be red rockets coming from the town. Red 1 who was then about three to four miles out turned and flew west parallel with the coast. He then spotted an aircraft also at sea-level gently weaving south, i.e. ahead and across his bows. He turned in pursuit and approaching from astern identified the aircraft as a FW 190. Closing to 300 yards, he gave several two-second bursts

†The air raid siren

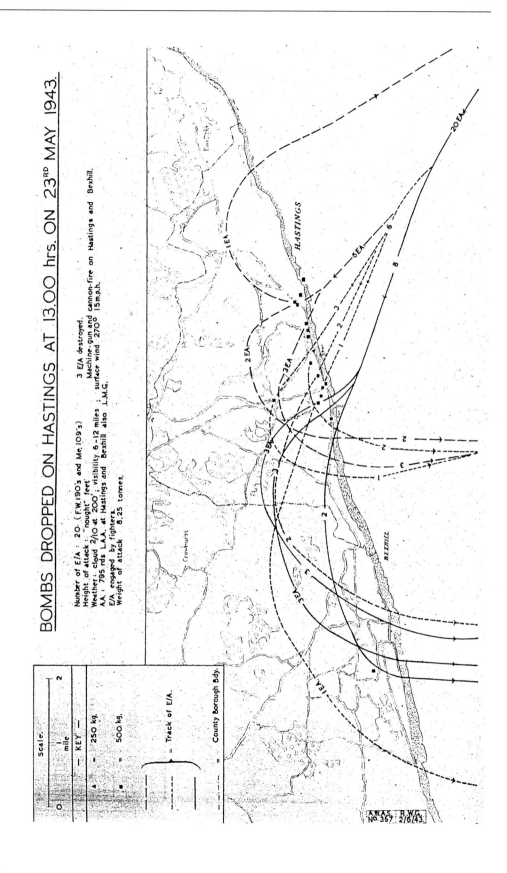

BOMBS DROPPED ON HASTINGS AT 13.00 hrs. ON 23ʳᵈ MAY 1943.

Number of E/A : 20. (F.W.190's and Me.109's)
Height of attack : "nought" feet
Weather : cloud 2/10 at 200 ; visibility 6-12 miles
AA : 795 rds L.A.A. at Hastings and Bexhill also L.M.G.
E/A engaged by fighters.
Weight of attack 8.25 tonnes,

3 E/A destroyed.
Machine-gun and cannon-fire on Hastings and Bexhill.
surface wind 270° 15 m.p.h.

Scale.
mile
KEY
▲ = 250 kg.
■ = 500 kg.
▬ ▬ ▬ = Track of E/A.
▬ ▬ = County Borough Bdy.

HASTINGS
BEXHILL
Crowhurst
Fairlight

A.W.A.S. R.W.G.
No 357 2/6/43

and saw strikes and as e/a started to climb, pieces flew off and the hood was jettisoned. Following in the steep climb, Red 1 continued firing, having to throttle back and weave to avoid overshooting. His ammunition exhausted, Red 1 called on Red 2 (Fg Off Watson) to have a crack but at that moment, when at 4,000 feet, pilot of e/a turned on his back and baled out. E/a was seen to crash into the sea and the pilot floating down in his parachute was alive…"

Both German pilots failed to survive and are still recorded as missing.

Meanwhile, further west, IV/*SKG* 10 was carrying out an identical attack on Bournemouth just four minutes after the first bombs exploded at Hastings. This time, the official report was a little more sombre:

"E/a approached at sea-level from the east-south-east with the sun half behind and flew out over the town flying in a westerly direction. All the bombs were dropped in a minute. Ample warning was received, the sirens sounding six minutes before the bombs were dropped. Considerable damage was done to property in the centre of the town. Two e/a were destroyed by AA."

Just one aircraft was lost – 21 year-old *Uffz* Friedrich-Karl Schmidt of 15/*SKG* 10 fell victim to a machine-gunner on the roof of the Eastcliffe Court Hotel, his aircraft then crashing into the St Ives Hotel at 34 Grove Road, Eastcliffe. Schmidt was killed in the crash which was later visited by Cpl Bill Hurley and his team who had been tasked to remove the wreckage:

15/SKG 10 immediately before the attack on Bournemouth. Standing L to R: Uffz Klaus Gehrke (+), Ofw Max Meixner (+21 Aug 44), Lt Werner Magarin (+27 Dec 43), Ofw Purps(groundcrew), Uffz Helmut Bächle, Uffz Karl Schmidt (+23 May 43), Lt Erhard Nippa (St Kap), Uffz Bernd Hofmeister (+23 Apr 44), Uffz Eugen Streich (+23 May 43), Uffz Rudi Agethen (+6 Mar 45). *Sitting/kneeling L to R:* Uffz Hans Müller, Gefr Karl Laue (+ 30 May 43), Uffz Ostermann. *Lying:* Uffz Herbert Kanngeter (POW 30 May 43) (Nippa)

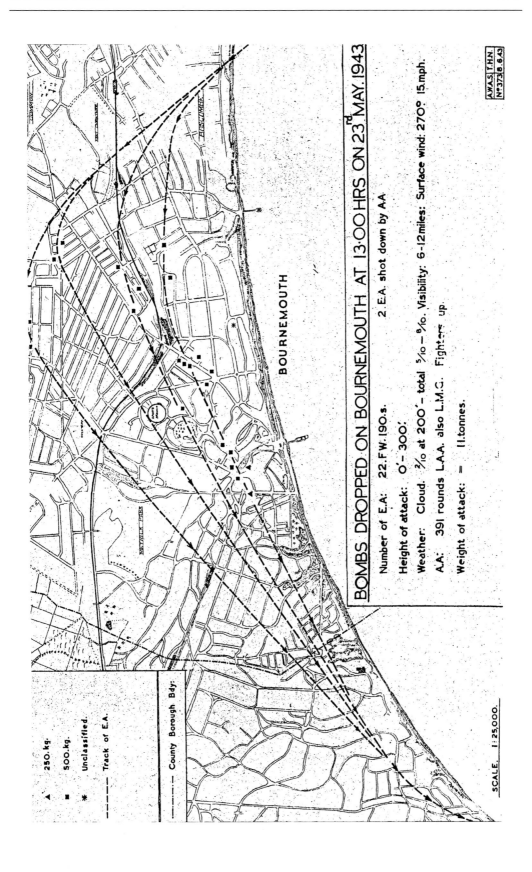

BOMBS DROPPED ON BOURNEMOUTH AT 13·00 HRS ON 23 MAY. 1943

Number of E.A.: 22.FW.190.s. 2. E.A. shot down by A.A.

Height of attack: 0´ – 300´:

Weather: Cloud. ²⁄₁₀ at 200´ – total ⁵⁄₁₀ – ⁸⁄₁₀. Visibility: 6 – 12 miles: Surface wind: 270° 15.mph.

A.A.: 391 rounds L.A.A. also L.M.G. Fighters up.

Weight of attack: = 11.tonnes.

BOURNEMOUTH

▲ 250.kg.
■ 500.kg.
✳ Unclassified.
– – – – Track of E.A.
——— County Borough Bdy.

SCALE. 1:25,000.

"We had been called out to travel to RAF Hurn (now Bournemouth Airport) to remove and transport the engine from a Mustang. On arriving we could see in the distance and coming from the centre of the town a big column of smoke and were then told of the German air raid that had taken place earlier. We were later given the order to go to Grove Road where we found that a German plane, almost intact, had crashed and embedded itself at an angle of about 45 degrees in the flat roof of what looked like an annex to the ground floor of the building. Some 15 to 20 feet away was a double fronted garage and at the bottom of one of the supporting posts was also embedded an unexploded bomb which a Bomb Disposal officer was trying to make safe..."

45 minutes later, the 500 kg bomb exploded, destroying the remains of the aircraft and the nearby houses. Schmidt's diary, found in the wreckage some time later, revealed not only his unit but that the attack on Bournemouth was his first operational flight.

Despite what the official report stated, the attack was both vicious and devastating. Although the approaching formation was detected, it was detected too late and the warning was not broadcast quickly enough. Initial reports after the raid stated that 20 civilians and six Service personnel had been killed, 25 seriously wounded and 44 slightly injured. Well over a year

The remains of Uffz Schmidt's FW 190

later, this figure was increased to 77 killed, 45 seriously wounded and 150 slightly wounded. However, in 1986, a letter to the Bournemouth Evening Echo written by Harry Mears, who on 23 May 1943 was the Bournemouth controller for Civil Defence, stated that 59 buildings were destroyed, 3,442 damaged, 77 civilians and 131 Service personnel killed. The exact figures of casualties are hard to ascertain. 34 RAF and RCAF personnel were killed or reported missing with an additional 38 wounded or injured. It is believed that the figure of 77 civilians is accurate but an unknown number of American servicemen are also thought to have lost their lives in the raid.

Scenes at Bournemouth Cemetery when the Service casualties were buried (Clarke)

Understandably, for those who experienced and survived the attack, memories are still crystal clear as the following accounts show:

> *"I was on duty at Parkstone Telephone Exchange. Several of my colleagues and I had just pressed the 'order wire button' and were waiting for the Bournemouth operator to allocate us lines. At this point, the alert had not sounded when we heard the noise of aircraft followed by a screech which we took to be a bomb falling. We could no longer hear the Bournemouth operator and we feared that the Exchange had been hit. We kept saying 'Are you there Bournemouth?' At last a very shaky voice replied saying that she couldn't see as they were temporarily blinded by dust but she felt that the bomb had fallen very close...*
>
> *"A strange coincidence occurred that day. The Restaurant manager and a colleague from Bobby's had been fire-watching and left their basement shelter to go for a drink in the Central Hotel and were killed there. At the same time, a bomb came through the ground floor window into the shelter whilst they were away. So whichever place they would have been in, a bomb seemed determined to get them!"*
>
> Margaret Cox

> *"I was given a few days leave before I had to return to 461 Squadron so called in on friends I had made in Bournemouth. I arrived on Saturday 22nd and on Sunday 23rd (it was a beautiful clear day) I was standing in the lounge at the front of the house when the windows started rattling. Wondering what it was, went to the window and peered out to see a FW 190, about 50 feet up, scattering cannon shells down the street. My only thought was glass! and found myself flat against the far wall. I had no recollection of moving but must have gone back in one hop! I raced into the dining room where the family were, yelled 'Air raid – into the shelter quick!' They wouldn't believe that a raid was on and wouldn't get into the shelter – the only one in it was Bonzo the dog. Finally, the air raid siren went but the raid was well and truly over by then – it only lasted a few seconds. I went outside and to my amazement, there were pillars of smoke coming up from all directions where the bombs had hit – and I hadn't heard one bomb explode!"*
>
> Peter Jensen

> *"I was four and a half years-old at the time and living in Christchurch. On this particular Sunday, a bright sunny day, I had just helped to lay the lunch table. I do not remember hearing the warning siren but I do recall clearly the windows vibrating to the roar of aircraft overhead. It sounded so close and so loud that it seemed as if they were going to crash into the building.*
>
> *"I ran out of the front door at the side of the flats and looked up just in time to see this aircraft, marked with a cross and its wings almost touching the chimney pots of the next block of flats. It was so low that I could see the pilot looking down at me.*
>
> *"Our upstairs neighbour rushed downstairs and whilst I was still gazing at*

the plane, she grabbed me and threw me into the hallway. I was most indignant, not understanding why, and then I heard her shouting at my mother 'Mrs Sims, Mrs Sims, that's a Jerry!'

"Then, within a few minutes, there was an almighty thud which shook the whole block. My grandmother who lived with us said 'My God, some poor devil has caught it.' Afterwards, we learned that Bournemouth had been bombed, in particular the Metropole Hotel and that a large number of airmen had died."

Patricia Di Girolamo

"Whilst my mother was preparing lunch, my brother, Dad and I went to visit a friend who lived across the road. We were all in the garden when the siren sounded and we heard the sound of approaching planes. I clearly remember looking up and saying 'Look Dad – I can see the man up there!'. Next thing I recall was Dad pushing me to the ground and lying on top of me. My brother was also on the ground with our neighbour lying on him.

"It all happened so suddenly. The planes were very, very low – it appeared that they flew just above the trolley bus cables in a line the length of Holdenhurst Road with the Metropole Hotel being at the far end..."

Mary Slater (nee Joy)

The Metropole before the attack (Clarke)

"On the fateful day, I was taking my daughter and another toddler to the Central Station to meet the London train. Whilst in the waiting room, the attack began. I don't remember if the siren gave warning. I dived under the seats and tried to cover the children. It seemed like hours but could have only been minutes. I was frozen with fear. After a while, when it was quieter, I crawled out and staggered outside. A taxi driver shouted get in – we must get out of the town. We drove to the Landsdowne when we were stopped by Police – we were outside the Metropole Hotel.

"I remember looking up and I saw an airman hanging out of the window. We told the rescue services who promptly put up ladders and brought him out. To our absolute horror, it was just a torso – I will never ever forget that."

Dorothy Walker

"It was a beautiful warm sunny day and peacefully quiet. I was sat on the small balcony of the Vale Royal Hotel – I could look out to sea through a gap to my left. All of a sudden there was an ear-shattering roar of aircraft engines. I looked and saw a line of German aircraft at roof top height. They immediately opened fired with cannon and released their bombs. I dived back into my room as cannon fire ripped into the hotel where the Bournemouth International Centre now stands. A bomb landed close to the Vale Royal which sent the hotel so far out of true that I expected the hotel to collapse. The raid was over in seconds – there had been no warning and the devastation was dreadful.

"I lost many Canadian friends particularly in the Metropole Hotel where I had been billeted a few weeks before. Bud Abbott† and I trained together – it was his habit to go to the gym and all that they found of his body was the torso. He could only be identified by his outstanding build. He lies buried with many others in Bournemouth."

Cyril Alright

"I had just sat down to lunch in the Osborne Hotel overlooking the Pleasure Gardens when the staccato rat-tat-tat of machine-gun fire flattened us to the floor. I glanced up through the window to see a Focke-Wulf pulling out of its dive over the Gardens. Then the window shattered and a stream of cannon shells embedded themselves along the wall of the dining room. When things quietened down, my first thoughts were to get back to HQ where my services would be urgently needed. As all the public transport was at a standstill, I had to make it across the town on foot, picking my way through masses of contents of shops littering the road when their windows had been blown out. As I approached the Landsdowne, the sight of what was left of the Metropole Hotel made my heart miss a beat, realising that some of my comrades were inside it. Then it suddenly dawned on me – had I not been promoted to Sergeant a few short weeks earlier, I too could well have been there when the bomb fell.

"Although I survived two near misses that day, I actually did not get off scot free. On my way back to HQ, an elderly lady, spying my RAF uniform, came bustling up to me brandishing her walking stick. 'Look what they have done to our beautiful town!' she screamed 'Why weren't you up there stopping them?' But before I could explain that I was only on the ground staff, she started walloping me about my head and shoulders, this unknowingly inflicting more damage to my person than Jerry had been unsuccessfully attempting over the past four years. Oh yes! I remember Bournemouth on that sunny Sunday in May 1943 all too well!"

Francis Lawford

"I was sitting in our beach hut which we had to remove from the Bournemouth cliffs and had erected on the garden lawn, doing some school homework. It was a month before my 17th birthday. I heard the noise of aircraft so I stood up and looking towards the house, saw a low-flying plane with a

†Believed to be Flt Sgt William Abbott

swastika on it passing just behind our chimney. There had been no siren warning. Suddenly there was a loud 'swish' and everything was obscured by dust and debris. I thought for a second that our house had been destroyed. However, it cleared and I ran towards our front door. My Mother had come up into the hallway but I could not reach her because of all the flying glass and debris...

"After a few minutes, things seemed to calm down and my Father, an ARP Warden, went off to his Warden's post and my Mother, a member of the Women's Voluntary Service, went to help where another bomb had done some damage to another house. I went to the bathroom to clean up some gashes on my legs and I then went to a school-friend's house to ask them if they had some more bandages which I could use on my legs.

"At the time, I thought that my injuries had been caused by flying debris but later investigation revealed two bomb fins on our lawn, one of which was very near to where I had been standing so I think it was that which caused the injuries. Also, it was clear that the bomb had caught the edge of the top floor wall of the house across the road, hit the pavement by our gate, bounced and caught the front wall of our house, continued upwards about a foot above my head, caught the top edge of the beach hut, gone through the sycamore trees behind and continued about a quarter of a mile over the Goods Yard (attached to Bournemouth Central Station), across the railway line and finally landed and exploded in Windham Road, severely damaging two houses..."

Gwendoline Read

All that the Germans said of the attack was that it had been a complete surprise and was aimed at the railway station and factories. Even *Lt* Leopold Wenger, now leading 13/*SKG* 10, only wrote that the raid was

13/SKG 10 three days after the Bournemouth attack, 'Poldi' Wenger is 2nd from the left (Wenger)

against the town centre, that he had experienced medium and heavy *Flak* and had spotted four Spitfires, probably reference to Spitfires of 616 Squadron which had been scrambled from the nearby airfield of Ibsley but failed to intercept. However, Wenger did manage to take a photo as he streaked over the town from east to west, looking down on a hotel. This hotel was recently identified by John Morley:

> *"It is the Cumberland Hotel on Bournemouth's East Cliff and it still looks today the same as it did when Lt Wenger took his audacious picture. One can count the number of windows along the back of the hotel; four rows each with 13 windows, and the drainpipes are even the same..."*

More amazing is that although it cannot be seen, there are three people on that roof as Lola Goodyear (nee Hayes) proves:

> *"It was a few days after my 19th birthday and my experience was just a fragment of the raid. I with Sgt Chapman and another member of the ATS was on fire piquet and we were checking equipment on the Cumberland's roof (sand bags, water buckets etc). A noise alerted us and to our horror a plane came out of the sun and roared quite low over the hotel. I am sure that the pilot was machine-gunning in the area. We left the roof in haste not daring to use the lift and ran down flights of stairs to safety."*

The Cumberland Hotel, 23 May 43 (Wenger)

Lola Hayes, May 43
(Goodyear)

Eugen Streich's funeral at Caen-Carpiquet (via Hall)

Uffz *Eugen Streich, of 15/SKG 10 killed in an accident on 23 May 43* (via Hall)

Two days later, the *Luftwaffe* tried raiding two more coastal towns. At 1220 hours, IV/*SKG* 10 sent 24 aircraft to attack Brighton. The British official report describes what happened:

> "*About 30 e/a made landfall between Roedean School and Rottingdean in line abreast. One section turned west over the town while the other headed NW towards Roedean Bottom where AA guns could not engage them. These e/a then circled the Whitehawk district, some acting as fighter escort at a height of 1,000 feet. Bombs were dropped near the railway and locomotive works and others appear to have been aimed, and with considerable success, at large buildings…*"

Tony Simmons was 13 at the time and kept a diary of what happened in Brighton from 1942 onwards and this is what he said about 25 May 1943:

> "*At about 1215 hours, Brighton had its worst raid yet. 25 planes came over machine-gunning and bombing. Was having Geography and had to get under a desk. I saw one Jerry swoop past the window – I was really scared. One boy went absolutely green. The house opposite was machine-gunned. At home Mummy got very scared and went under the shelter. Daddy, walking home, rushed inside a shop after seeing bombs falling out of several planes. Bombs were dropped at Eaton Place, Chichester Place, the other side of the hospital in Eastern Road (which was the worst). Bennett Road, St Marks School near the gas works, the gas works (all our gas went), the flats at Black Rock where a soldier was blown out to sea with his gun. The viaduct in London Road (one span was destroyed) and that's about all. Oh, and Arundel Road caught it and Hove was machine-gunned. In the evening I toured around the damage – it was awful.*"

For the inhabitants of Brighton, it was indeed an awful attack. 24 people were killed, 58 seriously injured and another 69 suffered lesser injuries. The damage to the town was considerable, the most spectacular bomb damage being seen by Estate Agent employee John Stoner:

> "*During the afternoon, I remember going to Argyle Road to see if any properties in which we were interested had been damaged. I saw where the enemy had had their luckiest strike. A bomb had gone through a garden wall, skidded across the road (I stood over the cuts in the tarmac) gone through a house, leaving a hole from front to back, and exploded under the arches of the viaduct carrying the railway line from Brighton to Lewes, the rails and sleepers were suspended across the gap.*"

The *Luftwaffe* again recorded the raid as a success, targets being the railway, gasometer and an electricity power station. *Lt* Leopold Wenger again took part and he was one of the pilots who attacked the Black Rock gasometer, proven by the spectacular photographs he took. However, despite the optimistic claims of the anti-aircraft gunners shooting down four fighter-bombers and RAF fighters claiming one, the only loss was *Uffz* Wilfried Braun of 14 *Staffel* whilst a second aircraft was slightly damaged. German

An aerial view of Brighton from Wenger's cockpit; the church to the left is St Marys (Wenger)

The same church in 2002 (Hall)

The view from the cockpit, Brighton, 25 May 43; in the distance and to the right is the Pier (Wenger)

The Blackrock gasworks 1943 (Wenger)

The same gasworks in 2002 (Hall)

records state that Braun was shot down by *Flak* but he could have been the victim of Sqn Ldr Desmond Scott, Commanding Officer of 486 Squadron. Scott and two other pilots had flown to Friston airfield to the east of Brighton and no sooner had they landed than they were scrambled to intercept the raid. The three New Zealand pilots were unable to intercept the attack before it happened but caught up with the formation as it was heading south. The port wing of the Focke-Wulf 190 Scott attacked was seen to clip the sea and the aircraft disintegrated on cartwheeling into the sea. Meanwhile, Flt Lt Spike Umbers was about to attack what he thought was a Messerschmitt 109 only to be bounced by another section of Typhoons from 486 Squadron who, mistaking his Typhoon for a Focke-Wulf 190, peppered his aircraft with cannon fire before realising the mistake.

However, the second raid of the day, carried out by the less experienced II/*SKG* 10, was a failure and showed what could happen if fighter-bomber attacks were successfully intercepted by RAF fighters.

The intended target was Folkestone which was to be attacked by 19 fighter-bombers at 2200 hours. As the formation approached the coast, they were detected and the warning passed to the airfield at Hawkinge, the new home of 91 Squadron, where Sqn Ldr Ray Harries and Plt Off John Round had just landed and were taxying in whilst Fg Off Jean Maridor and Plt Off Dennis Davy were about to land. 91 Squadron had recently been re-equipped with the superior Spitfire Mark XII which would make a difference in the ensuing combat; Jean Maridor's combat report relates what happened:

Fg Off Jean Maridor (Batten)

"I was about to land when I heard Control say that there were several e/a coming in towards Folkestone. I opened up straight out to sea and saw about 12 FW 190s at sea-level, one mile offshore, heading straight for Folkestone. I dived head-on at the leading formation with Blue 4 just behind me and to starboard. There were five e/a in a close box and the remainder were spread out behind them. Flak opened up from Folkestone. All the e/a panicked and jettisoned their bombs, turning towards the French coast. I selected one e/a and was about to attack when I saw Plt Off Round in a better position than I was. I took another e/a on the starboard side and closed to 300 yards without difficulty, giving him a four-second burst from astern without result. I closed to 250, giving another four-second burst seeing cannon hits on the fuselage. He began to smoke and I gave him a third burst, seeing further hits. I broke away on seeing some tracer going past my wings from astern and saw the e/a I had attacked go straight into the sea."

'Poldi' Wenger's Blue 12, Caen, 26 May 43 (Wenger)

486 Squadron – Gp Capt Paddy Crisham, Sqn Ldr Desmond Scott, Flt Lt Ian Waddy, Fg Off Allan Smith (via Thomas)

Sqn Ldr Harries claimed to have destroyed two of the fighter-bombers whilst Maridor, Davy and Round each claimed one destroyed. Albeit 91 Squadron had been instrumental in breaking up what could have been another devastating attack and justly deserve the credit (just one bomb fell on land – into the swimming pool at Folkestone), they were optimistic with their claims. The only aircraft shot down was that flown by the *Staffel Kapitän* of 6/*SKG* 10, *Oblt* Josef Keller; another Focke-Wulf 190 flown by *Lt* Walter Klein of 5/*SKG* 10 suffered slight damage and its pilot slightly wounded.

It would be another five days before both II and IV/*SKG* 10 ventured forth again. Yet again targets were chosen well away from each other – II *Gruppe* would attack Frinton-on-sea and Walton on The Naze in Essex in the evening whilst IV *Gruppe* would try a repeat performance of what they did at Bournemouth on 23 May only this time, it would be against 10/*JG* 2's once favoured target of Torquay.

Shortly before 1430 hours, at least 22 fighter-bombers were detected approaching Torbay. What happened next is left to those in the air and on the ground who were either involved or were witnesses:

> *"At the time of the attack, I was an 18 year-old aircrew cadet with No.1 ITW Babbacombe and was billeted in the Sefton Hotel. The day was a glorious one and after lunch I was one of a group of cadets who went onto the flat roof of the Sefton Hotel to revise for a forthcoming examination...*
>
> *"At about 1430 hours the sound of aircraft engines was heard coming from the direction of Torquay. I cannot be sure whether the air raid sirens had sounded. The noise increased and the sound of gunfire was heard. The aircraft were coming in our direction and it was obvious that the time to duck behind the parapet had come; we did so just in time. The attackers came in very fast, at rooftop height, and were firing their guns. Aircraft were passing to the front and rear of the hotel and directly over the roof; those passing overhead must have been only feet above us. The noise of the engines and guns was deafening, the roof of the Sefton seemed to shake and the slipstreams could be felt. We kept our heads down until the danger seemed to have passed, then there was an explosion. We regained our feet quickly and saw a column of dust and smoke rising above St Marychurch.*
>
> *"I don't recall whether anyone spoke – we just hastened in the direction of the dust and smoke. On arrival we were met with an appalling sight – the church (or most of it) lay in ruins. Someone said 'There are children under that lot'... No sound came from beneath the rubble, no cry for help, just silence. The horror of what had happened began to sink in – innocent children attending Sunday School were lying dead or dying beneath our feet, crushed by tons of shattered masonry, and we were powerless to help..."*

Walter Craine

> *"...A cadet who was our top man in aircraft recognition insisted that there were enemy aircraft coming in low over the sea. The corporal instructor said 'No way!'*

Torquay under attack, 30 May 43 (Wenger)

and then all hell broke loose. We made tracks for the shelters in the cliffs – I stood on the shelter steps and had a good view of the proceedings. I saw holes appearing in the white front walls of one of the hotels on the Front. The FW 190s were circling over Torquay and dropping bombs. There was an explosion over St Marychurch and within minutes, the enemy aircraft were belting back from whence they came. I

The remains of Gefr *Laue's FW 190* (via Irwin)

St Marychurch, 30 May 43 (via Irwin)

should mention that the Bofors gun on Petitor cliff only opened up when the FW 190s were going home, the siren went halfway during the raid. We had twin Brownings sited on the cliffs which we used for training. Live ammo we had none – the feed belts had wooden bullets…"

Roy Gowler

"At the time, I was 15 and Head Chorister at St Marychurch Parish Church. By all accounts I should have been in the church when the bomb dropped but I had decided earlier to miss on that occasion, not something I did very often. My purpose in playing truant from Sunday School was to visit Petitor to watch the making of a film starring Arthur Askey.

"I never did get to see it. As I left my home which overlooked the two towers of St Marychurch and the Roman Catholic church, the bomb dropped and I actually saw the church rise up and then disappear in a cloud of smoke and dust. I then went with my father to help the trapped children.

"The plane involved in the bombing of the church finally finished in Teignmouth Road, it crashed into and totally demolished the house of one of my friends (another choirboy). My view is that this particular bombing was a tragic accident rather than a deliberate targeting of the church. The plane was not in line for the church and my understanding has always been that its wing caught

The engine from Karl Laue's Jabo (via Irwin)

the 12 foot high cross on the Roman Catholic church, causing a change of direction (on course for the church). This in turn shook the bomb free (or it was released by the pilot to reduce weight). The plane then went out of control straight through my friend's house.

"Of the 21 children killed, seven were choirboys including a good friend I had walked home with after morning services. I had tried to persuade him to come with me to see the film being made but he declined. My last words to him were 'You won't get another chance – see you tonight then.'"

Gerald Thompson

"Being a Sunday, I with many other children went to Sunday School at St Marychurch. I was about to enter the church grounds when from the sound of low flying aircraft and gunfire, I knew another raid was in progress. I remember lying down in the gutter with my hands behind my neck in the approved manner until a bullet or something similar pinged against the wall very close to me. Thinking that this was just little more dangerous than usual, I ran towards better protection just as the church was hit with a bomb. The explosion lifted me bodily and just as quickly dropped me to the ground again.

"I think I was first on the scene of devastation and started to dig away debris from the sound of one of my schoolmates buried in the rubble (this was a lad called Eric Bartlett and was eventually rescued). Whilst digging away with my hands, I heard the sound of more aircraft approaching and immediately ran towards the cemetery where there were one or two graves with gravestones like tables. Crouching down between the stones, I looked up to see the fantastic sight of RAF fighters in hot pursuit...

"It was a sobering thought that if the timetables of events had been less than two minutes later, I would have been one of the children under tons of church debris. I thought this was enough for one day and ran home..."

Reginald Palk

Torquay after the attack. Clockwise: Union Street, Hartop School, Barton School and Installs Engineering (via Irwin)

Twenty-one bombs were dropped throughout the town, killing 45, seriously injuring 80 and slightly injuring another 77. At least 50 buildings were destroyed and over 3,250 suffered varying degrees of damage. Five RAF personnel were also killed and a further 11 wounded. By far the worst incident was the bombing of St Marychurch which resulted in the deaths of 21 children, the youngest nine, the oldest 14; 13 of those who died were orphans from the Erskine Home at Babbacombe.

From a German viewpoint, it had been both a successful and costly attack, led by *Hptm* Heinz Schumann and with all available pilots and aircraft taking part. One of the pilots involved was *Lt* Leopold Wenger who wrote:

> "On 30 May we again carried out a very heavy attack against Torquay. As usual in every large-scale effort, it worked well. The Flak was very much on the ball again and made it very difficult for us. Then we had air combat with the British and, for the first time, with American fighters [sic]. A good comrade of mine did not return this time…"

Another pilot was *Uffz* Hans Müller of 15/*SKG* 10 who as well as referring to the difficulty of the attack, also gives some idea of on what the bombs were dropped:

> "The attack on Torquay was my hardest sortie. The British radar had detected us although we were flying very low – and were waiting for us! Most of our bombs were jettisoned rather than being aimed at a special target. Of about 30 [sic] Fw 190s only 20 came back. I counted six AA hits in my aircraft. …
>
> "When I landed I did not know that my hometown Wuppertal† had been destroyed the night before, 29/30 May. Except for my relatives I lost everything I owned that night…"

German losses during this attack were much higher than normal. The pilot that collided with the church spire and then crashed into Teignmouth Road was *Gefr* Karl Laue of 15 *Staffel*. *Uffz* Erich Spät of 14 *Staffel* was hit by *Flak* and his Focke-Wulf 190 crashed into the sea just off Maidencombe Beach. *Uffz* Raimund Perlebach of 15 *Staffel* was last seen 70 kms south-east of Torquay and probably crashed due to *Flak* damage. These three pilots were killed – the only *Jabo* pilot lucky to be taken prisoner was *Uffz* Herbert Kanngeter of 15 *Staffel*:

> "On 30 May 1943 I was Rottenflieger to Fw Werner Magarin in No.2 Schwarm. We had been ordered to attack Torquay. The mission began at lunchtime. We crossed the Channel flying low-level and then climbed just before we reached the coastline. It had rarely happened ever before but this time we

---

†1,000 acres were destroyed by fire, approximately 3,400 people killed. It should not be overlooked that every week, pilots such as Hans Müller received letters from home or what had been their home telling them that friends and family had been killed by British bombs. One can probably understand therefore that some of them flew harbouring bitter feelings towards the British

Lt *Werner Magarin,* Uffz *Hans Müller,* Uffz *Klaus Gehrke,* Uffz *Rudi Agethen and* Fw *Franz Winter* (Nippa)

Rottenflieger Gefr Karl Laue (+ 30 May 43) and Uffz *Joachim Koch (+ with 10/JG 54, 2 Mar 43), Paris, Jun 42* (via Irwin)

received AA fire during our approach. Suddenly my plane shook and I saw lots of small holes in both wings; I had been hit. After jettisoning the bomb I turned back in the direction of the Channel and France. Via radio, I reported my situation and that I was trying to get as near to the French coast as possible.

"After a short time, the engine seized up; the propeller was still turning but the engine speed indicator did not show any revolutions. I was still flying at low-level and so it was impossible for me to pull up in order to bale out. I prepared to ditch – a procedure which had been discussed a thousand times and tested in theory before.

"I think a shell had hit the armoured engine cowling while I was climbing. Perhaps pieces of the armour plating were ripped off and shrapnel damaged both wings and some of the cylinder heads. Obviously the engine was losing oil and probably that was the reason why it seized up. I reported to my unit for the last time, disconnected the cable of my flying helmet and jettisoned the cockpit hood. There were only seconds left. While the Focke-Wulf was losing speed, I tried to maintain a horizontal flying attitude. When I noticed that the plane wanted to lose height suddenly I pulled the joystick so that the tail unit hit the water first. By doing this the aircraft did not turn over. I had previously undone the seat belts and braced my left arm against the instrument panel. When the Focke-Wulf went into the water nose first, I hit my head and only came to when I was already under water – still sitting in my plane. I escaped from the cockpit and swam to the surface. I was able to think, to move – so I was alive. I do not know what saved me – I must have had a guardian angel. After reaching the surface of the sea I inflated my dinghy and life-jacket and waited to see what fate would bring. Later two Hurricanes flew over me and reported my position. I was picked up and was treated very well. Of course this took some time but who counts the hours when you barely escape with your life. ..."

Herbert Kanngeter ditched 18 miles off Berry Head and was spotted by a Defiant flown by Fg Off Barry Hill and a Spitfire flown by Sgt A Kyle, both from the air-sea rescue unit 276 Squadron. They directed a Walrus, flown by Fg Off D McBrien, to Herbert and picked up what they described as 'a very exhausted German airman'. However, the Walrus was unable to take off again and had to be towed back into Torquay.

Flt Lt Barry Hill of 276 Squadron (+ 23 Jul 44) (Ewens)

The last moments of a Jabo *caught by Brian Calnan's camera gun* (Calnan)

One more German loss occurred, the only one to be shot down by the RAF. Five sections of Typhoons from 257 Squadron based at Warmwell were scrambled and all 10 fighters were vectored towards Torquay. However, as was normally the case, they arrived as the fighter-bombers were heading for home and even then, only Yellow Section, Flt Sgt Brian Calnan and Fg Off Tommy Clift, were able to catch up with the fleeing German aircraft:

> "…*After flying for about five minutes, Yellow Section saw a single aircraft at one o'clock about five miles distant at 300 feet and gave chase. After a further three minutes, Yellow 1 had closed the gap sufficiently to identify the aircraft as a FW 190. By this time, White 2 had joined up with Yellow Section.*
>
> "*The hostile had now approached the island of Guernsey and climbed to 1,000 feet to cross the coast. Yellow 1 gave full boost and revs and aircraft went into line astern. Speeds Typhoon 350 IAS FW 190 320 dropping to 300 estimated.*
>
> "*The chase continued across the Island and when Yellow 1 had closed in to 150 yards, he gave a 1½ second burst, seeing strikes on fuselage and wing roots. The FW 190 turned over onto its back and dived down, hitting a cliff, whereupon the aircraft exploded in a large sheet of orange flame…*"

Brian Calnan's Typhoon returned with a chunk of Focke-Wulf 190 cowling in his radiator. His victim is thought to have been Leopold Wenger's 'good comrade', *Lt* Hermann Müller. Both Wenger and Müller had joined *JG* 2 together back in December 1940, Wenger ending up in I *Gruppe* and Müller in III *Gruppe*. Müller was then posted to II/*JG* 53 and did not return to *JG* 2 until 23 March 1943.

At 1925 hours that same day, it was the turn of II *Gruppe* to attack Frinton-on-Sea and Walton on the Naze in Essex. 'Bunny' Burrows (now Edna Simpson) remembers the attack clearly:

"My room mate and I were in our bedroom on the second floor of the WAAF hostel and on hearing the sound of an aircraft overhead sounding very loud and very close, we naturally went to the window to see what was happening. We saw the plane alright, close enough for us to see the crosses on the wings. We instantly dived under the bed and heard the crunch of a bomb which, I believe, hit a nursing home on the street. It was close enough that the window shattered and our room was showered with debris from the falling plaster of our ceiling. I had been in Liverpool during the Blitz of 1941 and had lived through the horrors of the bombing there but the experience of actually seeing the plane responsible for the attack has lived on in my memory and I can still visualise the sight of that low flying aircraft and the cross on its wing."

Another eye-witness was Fred Daniels:

"It was customary on certain Sunday evenings for off duty personnel to be invited to the WAAF quarters recreation lounge for social get-togethers and musical concerts. A Scottish lass who was a very accomplished pianist would keep us entertained with a concert of classical music.

"I was making my way to the WAAF quarters when without any warning, a FW 190 flashed across in front of me at rooftop height and out to sea after just having dropped his bombs intended for Walton Tower†. He was one of at least six FW 190s reported on that raid – four made for the town where two civilians were killed and others injured. Of the two that were nearest the operational site, one we thought was aimed at the tower, fortunately missing it, and at the very low level he was flying, the bomb cut a furrow in the gravel of the road leading to the site, went over the cliffs and exploded on the beach below. At this stage my evening stroll changed to a smart run to the WAAF house where on finding the front door already open, I nipped into the recreation room to find all the 'bods' sheltering under the billiard table. After ascertaining that there were no more 'hostiles' in the offing, calm returned and the concert carried on without further interruption!"

The fighter-bombers had been seen to the north-east well out to sea, flying south, parallel to the coast, at 50 feet height. They then approached the coast in two groups, one from the south-east, the other from the south. After making landfall, the aircraft split into two clear groups, half attacking Walton, the other half attacking Frinton-on-sea. Again, the alert was not sounded but this was because there had been a breakdown in the system. Twenty bombs exploded in and around the two towns killing six and injuring 21, badly damaging the electricity transformer at Walton, disrupting gas and electricity supplies at three locations, damaging the main sewers, destroying six houses, badly damaging another 21 and slightly damaging hundreds more. The attackers did not get away without loss. Despite the anti-aircraft gunners claiming they had shot down five fighter-bombers, only two were lost. The aircraft flown by *Fw* Fritz Kessler

†Walton Tower was being used as a Chain Home Low operating station

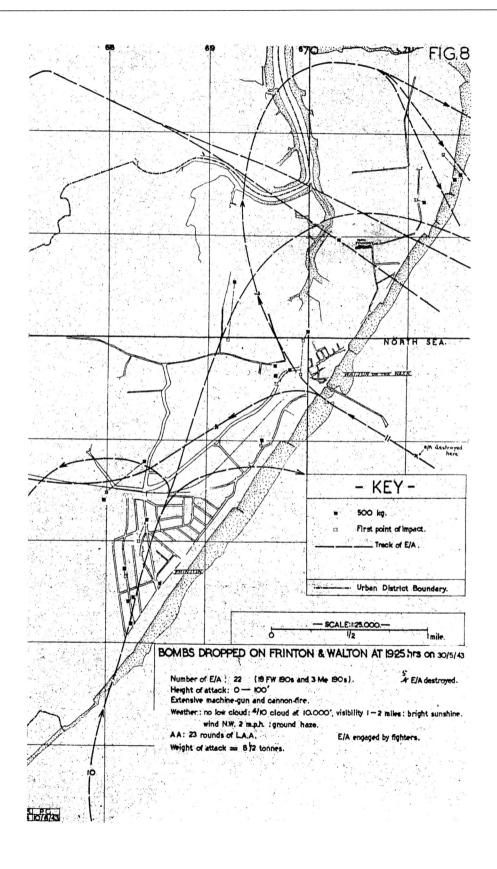

FIG.8

- KEY -

■   500 kg.

□   First point of impact.

———————   Track of E/A.

—·—·—·—   Urban District Boundary.

— SCALE:1:25,000.—

0   ½   1 mile.

BOMBS DROPPED ON FRINTON & WALTON AT 1925 hrs on 30/5/43

Number of E/A : 22   (19 FW 190s and 3 Me 190s).   E/A destroyed.
Height of attack: 0 — 100'
Extensive machine-gun and cannon-fire.
Weather: no low cloud; 4/10 cloud at 10,000', visibility 1 — 2 miles; bright sunshine.
        wind N.W. 2 m.p.h. ; ground haze.
AA: 23 rounds of L.A.A.   E/A engaged by fighters.
Weight of attack = 8½ tonnes.

of 5 *Staffel* was either shot down by a Bofors gun situated on the sea front on the approach to Walton or, as one eye-witness saw, crashed into the sea trying to avoid another Focke-Wulf 190. Kessler's aircraft crashed into the sea off Walton Pier and at dusk his body was recovered by the Walton lifeboat. The other German casualty was *Lt* Alois Harlos of 7 *Staffel*:

> "Soon after having left the coast my engine showed a thick trail of smoke. Nevertheless I kept on flying in the hope that I could reach the Belgian coast. However, after about 50 kms the engine suddenly stopped, perhaps because of a piston seizure. I suspect there was a problem with the oil supply of the engine. It is hard to say if this was a result of a technical problem or of British Flak.
>
> "Because I had suspected English fighters in the vicinity I was flying very low. I pulled the plane up but because of the low speed I could only reach a height of about 100 metres, so I did not think it wise to bale out. The surface of the sea was unusually smooth and I was able to ditch suffering only minor injuries. This happened towards evening, some time before sunset. The night was very impressive, the sea was full of marine phosphorescence. A ring of glowing creatures was floating around my dinghy. More than once I was able to observe porpoises obviously hunting fish.
>
> "From midday on the following day, I could hear aircraft flying along the English coast. Towards evening some fighter aircraft found me and called a Supermarine Walrus seaplane which picked me up in rough seas. The crew told me that they had been looking for a missing bomber whose emergency signals had been received. It was suspected that it had ditched or crashed in the area where they had found me but I had not noticed anything.
>
> "If they had not found me, there would have been only one chance of survival. The current could have taken me to the Danish coast, but that would have taken a lot of days and it is questionable if I could have survived it, especially because wind and swell were rising in the evening of 31 May and it began to become quite uncomfortable in my tiny dinghy. This way I survived this tragic war..."

Harlos had been very lucky to have been spotted as the 277 Squadron Operations Record Book entry for 31 May 1943 shows:

> "At 1800 hours, Operations informed the Flight that they had received a 'Mayday' from a Spitfire pilot of 402 Squadron†. At 1810 hours, WO Boddy and Sgt Granger were airborne from Martlesham Heath in Spitfires to act as escort to the Walrus which was airborne at 1815 hours piloted by WO Ormiston with Sgt Mann and Flt Sgt Errington. The Spitfires proceeded 140 degrees from base 55 miles at 5,000 feet. They spotted a dinghy and three Spitfires of 402 Squadron were in the vicinity circling the dinghy. Sgt Granger dropped another dinghy but this apparently failed to open correctly. WO Ormiston in the Walrus, having developed radio trouble failed to arrive at the correct position and WO Boddy asked for another Walrus accompanied by a

†Fg Off J G Torney of 402 Squadron who had been shot down by II/*JG* 1

Spitfire escort manned by Fg Off J M Edmiston and Flt Sgt Brodie. Meanwhile, WO Ormiston, finding his radio unserviceable and knowing the position of the pilot in the sea, decided to fly by dead reckoning and worked out an ETA on the way. Arriving over the position that he had plotted, there was nothing to be seen so he proceeded on for two minutes and then turned to return for base. After two minutes he spotted an airman in a dinghy waving to the aircraft. Dropping a smoke float, the Walrus landed on the water and the pilot, a Luftwaffe officer Leutnant Alois Harlos, who had been in the water for practically two days [sic], was taken aboard. All six aircraft landed at base at 1950 hours. The German airman thanked WO Ormiston for his effort and was taken to Station Sick Quarters for treatment…"

The morning after Alois Harlos was rescued, both Gruppen struck again. First of all, 13/*SKG* 10 attacked the western part of the Isle of Wight just before midday and then II/*SKG* 10 attacked Margate an hour and a half later. *Lt* Leopold Wenger led the first raid and wrote the following:

"…I have been over there today with my Staffel. I met a four-engined flying boat† just off the coast. We did shoot at it but couldn't waste time otherwise we could have had it 'for breakfast'. Then, however, we had to get rid of our bombs. Near St Catherine's Point, I scored a direct hit on a fuel or ammunition depot – everything went up with an enormous tongue of flame. A couple of places including a radio station were then attacked. The Flak livened up and fired at us. British fighter planes wanted to catch us as well but it was too late. Anyhow, this mission was a lot of fun…"

Wenger also reported that they had attacked a lighthouse. Ted Jones would remember this well:

"My father was a lighthouse keeper at St Catherine's Point and went off duty at midnight 31 May; the wind was then SSW Force 2. When Mr Tompkins went off duty at 0400 hours Tuesday 1 June, the wind had freshened to WSW Force 5. There had also been an Air Raid warning at 0130 hours with the All Clear at 0216 hours. Mr Grenfell came on duty at 0400 hours and should have been relieved by my father at 1300 hours. The last entry in the Journal at 0900 hours gives the wind still WSW Force 5 visibility clear. The three Keepers were then employed stowing bird perches in the engine room when the fighter-bombers came in at sea-level, under the radar hence no Air Raid warning. The first bomb hit the engine room, killing all three keepers. They then attacked Niton – one bomb hit the school playground killing a civilian. Another bomb hit the Undercliffe Hotel (it was a military HQ) killing two soldiers. Lloyds Wireless Station and an Observer Corps post were also attacked but there were no further casualties…"††

---

†Actually an unidentified Coastal Command Liberator
††The three lighthouse keepers who were killed were William Jones, Charles Tompkins and Richard Grenfell

Photographs taken by 'Poldi' Wenger showing the Liberator, radio station and lighthouse at Niton, 1 Jun 43 (Wenger)

Jim Crofts was serving in the radar unit at Niton at the time:

"Niton, known as RAF Blackgang, had proved to be a real thorn in the side of the Germans and had accounted for numerous enemy aircraft as well as a number of E-boats…

"It was customary for Blackgang to be switched off for maintenance and 1 June 1943 was no different to any other. The radar mechanics were busy checking the vital parts of the equipment and the non-technical staff were engaged on a general tidy up within the operations block whilst others were involved in a number of other tasks on other parts of the site.

Jim Crofts (standing, 3rd from left) and Sheila Barnard (kneeling, 2nd from right) (Crofts)

"We were about half way through our maintenance period when suddenly there was the roar of low-flying aircraft and the noise of explosions in the village of Niton just below the radar station where most of our personnel were billeted. We soon realised that this was an enemy low-level attack and everyone on the site grabbed their tin hats and ran for cover. A few more explosions were heard and in a very short time, all was quiet. We all emerged from our shelters to see a pall of smoke rising from the south of us.

"The first news of the attack on the village came from two of our airwomen. They had been on their way from the village to the site when they had to run for cover as the first enemy aircraft swept in from the sea. They reported that several houses had been hit, including the Undercliffe Hotel where a number of Army personnel were billeted.

"Our maintenance over, we were all desperate to finish our watch at 1300 hours and to find out for ourselves the extent of the damage to the village. A row of three houses had experienced a near miss but all of their windows were blown out and many slates were missing from their roofs. The undercliff seemed to have borne the brunt of the attack. The Undercliffe Hotel received a direct hit and had been demolished and it was understood that there had been a few casualties, some fatal. I talked with a lady who had been in one of the houses adjacent to the sea who actually saw the enemy aircraft approaching the coast and had witnessed one of the raiders circling the lighthouse at St Catherine's Point before dropping his bomb. It was later learned that all three Trinity House men who manned the lighthouse had been killed.

"Several other buildings sustained some slight damage but there was one remarkable incident. Personnel who manned the radar station at Blackgang used to use The Buddle Inn as their social HQ and on the morning in question, several of those off duty had been enjoying a quiet drink. One of our WAAFs, LACW Sheila Barnard, had just finished her drink and was leaving to return to her billet. She was half-way up some steps when one of the raiders dropped his bomb in the drive leading to The Inn. This did not explode on impact but instead skimmed the surface rather like a Dam Busters bomb. It continued straight ahead to where Sheila was standing and in its flight knocked her over. She fell against the stone wall and sustained a broken arm. As for the bomb, this continued on its merry way and exploded 200 yards further on. Surely there are not many people around today who can say that they were knocked over by a bomb and lived to tell the tale!"

Meanwhile, as one German formation was landing, another was taking off. Pat Sydes, who then lived at Broadstairs in Kent, witnessed what happened:

"I was watching some Typhoons with binoculars – they were fairly new on the scene then. There was a bang over Margate way and the Typhoons went out of sight. Next thing I saw was a line of FW 190s – all firing away – and a Typhoon seemed to be in the middle of them all. The Army was firing away as well – it was all very exciting to me as a young lad but a bit silly of me standing up like that in the middle of it all!"

The two Typhoons were from 609 Squadron and flown by Flt Lt Johnny Wells and Fg Off Idwal Davies; the Squadron Operations Record Book relates what happened:

"Seeing Margate gasometer blow up, Johnny Wells identifies 12 [sic] FW 190s. Engaging, he is promptly hit by light Ack-Ack but continues in pursuit of the enemy who streak out to sea almost touching the waves. Deciding it is important to attack the leading 'vic' of three, he finds the rest of the enemy formation flying innocuously on either side of him. Then, as he opens fire at 200 yards, one of the leaders dips a wing and goes in. Flying through the spray, he attacks the second which responds with a skid to starboard. Closing up, he fires

Flt Lt Johnny Wells, 609 Squadron

Fg Off Idwal Davies

again and this aircraft also plunges into the sea. At last, his 'escorts' open fire on him but ignoring this, Johnny attacks the third only to find his ammo exhausted. A steep climbing turn and his 'escorts' pass beneath. Score : Two.

"Davies attacks four FW 190s which are gunning the streets of Broadstairs. Chasing down after them between the houses, with his owns guns blazing, he just has time to see one pull up and its pilot bale out before giving chase to another six which are headed out to sea – five in a 'vic' with one in the 'box'. Firing on the last one from 600 yards, this aircraft obliges by weaving and closing the range, he fires twice more and it crashes into the sea in a great fountain of water. He then has to turn sharply on seeing tracer flash over his wings. On completing his turn, he is alone but resuming his original course at full boost, spots another pair of 190s with a third to port. Saving his last second's worth of ammo till he is well within range, he attacks the last and it bursts into flames. They are now exactly over Ostend and the others turn to counter attack. Time to go home. Score: Three."

The attack was assessed by the British as being 100% effective. Damage was extensive and yet another church, this time the Holy Trinity Church in Margate, was destroyed (and later demolished). There was also great damage caused to the rest of the town with 10 civilians and an unknown number of military personnel killed. Typical of wartime reporting, the 'Isle of Thanet Gazette' reported the attack under the banner 'Sneak Raiders Lightning Attack' saying:

> *"Sneak raiders of the Luftwaffe paid their heaviest price so far in their attacks when they bombed and machine-gunned a south-east coast town shortly after midday on Tuesday for 50 percent of the force of 12 bomb-carrying FW 190s were destroyed.*
>
> *"Light anti-aircraft gunners on the sea front claimed the first, peppering the fuselage as it approached the coast. With smoke belching from it, the plane roared over the town, dropping its bombs, and crashed near golf links at the rear. The pilot was killed. RAF Typhoon fighters swooped on the others as they made their way back and shot five into the sea.*
>
> *"The raid was the first the town had experienced for several months and lasted barely a minute. Damage was mainly confined to houses, a number of working class dwellings being destroyed, causing casualties, some of which were fatal. A church, a mission hall and a thrice-bombed cinema were among the buildings hit while many of the houses damaged had suffered in previous raids and still had first-aid material to their windows. Some shops were also hit and an infants school was damaged but, being the lunch hour, they were closed otherwise casualties would have been heavy…"*

Pilots of 609 Squadron investigating the crash of Uffz Zügenrücker's *FW 190*

The German version was actually much nearer the truth:

> *"Margate – success with complete surprise by fighter-bombers. Bombs hit a factory which began to burn and fuel tanks in a fairly large storage station set alight by machine-gun fire. One aircraft missing."*

It would appear that British claims of six aircraft shot down were wildly over-optimistic. Surviving German records make no mention of any fighter-bombers suffering substantial damage and the only casualty was *Uffz* Otto Zügenrücker of 5/*SKG* 10. He had already dropped his bomb and was turning back for home when he was both attacked by Idwal Davies and engaged by light anti-aircraft fire; Zügenrücker baled out but his parachute failed to open and he was killed; his aircraft crashed two miles west of Broadstairs.

Early the following morning, II/*SKG* 10 struck again, this time against Ipswich in Suffolk. The German report of the attack stated:

> *"Ipswich-harbour area and railway installations attacked with bombs and machine-guns from low altitude. At the same time another formation of fighter-bombers approached Felixstowe. While still out to sea, they encountered strong opposition from patrol boats but effectively broke through the Flak and Felixstowe's balloon barrage and attacked military objectives in the town."*

British records acknowledge that both Felixstowe and Ipswich were attacked just after dawn. Three bombs were dropped on Ipswich and another 13 in and around Felixstowe, hitting an iron foundry, setting alight yet another gas holder and machine-gunning an anti-aircraft site. The three aircraft that attacked Ipswich were flying extremely low, so low in fact that *Lt* Hans Schate of 7/SKG 10 either collided with a crane in Ipswich Docks or lost control trying to avoid high-tension cables; Schate was killed instantly.

It is interesting to note that for this attack, the *Jabos* were escorted by II/*JG* 26. *Ofw* Adolf Glunz of 4/*JG* 26 recorded in his logbook that he had taken off from Vitry at 0508 hours on a 'fighter escort for *Jabos* carrying out a *Terrorangriff* against Ipswich.' He landed again at 0621 hours, noting that the flight was uneventful.

Only two more 'tip and run' attacks would occur, both of them being aimed at Eastbourne with both raids being assessed by the British as 100% effective. The official British report stated:

> *"These raids demonstrated how the enemy varies his tactics in successive attacks on the same target. On 4 June, the e/a made landfall between Birling Gap and Beachy Head and turned east to attack Eastbourne; on 6 June, they reversed the procedure approaching from the east and going out over Beachy Head. The high ground at Beachy Head, to SW of the town, is thus used to provide cover either for approach or for departure.*
>
> *"Damage in these raids was confined mostly to shops, hotels and other large buildings. There was widespread machine-gunning and cannon fire in the*

town in both attacks. A Bofors gunsite was shot up on the 4th and the pier and two small naval launches anchored offshore on the 6th. "

The first attack by 18 fighter-bombers took place just before midday on 4 June 1943 and would be the last raid flown against the United Kingdom by IV/*SKG* 10. *Lt* Leopold Wenger took part:

"Today we attacked the town of Eastbourne with strong forces flying at low-level. We achieved considerable destruction. Certainly the Flak fired considerably better than usual and I was hit by 2cm Flak behind the engine which went through the whole aircraft. Several instruments failed and a small splinter went into my leg. I had more than enough trouble to bring my 'kite' home in one piece."

In addition to the extensive damage caused to the town by bombs and machine-gun fire, seven civilians were killed and 33 suffered varying degrees of injury. Two Spitfires of 41 Squadron flown by Fg Offs Jan Solak and Donald Smith managed to claim one Focke-Wulf 190 destroyed by Solak and another damaged by Smith just south of Beachy Head. Just one Focke-Wulf 190 was lost, that flown by the *Gruppen Adjutant* of IV/*SKG* 10, *Oblt* Kurt Hevler. Hevler was an experienced pilot, having flown with 7/*JG* 77 from 1940 to 1942, where he had gained *Jabo* experience, before becoming a fighter instructor in *Jagdgruppe Süd*, returning to operational flying in 1943, first with *JG* 27 and then IV/*SKG* 10. However, it would appear that his loss was not due to the two 41 Squadron pilots as the Bexhill Observer recorded:

"Gunners of a light AA unit, all Scotsmen, and who had taken over their site only a few days previously, are elated at their success in bringing down a FW 190, one of a force which raided a south coast town, dropping bombs and causing casualties.

"This was their first actual operational duty since coming from a course of intensive training. Besides this plane, which crashed on deserted marshland at

Eastbourne under attack, 4 Jun 43 (Wenger)

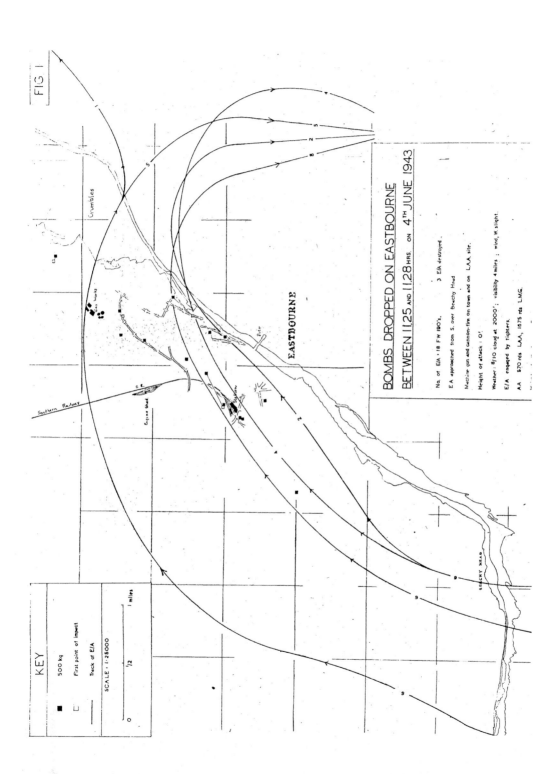

FIG I

KEY

500 kg
First point of impact
Track of E/A

SCALE 1:25000

0   ½   1 miles

BOMBS DROPPED ON EASTBOURNE
BETWEEN 1125 AND 1128 HRS. ON 4TH JUNE 1943

No. of E/A : 18 F W 190's.   3 E/A destroyed.

E.A. approached from S. over Beachy Head.

Machine gun and cannon-fire on town and on L.A.A. site.

Height of attack : 0'.

Weather : 8/10 cloud at 2000'; visibility 4 miles ; wind, W. slight.

E/A engaged by fighters.

AA   570 rds LAA, 1575 rds LMG.

EASTBOURNE

Crumbles

Southern Railway

Engine Shed

Normans Bay, the pilot of which was picked up dead, another gun crew is credited with the destruction of a second member of the raiding force and a third goes to the bag of an RAF fighter.

"After dropping their bombs, several of the raiders flew away from the town and approached the gunners. The barrage put up was considerable and drove the enemy seawards. As they turned it became evident that one had been hit.

"Those on the spot saw it falter, break away from the others and turn inland. It then suddenly dived headlong, nose first to the ground. The impact of the crash smashed off one wing and the rest of the machine rebounded some yards away to come to rest shattered and twisted, on its back. The pilot was thrown out when it first touched the ground – he had received a severe head wound from gunfire."

The second attack on Eastbourne occurred at 1338 hours two days later and was carried out by II/*SKG* 10. A report filed by Superintendent H D Archer very accurately relates what happened during what was a classic 'tip and run' attack:

"...at 1338 hours, Sunday 6 June 1943, 14 Focke-Wulf 190s dropped 13[sic] bombs on the town. These aircraft approached the coast at between 0 and 100 feet flying in a WNW direction, making landfall between Langney Point and Eastbourne Pier. One formation kept close to the coastline whilst the remainder flew inland for about a mile, wheeling to drop their bombs in the Upperton district.

"Eight aircraft passed out to sea over Birling Gap and six over Beachy Head Signal Station, flying due south. Ground defences engaged the raiders and several hits are claimed but there is no verification of aircraft being brought down by ground fire. One plane is reported as being shot down by the RAF.

"Five civilians were killed and one is missing, five service personnel were killed. 24 civilians were detained in hospitals and five service personnel."

Considerable damage was caused both by bombs at 14 locations throughout the town and machine-gun fire. Just one German aircraft was lost, that flown by *Lt* Dominikus Miller of 7/*SKG* 10. Yet again, he was shot down after he had dropped his bomb by two Spitfires of 91 Squadron flown by Plt Off Dennis Davy and Sgt John Watterson. John Watterson's combat report confirms the kill:

Dennis Davy, 91 Squadron (Batten)

SATURDAY, JUNE 12, 1943

END OF A SNEAK RAIDER

od shooting. This F.W. 190, seen lying on its back, was brought down by Ack-Ack fire at Normans Bay during a recent raid on the South-East Coast.

Some of the gun crew, who shot down the plane, examining the wreckage.

The only known photographs of Oblt *Hevler's* Jabo *(via Burgess)*

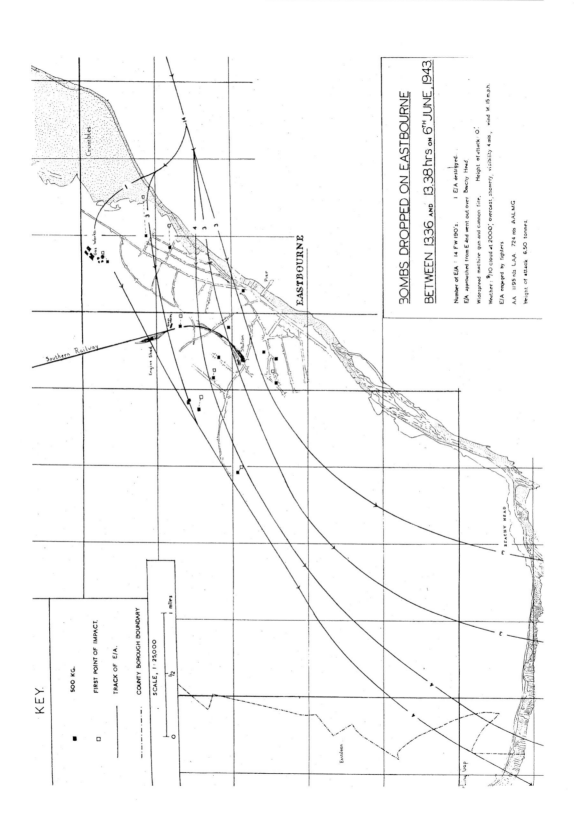

KEY.

■   500 KG.

□   FIRST POINT OF IMPACT.

    TRACK OF E/A.

—·—·—   COUNTY BOROUGH BOUNDARY

SCALE, 1:25,000

BOMBS DROPPED ON EASTBOURNE
BETWEEN 13.36 AND 13.38 hrs on 6TH JUNE, 1943

Number of E/A : 14 FW 190's.   1 E/A destroyed.

E/A approached from E and went out over Beachy Head.

Widespread machine gun and cannon fire.   Height of attack 0'.

Weather : 9/10 cloud at 2000', overcast, showery, visibility 4 mls, wind W 15 m.p.h.

E/A engaged by fighters

AA   1195 nds LAA   724 nds AALMG

Weight of attack 6.50 tonnes.

"I was Blue 2 in a section of three being led by Plt Off Davy on patrol south of Hastings. We were told there were 12 plus e/a at Pevensey and then saw bombs exploding in Eastbourne. I followed Blue 1 when he altered course to intercept the raid on the way out. We spotted one FW 190 about three miles away at sea-level and closed steadily until Blue 1 was able to attack with several bursts of cannon and machine-guns. I saw strikes during these attacks. The e/a was taking mild evasive action and, during one or two of his gentle turns, I fired several short bursts with about 10 degrees deflection observing strikes. After Blue 1 had made another attack and scored a good strike to starboard on the e/a, so that black smoke issued, I was able to close to about 100 yards and give a three second burst which resulted in strikes all over the aircraft. The e/a hit the sea and broke up and I could not avoid passing through some of the wreckage thrown up so that I sustained minor damage to my aircraft..."

As II/*SKG* 10 retreated to France, southern Britain yet again counted the cost and waited for the next attack, where ever and whenever that would be but, in the days that followed the 6 June 1943 raid, only nuisance – simply using gun-fire rather than bombs – as opposed to 'tip and run' attacks were carried out which continued to tie up the British defences. For example, on 6 July 1943 two Focke-Wulf 190s from 2/*JG* 1 strafed Ludham, Marham and Horsley in Norfolk. Two Typhoons of 56 Squadron were on cockpit readiness at Ludham airfield waiting for 'tip and run' raiders that had recently failed to materialise. One of the pilots was Flt Sgt 'Vic' Plumb:

"I was waiting in my Typhoon alongside my wingman, Flt Sgt Joe Clucas. Engines were constantly warmed up for instant take off and radios switched on. Suddenly we heard cannon-fire and saw two fighter aircraft diving down and firing at something on the ground in the vicinity of Ludham village. Not wishing to be caught on the ground, we took off and in doing so lost sight of the enemy machines which were Focke-Wulf 190s.

"Vectored out to sea by Neatishead controller, who was surprised to find us already airborne, I was told that the 190s were slightly ahead of us but faster. The information was repeated until we were almost out of radio contact at low altitude. The controller ordered us to proceed for another 15 minutes before abandoning the chase and I eventually decided to return. Climbing to 1,000 feet for a homing bearing to base, I looked across to my No.2 and saw a FW 190 behind him! Realising that the 190s had been behind us all the time, I shouted for Clucas to break. I pulled round for a head on attack on Clucas's 190 and as I did so, I saw that the second 190 was behind me. I fired at my wingman's attacker although I didn't see any hits. At the same time, the 190 behind me hit my wings with two cannon shells. Clucas's Typhoon went into a shallow dive pouring smoke from the fuselage and struck the water†. I now had the undivided attention of both 190s. I knew that the pilots of the 190 did not like to fly steep

†Clucas was shot down by *Uffz* Hans Vorhauer of 2/*JG* 1

*turns at low level, owing to its vicious high speed stall so flying just above the sea
I steep turned into my opponent's attacks. After a number of these manoeuvres, I
shook off my pursuers and returned to Ludham. The ground crew saw that
cannon shells had damaged the Typhoon's wings and when they took the cover
off one cannon bay, a fire was discovered in the wing. The Typhoon was written
off and to my great sorrow, Flt Sgt Clucas was never found."* †

However, the *Jabos* still did not come and the longer Britain waited, the
clearer it became that as suddenly as they had started, inexplicably 'tip and
run' attacks had finished.

After 15 months, the 'tip and run' campaign was finally over.

†Typhoon R8224 named 'Woman's Land Army' was declared Category B. On 13 September
1943, it was written off when overstressed during aerobatics whilst with 609 Squadron

Postscript

It was assumed that 'tip and run' raids in June 1943 would have continued in the same vein. The anti-aircraft guns were still loaded, Observer Corps posts still manned and the RAF still flew its 'anti-Rhubarb' patrols. The *Luftwaffe's* fighters did occasionally stray over the United Kingdom but did not carry bombs, preferring to carry out the occasional nuisance attack using guns.

The reason for the sudden cessation of 'tip and run' attacks has never been satisfactorily explained. The Observer Corps Narrative tries to explain it by saying:

> "...at the end of the first week in June [1943], these 'tip and run' raids ceased. Undoubtedly, the enemy had found it increasingly dangerous to make daylight sorties over this country..."†

Another source supports this explanation by saying

> "...Göring decided that the losses were too great and in June [1943] the...attacks petered out..."††

Contrary to the above, 'tip and run' raids had met with considerable success, especially for much of 1943, by normally hitting the designated target whilst keeping fighter-bomber losses to a minimum. There were a very few exceptions to this and in particular, the attacks carried out in June 1943 were seen by the British as being 100% successful.

There are three simple reasons why 'tip and run' attacks stopped. Firstly, German post-attack intelligence, normally quite poor throughout the war, underestimated what the raids had achieved; even the German radio broadcasts were unusually non-committal about the achievements†††.

Secondly, the *Luftwaffe* mistakenly believed that by using the fighter-bomber at night, similar results could be achieved whilst the darkness would help protect the aircraft. However, advances in British air-to-air radar technology and the superiority of British night fighters proved that that darkness was no protection, German losses were high and effectiveness very poor. As *Maj* Kurt Dahlmann, *Staffel Kapitän* of 2/*SKG* 10 in the Summer of 1943 and who later commanded I/*SKG* 10††††, flying nocturnal Focke-Wulf 190 attacks in the west to the end of the war made clear:

†*Royal Observer Corps Narrative 1943* pp.101 – 102
††Routledge, N W (1994) p.404
†††*Diary of Day Raiding – April and May 1943*
††††In August 1944, I/*SKG* 10 was re – designated III/*KG* 51 which itself was re-designated *Nachtschlachtgruppe* 20 in November 1944

A captured nocturnal Jabo *of 1/SKG 10, which landed at Manston, 22 Jun 43*

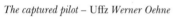

The captured pilot – Uffz Werner Oehne

Maj *Kurt Dahlmann* (Putz)

> *"...the night action of the Focke Wulf 190 against London was not very successful. It was a real makeshift. This type of aircraft was neither designated for this kind of mission nor was it suitable for this task..."*

The final reason why the attacks stopped was far simpler in that there were no fighter-bombers available for 'tip and run' missions left in north-west Europe by the middle of June 1943. On 12 May 1943, German forces had surrendered in North Africa and it was clear that the Allies would soon invade southern Europe. The Germans thought that the greater threat was now in the Mediterranean, the 'soft underbelly of Europe', so in order to reinforce III/*SKG* 10, II *Gruppe* was rushed from France to southern Italy in the second week of June 1943 whilst IV *Gruppe* was also withdrawn from France and operational from Italy by the end of June 1943. By then, the only fighter-bomber unit still in northern France was the nocturnal I/*SKG* 10.

So what was the impact of the German 'tip and run' campaign? The Germans had discovered a unique use for its fighter aircraft and after much trial and error (and even outright opposition), the fighter-bomber proved to be a very effective weapon against shipping. Extending its usage to coastal targets was also a success and the British defences had great difficulty in preventing many devastating attacks on numerous coastal towns and latterly inland targets.

For much of the 15 months that 'tip and run' attacks occurred, the Germans could only muster a maximum of 28 aircraft to attack targets on a coastline which stretched from Great Yarmouth to the Lizard, a distance in excess of 1,300 kilometres. However, this length of coastline and uncertainty of what would be attacked also played into the German's hands. There were insufficient anti-aircraft guns of the correct calibre to counter a low-flying high-speed threat, whilst:

> *"...the RAF could offer no positive defence against these fast, low-flying fighter-bombers which achieved an effect out of all proportion to the effort they represented. The Chain-Home and Chain-Home Low radar stations...were unable to plot the movements of the Jabos on account of their low altitude and Fighter Command was forced to mount standing patrols in order to counter the threat..."*[†]

It is interesting to note that wartime analysis stated anti-aircraft guns accounted for 55 'tip and run' attackers during the period March 1942 to 6 June 1943; fighters were said to have accounted for a further 51.[††] Analysis tells a different story – anti-aircraft fire actually accounted for 28 fighter-bombers, fighters a further 28, one aircraft was shared whilst a further five either collided with buildings, high-tension wires or other aircraft. It is clear that to lose 62 aircraft and 62 pilots over a 15 month period was high but at this stage of the war, this was sustainable. Furthermore, these losses should be

[†]Wood, T & Gunston, B (1977) p.62
[††]Routledge, N W (1994) p.404

IV/SKG 10 en route to the Mediterranean; LeO 452's transporting the groundcrew seen at Albenga, Italy (Feiger)

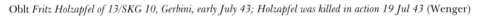

Oblt *Fritz Holzapfel of 13/SKG 10, Gerbini, early July 43; Holzapfel was killed in action 19 Jul 43* (Wenger)

A burnt out Jabo *of IV/SKG 10, Marsa del Oro, Sicily after an attack on the airfield, 7 Jul 43* (Wenger)

compared against a comparable German twin-engined *Kampfgeschwader*, *KG* 2 which, for the same period, lost 122 aircraft in attacks on Britain, costing in the region of 480 aircrew killed, missing or prisoners of war.

From a military viewpoint, 'tip and run' attacks did result in many more anti-aircraft guns and associated personnel being dedicated to defend potential targets. Furthermore, Fighter Command was forced to dedicate many aircraft to try and prevent the fighter-bombers from dropping their bombs, something normally met with little success. These assets could have been better used.

What of the impact on the civilian population and the Government? The inability to prevent such raids was a great worry to those living on the south coast. For example, Torquay was attacked eight times over the 15 months, two of these being severe and resulting in considerable loss of life. Two raids in 1943 so incensed civilians living in the towns affected that petitions were written and questions asked in the House of Commons. However, it would appear from the non-committal responses that 'tip and run' problems were left purely to the military and the attacks remained a constant irritation to civilians living on or near the south coast.

What then of the value of the 'fighter-bomber' as a weapon? The Germans did indeed develop the idea but the Allies copied and perfected it. Every Allied fighter introduced later during the war had to have, with minimum modification, the capability of carrying a bomb and the best example of this was the Hawker Typhoon. In the second half of 1943, the Typhoon found a new role as an all weather intruder and then close support aircraft, armed with bombs and rockets. In the battle for Normandy in the Summer of 1944, the Typhoon made a name for itself as a first-class anti-tank, anti-vehicle, anti-building and anti-strongpoint weapons platform, something the Germans never really managed to achieve after their early successes of the war.

'Tip and run' attacks did therefore have an impact on both the British

Jabos *of I/SG 5, Finland, 1944* (Diekwisch)

military and, to a lesser extent, the civilian population living on Britain's southern coast but there is scant evidence that the Government was overly concerned, unless a Member of Parliament's constituency was a regular target. From the German viewpoint, they underestimated what they were achieving with what was a very small force of fighter-bombers, a force which was too small to cause massive damage. The decision made in 1943 to use the fighter-bomber at night was misguided and even when the *Luftwaffe* had a massive fighter-bomber force at its disposal, it failed to utilise it in a way that would have swamped British defences and allowed the fighter-bombers to attack more targets, further inland, with virtual impunity.

As a result, the second 'tip and run' campaign has been largely forgotten or overlooked but for those on the receiving end, the memory of those attacks is still today burned into their memories with a vivid, still terrifying, clarity.

What could have been the ultimate Jabo – *a Messerschmitt 262A-2a seen at the end of the war* (Griehl)

Appendix 1
Jabostaffeln September – December 1940

Jabostaffel	Staffelkapitän	In Post
2/JG 2†[1]	*Oblt* Siegfried BETHKE	
6/JG 2	*Oblt* Frank LIESENDAHL	
7/JG 2	*Oblt* Werner MACHOLD	
2/JG 3	*Oblt* Helmut MECKEL	From 15 Sep 40
5/JG 3	*Oblt* Herbert KIJEWSKI	
7/JG 3	*Oblt* Erwin NEUERBURG	To 14 Dec 40
3/JG 26	*Hptm* Johannes SEIFERT	
4/JG 26	*Oblt* Hans KRUG	POW 7 Sep 40
	Oblt Kurt EBERSBERGER	
9/JG 26	*Oblt* Heinz EBELING	POW 5 Nov 40
	Oblt Kurt RUPPERT	From 12 Nov 40
6/JG 27†[2]	*Oblt* Werner SEYFERT	
	Hptm Hans-Joachim GERLACH	
7/JG 27†[3]	*Oblt* Erhard BRAUNE	
2/JG 51	*Oblt* Viktor MÖLDERS	POW 7 Oct 40
	Oblt Wilhelm HACHFELD	
5/JG 51	*Oblt* Hans KOLBOW	
9/JG 51	*Oblt* Karl-Heinz SCHNELL	From 30 Sep 40
1/JG 77†[4]	*Oblt* Hans-Karl KEITEL	
3/JG 53	*Oblt* Walter RUPP	POW 17 Oct 40
	Hptm Werner URSINUS	From 27 Oct 40
4/JG 53	*Oblt* Richard VOGEL	+ 10 Oct 40
	Oblt Kurt LIEDKE	
8/JG 53	*Oblt* Walter FIEL	POW 2 Oct 40
	Hptm Ernst-Günther HEINZE	
6/JG 54	*Oblt* Franz ECKERLE	
8/JG 54	*Oblt* Leo EGGERS	To 27 Oct 40
	Oblt Hans-Ekkehard BOB	4 Nov – 14 Dec 40
	Oblt Richard HAUSMANN	from 14 Dec 40
9/JG 54	*Oblt* Richard HAUSMANN	To 14 Dec 40
	Oblt Hans-Ekkehard BOB	From 14 Dec 40
3/Erpr.Gr 210	*Oblt* Otto HINTZE	POW 29 Oct 40
	Oblt Peter EMMERICH	
1(J)/LG 2†[5]	*Oblt* Adolf BUHL	+ 27 Sep 40
2(J)/LG 2	*Oblt* Friedrich-Wilhelm STRAKELJAHN	
3(J)/LG 2	*Oblt* Werner TISMAR	
4(S)/LG 2	*Oblt* Heinrich VOGLER	+ 5 Dec 40
	Oblt Alfred DRUSCHEL	
5(S)/LG 2	*Oblt* Bruno von SCHENK	+ 29 Oct 40
	Oblt Georg DÖRFFEL	
6(S)/LG 2	*Oblt* Werner DÖRNBRACK	

N.B If no dates are specified, the post was occupied for the entire period.

†[1] There is no evidence that *JG* 2 flew *Jabo* sorties during 1940
†[2] Transferred to Germany 6 Nov 40
†[3] Transferred to Germany 11 Nov 40
†[4] Redesignated 10/JG 51 21 Nov 40
†[5] I (J)/LG 2 was transferred to Germany 5 Nov 40

Appendix 2

Pilots of 13 & 10/Jagdgeschwader 2 November 1941 – 16 April 1943

St Kap	*Oblt/Hptm* Frank LIESENDAHL	11 Nov 41 – +17 Jul 42. Awarded *Ehrenpokal* 29 Jan 42, *DKiG* 5 Jun 42, RK 4 Sep 42
	Oblt Fritz SCHRÖTER	18 Jul 42– Dec 42; survived. Awarded *DKiG* 21 Aug 42, RK 24 Sep 42
	Oblt Heinz SCHUMANN	11 Dec 42 – 16 Apr 43; + 8 Nov 43 with *Stab/SG* 10. Awarded *Ehrenpokal* 15 Sep 41, *DKiG* 22 Jan 42, *RK* 18 Mar 43
Pilots	*Oblt* Fritz SCHRÖTER	Nov 41 – to *St Kap* 18 Jul 42
	Lt Kurt ECKLEBEN	21 Sep 42 – + 25 Nov 43 with Stab II/*SG* 10
	Lt Josef 'Sepp' FRÖSCHL	Nov 41 – POW 27 May 42; awarded *DKiG* 10 Jul 42
	Lt Fritz HOLZAPFEL	+ with 13/SKG 10, 19 Jul 43
	Lt Gerhard LIMBERG	Nov 41; Survived. Awarded *Ehrenpokal* 26 Jul 43, *DKiG* 20 Mar 44
	Lt Erhard NIPPA	Nov 41; Survived. Awarded *DKiG* 29 Apr 43, *RK* 26 Mar 44
	Lt Hans-Joachim SCHULZ	28 Mar 42 – +16 May 42
	Lt Leopold WENGER	Nov 41; 10 Apr 45 with 6/*SG* 10. Awarded *DKiG* 17 Oct 43, *RK* 14 Jan 45
	Ofw Herbert KORTH	+12 Mar 43
	Fw Joachim Von BITTER	28 Mar 42 – +10 Jan 43
	Fw Karl BLASE	6 May 42 – +26 Jan 43; awarded *DKiG* 23 Feb 43
	Fw Josef NIESMANN	Nov 41 – Survived
	Fw Hermann ROHNE	+26 Feb 43
	Uffz Kurt BRESSLER	+ 26 Feb 43
	Uffz Bruno GÖRENDT	+8 May 42
	Uffz Walter HÖFER	26 Jun 42 – + 4 Sep 42
	Uffz Ernst LÄPPLE	+1 Mar 43
	Uffz Werner MAGARIN	+27 Dec 43 with 5/*SG* 10. Awarded *DKiG* 17 May 43
	Uffz Max MEIXNER	+ 21 Aug 44 with 6/*SG* 10
	Uffz Walter PEILER	+ 1 Jun 44 with 4/*SG* 10
	Uffz Rudolf RADLEWSKI	+ 7 Apr 43
	Uffz Rudolf SCHWARZER	+31 May 42
	Uffz Hans-Walter WANDSCHNEIDER	+17 Sep 42
	Uffz Gottfried WEISER	+31 Mar 42
	Uffz Günter ESCHENHORN	+7 Apr 43
	Ogefr Franz LANGHAMMER	+21 Apr 42

Pilots of 10/Jagdgeschwader 26 & 10/Jagdgeschwader 54 March 1942 – April 1943

St Kap	*Hptm* Karl PLUNSER	10 Mar – 12 Jul 42 (believed to *JG* 106)
	Oblt Fritz SCHRÖTER	From 10/*JG* 2 13 Jul 42; returned to 10/*JG* 2 17 Jul 42. Survived
	Oblt Joachim-Hans GEBURTIG	From 8/*JG* 26 18 Jul 42 – POW 30 Jul 42
	Oblt Paul KELLER	From *Stab* II/*JG* 26 1 Aug 42 to 4/*JG* 26 4 Nov 42. Awarded *DKiG* 27 Nov 42; + 24 Mar 43
	Oblt Kurt MÜLLER	From *JFS* 2 (?) 4 Nov 42 – +19 Dec 42
	Oblt Paul KELLER	From 4/*JG* 26 20 Dec 42 – +24 Mar 43. Awarded *DKiG* 27 Nov 42
	Oblt Erwin BUSCH	25 Mar – 15 Apr 43. Awarded *DKiG* 29 Apr 43
Pilots	*Ofw/Lt* Erwin BUSCH	From 9/*JG* 26 10 Mar 42, to *St Kap* 25 Mar 43
	Oblt Hans RAGOTZI	From 8/*JG* 26 14 Mar 42 – +9 Jun 42
	Oblt Siegfried STORSBERG	Survived (on 5/*SG* 10 May 45)
	Lt Otto-August BACKHAUS	+9 Apr 43
	Lt Arnd FLOCK	21 Jun 42 – +1 Aug 42
	Lt Hermann HOCH	From *Stab* I/*JG* 26 – POW 20 Jan 43
	Ofw Werner KASSA	16 Apr 42 – +26 Aug 42
	Ofw Karl-Heinz KNOBELOCH	Awarded *Ehrenpokal* 25 Jun 43, *DKiG* 29 Mar 44; +28 Oct 44 with 6/*JG* 26
	Ofw Heinrich WAGNER	24 Jun 42 – +1 Sep 42
	Fw Emil BÖSCH	+12 Mar 43. Awarded *DKiG* 29 Apr 43
	Fw Hans-Jürgen FRÖHLICH	From 2/*JG* 26 10 Mar 42 – +24 Apr 42
	Fw Otto GÖRTZ	From 5/*JG* 26 29 Mar 42 – +6 Jun 42
	Fw Herbert MÜLLER	+4 Jan 43
	Fw Hermann NIESEL	11 Jun 42 – +17 Oct 42
	Uffz Karl BAUMGARTNER	Fate unknown
	Uffz Fritz Von BERG	7 Aug 42 – +19 Aug 42
	Uffz Herbert BÜTTNER	+5 Feb 43
	Uffz Fritz EBERT	+3 Apr 43
	Uffz Oswald FISCHER	From 7/*JG* 26 10 Mar 42 – POW 20 May 42
	Uffz Karl-Heinz GAYKOW	Fate unknown
	Uffz Karl HECK	+9 Apr 43
	Uffz Alfred IMMERVOLL	+23 Jan 43
	Uffz Joachim KOCH	+29 Mar 43
	Uffz Werner SCHAMMERT	POW 7 Oct 42
	Uffz (Erich?) SCHWARZ	Fate unknown
	Ogefr/Uffz Richard WITTMANN	1 Jul 42 – 1 Dec 42. Awarded *DKiG* 5 Feb 45 with 2/*NSG* 20. Survived

Appendix 4

Executive Officers of I, II & IV Schnellkampfgeschwader March – June 1943

Rank	Officer	Details
Gesch Komm	Maj Günther TONNE	From II/ZG 1 1 Feb 43 – +15 Jul 43. Awarded *RK* 5 Oct 41, *EL* 24 Oct 44
Gr Kdr I Gruppe	Maj Heinrich BRÜCKER	From *RLM* 1 Dec 43 – 30 May 43. Survived. Awarded *DKiG* 15 Apr 44, *RK* 22 Jun 41
	Hptm Wilhelm SCHÜRMANN (?)	Unknown
Gr Adj	Hptm Edmund KRAUS	From 1/*SKG* 10 Jun 43 – 30 Jul 43. Survived. Awarded *DKiG* 27 Oct 43
Gr Ia	Oblt Karl-Heinz STÜRMER	From *Erpr St* 110 27 May 43. + with 8/*KG* 51 1 Sep 44
Gr Ic	Hptm HILLBRECHT	From III/*KG* 30
Gr TO	Maj SARRE-NOEL (?)	Unknown
Gr NO	Oblt Alfons FRANZ	Possibly *Gr Adj* in late 1943
1 St Kap	Oblt HOYER (?)	Unknown
	Hptm Edmund KRAUS	To *Gr Kdr* Jun 43
	Hptm Wolrad GERLACH (?)	To 28 Jul 43
2 St Kap	Oblt Kurt KLAHN	From *Erprobungs und Lehrstaffel He* 177 18 Dec 42 – +16 Apr 43. Awarded *Ehrenpokal* 25 May 43
	Oblt Paul ANTWERPEN (?)	From *KG* 101. + 18 May 43
	Hptm Kurt DAHLMANN	From 9/*KG* 30 11 Jun 43. Survived. Awarded *DKiG* 15 Feb 43, *Ehrenpokal* 19 Jan 42, *RK* 11 Jun 44, *EL* 24 Jan 45
3 St Kap	Oblt Rudolf TRENN	From 8/*StG* 77 20 Feb 43 – +16 Apr 43. Awarded *DKiG* 2 Jul 42, *RK* 25 May 43
	Hptm Kurt GEISLER	From *Transportgruppe Don* 15 Jun 43. +6 Sep 43. Awarded *RK* 24 Jan 43, *Ehrenpokal* 1 Feb 43
4 (Erg) St Kap	Hptm Walter KELLENBERGER (?)	From *Zerstörerschule* 2 3 Apr 43 – +17 Apr 43
	Hptm Lothar KRUTEIN	From *KSG* 3
Gr Kdr II/SKG 10	Oblt/Hptm Helmut VIEDEBANTT	From 5/*ZG* 1 1 Feb 43 – 15 Aug 43. +1 May 45. Awarded *Ehrenpokal* 19 Oct 42 *RK* 30 Dec 42
Gr Ia	Hptm Karl-Friedrich BÖTTGER	From IV/*Zerstörerschule* 2 15 Feb 43. Survived
Gr Adj	Oblt Oswald LAUMANN	+23 Mar 43
	Oblt Gerhard WALTHER	From Jun 43. Awarded *DKiG* 14 Nov 42 *RK* 26 Mar 44. + with II/*SG* 4 18 May 44
Unknown Stab II	Hptm Horst HINGST	+6 Mar 43
	Hptm Hans Curt GRAF Von SPONECK	Survived
5 St Kap	Hptm Herbert WIESE (?)	Jun – Aug 43. Believed survived

Rank	Officer	Details
6 *St Kap*	*Oblt* Josef KELLER	+25 May 43
	Oblt Götz BAUMANN	Awarded *DKiG* 24 Apr 42. Survived
7 *St Kap*	*Oblt* Werner DEDEKIND	Awarded *Ehrenpokal* 9 Aug 43, *DKiG* 26 Nov 43. Survived
Gr Kdr IV/SKG 10	*Hptm* Heinz SCHUMANN	+8 Nov 43 with *Stab/SG* 10. Awarded *Ehrenpokal* 15 Sep 41, *DKiG* 22 Jan 42, *RK* 18 Mar 43
Gr Adj	*Oblt* Kurt HEVLER	From *Jagdgruppe Süd* 1 May 43 – +4 Jun 43
Gr TO	*Oblt* HAHN (?)	Unknown
13 *St Kap*	*Lt/Oblt* Leopold WENGER	+ 10 Apr 45 with 4/SG 10. Awarded *DKiG* 17 Oct 43, *RK* 14 Jan 45
14 *St Kap*	*Oblt* Erwin BUSCH	Survived. Awarded *DKiG* 29 Apr 43
	Maj Gerhard VON KALDENBERG	(*Stellvetreter*) +10 Jul 43
15 *St Kap*	*Lt* Erhard NIPPA	Survived. Awarded *DKiG* 29 Apr 43, *RK* 26 Mar 44

Appendix 5

Jabo Losses Suffered By Jagdgeschwader 2 May 1941 – April 1943

Date	Aircraft Details	Pilot	Details
17 May 41	Bf 109 E-7, 3816	*Uffz* Helmut RIES – +	6/JG 2. Shot down by *Flak* off Shoreham
19 May 41	Bf 109 E-7, 6506	*Uffz* Kuno DOLLENMAIER – uninjured	Suffered mechanical failure on return from *Jaboangriff* against a convoy off Portland
9 Jun 41	Bf 109 E-7, 5983, White 15	*Oblt* Werner MACHOLD – *St Kap* – POW	7/JG 2. Shot down by flak from HMS *Blencathra* and crash-landed near Swanworth Quarries, Worth Matravers, 1427 hrs
13 Staffel			
8 Feb 42	Bf 109 E-7/B, 1556	*Lt* Josef FRÖSCHL – inj	Suffered engine failure during non-operational flight and crash-landed at Quillebeuf-sur-Seine, 80% damage
31 Mar 42	Bf 109 F-2, 8171	*Uffz* Gottfried WEISER – missing	Hit by flak during attack on shipping off Brixham, and ditched 30 kms north of Alderney/52 miles NW Cherbourg/PIQ 15W/3024, 1345 hrs
10 Staffel			
21 Apr 42	Bf 109 F-4, 13005, Blue 12	*Ogefr* Franz LANGHAMMER – missing	Shot down by *Flak* off Portland, PM
8 May 42	Bf 109 F-4, 7053, Blue 9	*Uffz* Bruno GÖRENDT – missing	Shot down by Adjutant A G Y Debec, 340 Squadron, 15-20 kms south of Worthing, 1235-1255 hrs
16 May 42	Bf 109 F-4, 13014, Blue 8	*Lt* Hans-Joachim SCHULZ – +	Shot down by *Flak* from HMSs CLEVELAND and BROCKLESBY off Plymouth and crashed into the sea at Cawsand Bay, 1252 hrs. Body recovered 2 Jun 42
27 May 42	Bf 109 F-4, 7626, Blue 4	*Lt* Josef FRÖSCHL – POW	Shot down by Flt Lt D W Wainwright, 41 Squadron during attack on shipping in the Solent and crashed at Yaverland Manor Farm, Brading, Isle of Wight, 1505 hrs

Date	Aircraft Details	Pilot	Details
31 May 42	Bf 109 F-4, 7610	*Uffz* Rudolf SCHWARZER – missing	Shot down by *Flak* attacking shipping off Bognor Regis, c. 1800 hrs
13 Jul 42	FW 190 A-2, 2075	Uninjured	Force-landed at Caen-Carpiquet due to technical problems, 40% damage
17 Jul 42	FW 190 A-2, 0439, Blue 14	*Hptm* Frank LIESENDAHL – *St Kap* – +	Shot down by *Flak* attacking shipping off Brixham, 1245 hrs. Pilot's body found 6 miles east of Berry Head, 6 Sep 42 and buried at sea
18 Jul 42	FW 190 A-2, 2087	(Possibly) *Oblt* Fritz SCHRÖTER – *St Kap*	Damaged in combat with Sous Lt M Albert, 340 Squadron, – uninjured south of Littlehampton, 0625 hrs; force-landed near Dieppe with 60% damage
31 Jul 42	FW 190 A-2, Blue 2	*Lt* Leopold WENGER – uninjured	Undercarriage collapsed, Ste Andre
3 Aug 42	FW 190 A-3, 2239	Uninjured	Landing accident, Ste Andre, 45% damage
19 Aug 42	FW 190 A-2, 5299	*Lt* Leopold WENGER – uninjured	Undercarriage collapsed, Caen-Carpiquet, 30% damage
19 Aug 42	FW 190 A-2, 0272	*Uffz* Werner MAGARIN – uninjured	Force-landed near Paluel after being damaged by *Flak* over Dieppe, 30% damage
19 Aug 42	FW 190 A-2, Blue 16	*Lt* Leopold WENGER – uninjured	Suffered slight damage in combat with Spitfire flown by Gp Capt H Broadhurst, Deputy Senior Air Staff Officer, HQ 11 Gp, 1350 – 1443 hrs
2 Sep 42	FW 190 A-2, 2113	Uninjured	Tyre burst on landing at Caen-Carpiquet, 30% damage
4 Sep 42	FW 190 A-3, 2242	*Uffz* Walter HÖFER – +	Shot down by light *Flak* during attack on Torquay/Paignton and crashed at Tor Abbey Sands, 1851 hrs
9 Sep 42	FW 190 A-2, 2112	Uninjured	Undercarriage collapsed, Ste Andre, 25% damage
15 Sep 42	FW 190 A-2, 5387	Uninjured	Force-landed, Ste Andre, 10% damage
17 Sep 42	FW 190 A-2, 215	*Uffz* Hans-Walter WANDSCHNEIDER – M	Shot down by Plt Off L W Powell, 412 Squadron after attacking Worthing and crashed PIQ 15W/1180, 1540-1545 hrs
17 Sep 42	FW 190 A, Blue 14	*Lt* Leopold WENGER – uninjured	Damaged by Plt Off W B Needham, 412 Squadron after attacking Worthing, 1540-1545 hrs

Date	Aircraft Details	Pilot	Details
26 Oct 42	FW 190 A-3, 2177, Blue 7	*Lt* Kurt ECKLEBEN – injured	Engine failure and force-landed near Mezidon, 35% damage
3 Nov 42	FW 190 A-3, 2239	Uninjured	Ran out of fuel and force-landed at Briquebec, 30% damage
17 Nov 42	FW 190 A-3	*Lt* Leopold WENGER – uninjured	Suffered engine failure on non-combat flight and force-landed near Givors
10 Jan 43	FW 190 A-3, 5424	*Fw* Joachim Von BITTER – +	Shot down by Fg Off J Small, 266 Squadron into sea 500 yds off Teignmouth, 1435 hrs. Pilot's body washed ashore at Dawlish Warren, 13 Jan 43
10 Jan 43	FW 190 A-3, 2234	*Lt* Kurt ECKLEBEN – uninjured	Accident at Théville on returning from attack on Teignmouth, 50% damage
10 Jan 43	FW 190 A-3, 467, Blue 12	*Lt* Leopold WENGER – uninjured	Reportedly damaged by *Flak* during attack on Teignmouth but probably damaged by Fg Off S J P Blackwell, 266 Squadron, 1435 hrs
26 Jan 43	FW 190 A-4, 5680, Blue 7	*Fw* Karl BLASE – missing	Shot down by Fg Off C R M Bell, together with Sgt N V Borland, of 266 Squadron, 12 miles SE of Start Point, 1616 hrs
26 Feb 43	FW 190 A-4, 735	*Fw* Hermann ROHNE – missing	Shot down by Sqn Ldr C L Green and a second FW 190 shared with Sgt R K Thompson, 266 Squadron, 50 miles SSE of Exmouth/PlQ 15W/4169 – 3154, 1215 hrs
26 Feb 43	FW 190 A-5, 2588	*Uffz* Kurt BRESSLER – missing	See above
1 Mar 43	FW 190 A-5, 1106, Blue 11	*Uffz* Ernst LÄPPLE – +	Shot down by Flt Sgt W B Tyerman, 486 Squadron, 4 miles south of Bognor Regis/PlQ 15W/113, 1215 hrs
12 Mar 43	FW 190 A-5, 7216	*Ofw* Herbert KORTH – +	Damaged by either 2/Lt B Bjornstad & Flt Sgt Olsen or Capt S Lundsten or Lt H Sognes of 331 Squadron or Plt Off M Edwards of 122 Squadron during attack on London, 0750 hrs and crashed near Coxyde
13 Mar 43	FW 190 A-5, 2275	Uninjured	Force-landed at Coxyde with 15% combat damage. No Allied claims but could be 12 Mar 43 (see above)
26 Mar 43	FW 190 A-5, 1094	Uninjured	Damaged by friendly *Flak* and force-landed at Wenye (?), 80% damage

Appendix 6

Losses suffered by 10/Jagdgeschwader 26 & 10/Jagdgeschwader 54 March 1942 – April 1943

Date	Aircraft Details	Pilot	Details
18 Mar 42	Bf 109 E 7, 5065	Uninjured	Landing accident, Théville; 30% damage
8 Apr 42	Bf 109 F-4, 8345	Uninjured	Force-landed Arques, 10% damage
10 Apr 42	Bf 109 F-4, 8353	Uffz Karl-Heinz GAYKOW – injured	Suffered engine failure during operational sortie and force-landed at Arques, 65% damage
24 Apr 42	Bf 109 F-4, 7196	Fw Hans-Jürgen FRÖHLICH +	Shot down by Flak attacking Folkestone, 0840 hrs
17 May 42	Bf 109 F-4, 8353	Uninjured	Take off accident, Arques, 10% damage
17 May 42	Bf 109 F-4, 8361	Uninjured	Suffered engine failure and ditched off Boulogne
20 May 42	Bf 109 F-4, 7232, White 11	Uffz Oswald FISCHER – POW	Hit by Flak and force-landed at Beachy Head, 1205 hrs
6 Jun 42	Bf 109 F-4, 8532, White 2	Fw Otto GÖRTZ – +	Shot down by Flak and crashed 3 miles south of Bournemouth, 1720 hrs
8 Jun 42	Bf 109 F-4, 7223	Uninjured	Crash-landed at St Omer due to pilot error, 20% damage
9 Jun 42	Bf 109 F-4, 8344, White 7	Oblt Hans RAGOTZI – +	Shot down by Plt Off K A H Mason, 131 Squadron and crashed 50 kms west of the Somme Estuary, 2120 hrs
17 Jun 42	Bf 109 F-4, 7342	Uninjured	Engine failure and crash-landed at Wizernes, 50% damage
30 Jun 42	Bf 109 F-4, 7229	Uninjured	Take off accident, Le Bourget, 15% damage
30 Jul 42	FW 190 A-3, 7003, Black 1	Oblt Joachim-Hans GEBURTIG – St Kap – POW	Shot down by Flak and ditched 2 miles SE of Littlehampton, 1210 hrs
1 Aug 42	FW 190 A-2, 5253, White 5	Lt Arnd FLOCK – +	Shot down by Plt Off G G Davidson, 412 Squadron off Newhaven, 1050 hrs
19 Aug 42	FW 190 A-3, 2240	Uffz Fritz Von BERG – +	Crashed after take off 4 kms north of Hesdin
26 Aug 42	FW 190 A-2, 2080, Black 13	Ofw Werner KASSA – +	Shot down by Pte E G Johnstone and crashed at Lottbridge Drove, Eastbourne, 0934 hrs
26 Aug 42	FW 190 A	Ogefr Richard WITTMANN – uninjured	Ac slightly damaged in attack on Eastbourne, 0930 hrs
1 Sep 42	FW 190 A-2, 5315, Black 4	Ofw Heinrich WAGNER – +	Believed damaged by Flak during attack on Dungeness and ditched in the Channel between Dungeness and Cap Gris Nez. Possibly crashed due to engine failure

Date	Aircraft Details	Pilot	Details
4 Oct 42	FW 190 A-3, 0248	*Uffz* Karl BAUMGARTNER – injured	Suffered engine malfunction on taking off on an operational mission and crashed south of Campagne
10 Oct 42	FW 190 A-3, 0420, BO+UT/Black 7	*Uffz* Werner SCHAMMERT – POW	Shot down by *Flak* and crashed at Wellington Crescent, Ramsgate, 0755 hrs
17 Oct 42	FW 190 A-4, 2403, Black 14	*Fw* Hermann NIESEL – +	Shot down by Plt Off G G Thomas & Sgt A N Sames, 486 Squadron, 9 miles south of Hastings, 1430 hrs
19 Dec 42	FW 190 A-4, 712, White 9	*Oblt* Kurt MÜLLER – *St Kap* – +	Damaged by *Flak* and then shot down by Fg Off R Lallemand, 609 Squadron 1 mile ENE of Deal, 1412 hrs
4 Jan 43	FW 190 A-4, 2439, Black 4	*Fw* Herbert MÜLLER – +	Damaged by light AA fire from soldiers of the Royal Welch Fusiliers and then hit power cables and crashed at Castle Farm House, Winchelsea, 1256 hrs
20 Jan 43	FW 190 A-4, 2409, Black 2	*Lt* Hermann HOCH – POW	Damaged by *Flak* during attack on London and force-landed at Capel, 1400 hrs
23 Jan 43	FW 190 A-4, 5636, Black 14	*Uffz* Alfred IMMERVOLL – +	Shot down by Pte J Andros and Pte C Darrock, No.1 Post Beachy Head and crashed into the sea off Beachy Head, 0955 hrs
5 Feb 43	FW 190 A-4, 2435, Black 1	*Uffz* Herbert BÜTTNER – +	Shot down by Fg Off P J Nankivell, 609 Squadron, 30 miles south of Beachy Head, 0940 hrs
Redesignated 10/JG 54 17 Feb 43			
12 Mar 43	FW 190 A-5, 0829, Black 12	*Fw* Emil BOESCH – +	Shot down by either 2/Lt B Bjornstad, Sgt F Eitzen, 2/Lt R Engelsen or Lt H Sognnes of 331 Squadron, 10-20 kms north of Dunkirk, 0750 hrs
24 Mar 43	FW 190 A-5, 2587, Black 7	*Oblt* Paul KELLER – *St Kap* – +	Exploded over Ashford and crashed at Godinton Road, Ashford, 1010 hrs
29 Mar 43	FW 190 A-5, 2576, Black 4	*Uffz* Joachim KOCH – +	Shot down by Fg Off F Venesoen, 610 Squadron off Brighton, 1215 hrs
29 Mar 43	FW 190 A-5, 0834	Uninjured	Damaged by Fg Off F Venesoen, 610 Squadron 1215 hrs and ditched in the Channel; pilot rescued
3 Apr 43	FW 190 A-5, 0835, Black 11	*Uffz* Fritz EBERT – +	Shot down by *Flak* off Eastbourne, 1145 hrs
9 Apr 43	FW 190 A-5, 0831, Black 14	*Uffz* Karl HECK – +	Shot down by *Flak* and ditched 20 kms NW of Cap Gris Nez, 1800 hrs
9 Apr 43	FW 190 A-5, 7290, Black 12	*Lt* Otto-August BACKHAUS – +	Probably shot down by Flt Lt E Haabjoern, 609 Squadron off Boulogne, 1915 hrs whilst on air-sea rescue mission for *Uffz* Heck

Appendix 7

Daytime Losses suffered by III/Zerstörergeschwader 2 & Schnellkampfgeschwader 10 North-West Europe November 1942 – 6 June 1943

Date	Unit	Aircraft Details	Pilot	Details
3 Nov 42	8/*ZG* 2	FW 190 A-3, 2150, Black 3	*Lt* Hermann KENNEWEG – +	Shot down by Fg Off G F Ball & Plt Off P G Scotchmer, 257 Squadron off Guernsey, 1210 hrs
3 Nov 42	8/*ZG* 2	FW 190 A-2, 0503, Black 6	*Uffz* Johann Hannig – +	See above
17 Feb 43	II/*SKG* 10	FW 190 A-5, 7185	Uninjured	Ran short of fuel and crash-landed at Rennes, 60% damage
6 Mar 43	*Stab* II/*SKG*	FW 190 A-5, 2562	*Hptm* Horst HINGST – +	Suffered engine fire during high-altitude flight and crashed at L'Hermitage, 20 kms west of Rennes
6 Mar 43	5/*SKG* 10	FW 190 A-4, 5827	*Uffz* Max MÖLLER – +	Crashed into the River Gironde at Le Verdon during training flight
8 Mar 43	5/*SKG* 10	FW 190 A-4, 7184, White H	*Fw* Hans HINZ – missing	Crashed near Rennes after intercepting attack by B-17s of 1st Bombardment Wg on Rennes Marshalling Yard
8 Mar 43	II/*SKG* 10	FW 190 A-5, 1079	*Uffz* Karl JONAS – wounded	Shot down in combat with B-17s of 1st Bombardment Wg, pilot baled out and ac crashed at St Lo
11 Mar 43	6/*SKG* 10	FW 190 A-5, 0820	*Fw* Kurt BARABASS – +	Damaged by *Flak* during attack on Hastings and crashed into sea 3 kms east of Coxyde, 1545 hrs
13 Mar 43	5/*SKG* 10	FW 190 A-5, 2356, White B	*Ofw* Hermann SCHORN – +	Shot down by Fg Off J H Deall & Sgt D S Eadie of 266 Squadron 15-20 miles south of Start Point, 1225 hrs
13 Mar 43	5/*SKG* 10	FW 190 A-4, 7153, White E	*Uffz* Erwin ZIEGLER – missing	See above
23 Mar 43	*Stab* II/*SKG*	FW 190 A-5, 2544, Green H	*Oblt* Oswald LAUMANN – *Gr Adj* – +	Shot down by *Flak* and crashed at Strete, Dartmouth, 1915 hrs

Date	Unit	Aircraft Details	Pilot	Details
7 Apr 43	13/SKG 10	FW 190 A-5, 2586	*Uffz* Rudolf RADLEWSKI – missing	Probably ac shot down by Fg Off P F Steib, 257 Squadron and crashed 30 miles south of the Isle of Wight, 0715 hrs
7 Apr 43	13/SKG 10	FW 190 A-5, 7209	*Uffs* Günther ESCHENHORN – +	Probably ac that was shot down by *Flak* and exploded off the Isle of Wight, 0715 hrs
11 Apr 43	Stab/SKG 10	FW 190 A-5, 0850	Uninjured	Ground collision, 80% damage
15 Apr 43	II/SKG 10	FW 190 A-4, 7157	Uninjured	Engine fire, Rennes, 80% damage
23 Apr 43	II/SKG 10	FW 190 A-5, 0821	Uninjured	Hit sea off Start Point during operational flight, 30% damage
25 Apr 43	14/SKG 10	FW 190 A-5, 0832	*Uffz* Walter KÄLBERER – +	Crashed into sea off Carbourg on training flight
1 May 43	IV/SKG 10	FW 190 A-5, 7207	*Ogefr* Ernst PFAFFENEDER – +	Crashed into Seine Estuary due to pilot error
2 May 43	IV/SKG 10	FW 190 A-5, 2590	Uninjured	Engine malfunction and force-landed at Caen, 10% damage
7 May 43	7/SKG 10	FW 190 A-5/U8, 2526, Yellow A	*Oblt* Willi FREUDENREICH – +	Hit telegraph pole and crashed into sea off Newport, Norfolk, 0715 hrs
11 May 43	5/SKG 10	FW 190 A-5/U8, 0822	*Lt* Joachim-Peter GIERMANN – missing	Believed shot down by Fg Off J R C Townsend, 613 Squadron, 10 miles off Dutch Coast/PIQ 05W/2347, 0846 hrs
13 May 43	IV/SKG 1	FW 190 A-5, 7211	Uninjured	Technical problems & force-landed at Caen, 10% damage
15 May 43	7/SKG 10	FW 190 A-4, 5820	*Fw* Bernhard MAASSEN – uninjured	Crashed at Maasluis, Holland probably after combat with Plt Off W Kirchner and Plt Off T Tarnowicz of 317 Squadron, 10 miles east of Orfordness, 2210 hrs
15 May 43	Stab/SKG 10	FW 190 A-5, 50892	*Fw* Hans BURKHARD – missing	Reported shot down by *Flak* 10 kms east of Southwold; possibly shot down in combat with 317 Squadron (see above)
17 May 43	II/SKG 10	FW 190 A-5, 1075	*Fw* Karl ARNDT – +	Crashed at St Avé, near Vannes, 1200 hrs probably after combat with B-17s of 1st Bombardment Wg during attack on Lorient
18 May 43	Stab/SKG 10	FW 190 A-5, 0892	–	Destroyed in air raid on Poix
18 May 43	IV/SKG 10	LeO 451, 484	–	Destroyed in air raid on Poix
23 May 43	6/SKG 10	FW 190 A-4/U8, 7156, Black K	*Fw* Adam FISCHER – missing	Shot down by *Flak* off Hastings, 1300 hrs

Date	Unit	Aircraft Details	Pilot	Details
23 May 43	5/SKG 10	FW 190 A-4/U8, 5834, White L	*Ofw* Herbert DOBROCH – missing	Probably shot down by Flt Sgt W H Ramsey, 1 Squadron, 15 miles south of Hastings, 1315 hrs
23 May 43	II/SKG 10	FW 190 A-5, 1381	Uninjured	Taxiing accident at Amiens whilst taking off on an operational mission, 20% damage
23 May 43	II/SKG 10	FW 190 A-5, 2525	Uninjured	Ran out of fuel during operational flight and force-landed at St Pierre, 20% damage
23 May 43	14/SKG 10	FW 190 A-5, 1368, Black K	*Lt* Erwin BUSCH – *St Fhr* – wounded	Crashed at Caen, 35% damage
23 May 43	15/SKG 10	FW 190 A-5/U8, 840189	*Uffz* Eugen STREICH – +	Hit tree during training flight and crashed at Carpiquet
23 May 43	15/SKG 10	FW 190 A-5/U8, 0136, Yellow H	*Uffz* Friedrich-Karl SCHMIDT – +	Shot down by *Flak* and crashed at 34 Grove Road, Eastcliffe, Bournemouth, 1300 hrs
25 May 43	14/SKG 10	FW 190 A-5, 1377, Black L	*Uffz* Wilfried BRAUN – missing	Reported to have been shot down by *Flak* during attack on Brighton; probably shot down by Sqn Ldr D J Scott of 486 Squadron 30 miles south of Brighton, 1230 hrs
25 May 43	IV/SKG 10	FW 190 A-5, 1359	Uninjured	Suffered engine failure on training flight and crashed at Caen
25 May 43	IV/SKG 10	FW 190 A-5, 840056	Uninjured	Suffered 15% damage in combat, probably during attack on Brighton
25 May 43	6/SKG 10	FW 190 A-5/U8, 2521, Black M	*Oblt* Josef KELLER – *St Kap* – missing	Shot down by either Sqn Ldr R H Harries, Fg Off J P Maridor and Plt Off J A Round of 91 Squadron 2 miles off Cap Gris Nez, 2200 hrs or Plt Off D E Davy, 91 Squadron, 2200 hrs, 4-5 miles north of Cap Gris Nez
25 May 43	5/SKG 10	FW 190 A-5/U8, 1361	*Lt* Walter KLEIN – wounded	Suffered 10% damage in combat with Spitfires of 91 Squadron (see above)
29 May 43	II/SKG 10	FW 190 A-5, 2717	Uninjured	Written off in crash-landing at Vannes following combat with B-17s of 1st Bombardment Wg attacking St Nazaire
29 May 43	IV/SKG 10	FW 190 A-5, 840046	–	10% damage during air raid on Caen-Carpiquet
29 May 43	IV/SKG 10	FW 190 A-5, 1367	–	15% damage during air raid on Caen-Carpiquet
30 May 43	IV/SKG 10	FW 190 A-5, 840048	Uninjured	10% combat damage, landed Caen Carpiquet
30 May 43	13/SKG 10	FW 190 A-5/U8, 1412, Blue F	*Lt* Hermann MÜLLER – missing	Probably shot down by Flt Sgt B J C Calnan, 257 Squadron and crashed on Alderney, 1510 hrs

Date	Unit	Aircraft Details	Pilot	Details
30 May 43	14/SKG 10	FW 190 A-5/U8, 840050, Black A	*Uffz* Erich SPÄT – +	Shot down by *Flak* and crashed off Maidencombe Beach, Torquay, 1445 hrs
30 May 43	15/SKG 10	FW 190 A-5, 1334, Yellow J	*Uffz* Hans MÜLLER – uninjured	10% damage due to *Flak*
30 May 43	15/SKG 10	FW 190 A-5/U8, 1363, Yellow F	*Uffz* Herbert KANNGETER – POW	Shot down by *Flak* and ditched 18 miles off Berry Head, 1445 hrs
30 May 43	15/SKG 10	FW 190 A-5/U8, 1365	*Gefr* Karl LAUE – +	Collided with a church spire and crashed into a house in Teignmouth Road, Torquay, 1441 hrs
30 May 43	15/SKG 10	FW 190 A-5/U8, 840059, Yellow D	*Uffz* Raimund PERLEBACH – missing	Damaged by *Flak* and ditched 70 kms SE of Torquay, 1451 hrs
30 May 43	II/SKG 10	FW 190 A-4, 7158	Uninjured	Crashed at Coxyde due to pilot error after attack on Frinton-On-Sea, 45% damage
30 May 43	7/SKG 10	FW 190 A-5/U8, 0824, Yellow H	*Lt* Alois HARLOS – POW	Crashed in sea off The Naze, 1930 hrs
30 May 43	5/SKG 10	FW 190 A-5, 0910, White L	*Fw* Fritz KESSLER – +	Crashed off Walton Pier, 1930 hrs either due to *Flak* or pilot error
1 Jun 43	5/SKG 10	FW 190 A-5/U8, 2529, White R	*Uffz* Otto ZÜGENRÜCKER – +	Shot down by *Flak* and Fg Off I J Davies of 609 Squadron and crashed at Lydden, Margate, 1310 hrs
2 Jun 43	5/SKG 10	FW 190 A-5/U8, 51375, White B	*Lt* Hans SCHATE – +	Collided with crane or hit ground trying to avoid high tension cables, Ipswich Docks, 0525 hrs
4 Jun 43	*Stab IV/SKG*	FW 190 A-5/U8, 51353, < + ~	*Oblt* Kurt HEVLER – *Gr Adj* – +	Shot down by *Flak* and crashed at Norman's Bay, Bexhill, 1130 hrs. Possibly claimed by Fg Off J Solak, 41 Squadron, off Bexhill, 1130 hrs and Fg Off D H Smith, 41 Squadron, 10 miles south of Beachy Head, 1125 hrs
4 Jun 43	13/SKG 10	FW 190 A, Blue E	*Lt* Leopold WENGER – *St Kap* – wounded	Damaged by *Flak* during attack on Eastbourne; wounded pilot slightly wounded in leg
6 Jun 43	7/SKG 10	FW 190 A-5/U8, 1376, Yellow G	*Lt* Dominikus MILLER – missing	Either shot down by *Flak* off Eastbourne or by Plt Off D E Davy and Sgt J T Watterson of 91 Squadron off Le Treport, 1329 hrs

Appendix 8

Confirmed 'Tip And Run' Attacks March 1942 – June 1943

Only those attacks positively identified as 'tip and run' attacks have been included. Likewise, only when the unit involved has been positively identified has it been included.

Take off times are in Central European Time; attack times are in local time.

Date	Unit	Aircraft	Details
5 Mar 42	?	Bf 109	Isle of Wight/Freshwater Bay: Convoy off the Needles, PM; 2 bombs dropped at Freshwater, 1519 hrs; MV *Alacrity* damaged 7 miles NW Bishops Rock
7 Mar 42	?	4 Bf 109	Exmouth-Teignmouth area, 0935 hrs; Spitfire of 317 Squadron attacked on take off from Bolt Head airfield by 2 Bf 109s & crash-landed
	?		Portland 0927 hrs
8 Mar 42	?	2 Bf 109	Hayling Island/Christchurch area, 1803-1840 hrs
18 Mar 42	?	4 Bf 109	Torquay, 1150 hrs
19 Mar 42	?	2 Bf 109	Convoy WATCH & MEADOW 4½ miles off Poole, 1531 hrs
	?	2 Bf 109	Portsmouth, 1050 hrs, 2 inj
24 Mar 42	13/JG 2	? Bf 109	Ship damaged, 1340 hrs (*Oblt* Liesendahl involved)
27 Mar 42	13/JG 2	4 Bf 109	Torquay & Brixham, 1650 hrs. Staghound sunk by *Oblt* Liesendahl at Torquay
31 Mar 42	13/JG 2	2 Bf 109	Brixham, 1343 hrs; Collier *London City* (3000 ton) sunk by *Oblt* Liesendahl
5 Apr 42	?	6 Bf 109	Bognor Gas Works, 0815-0824 hrs
6 Apr 42	?	3 Bf 109	Worth Matravers Telecommunications Research Establishment, 1909 hrs
8 Apr 42	10/JG 26	? Bf 109	?
	?	3 Bf 109	Worth Matravers Telecommunications Research Establishment, 1328 hrs; cookhouse hit 2 + 6 inj
9 Apr 42	?	1 Bf 109	Ship damaged off Swanage, 0908 hrs
13 Apr 42	?	2 Bf 109	Worthing,0747 hrs
17 Apr 42	?	4 Bf 109	Weymouth, 0736 hrs
19 Apr 42	?	3 Bf 109	Exmouth & Budleigh Salterton, 1325 hrs
20 Apr 42	10/JG 26	4 Bf 109	Dungeness Lighthouse, Bexhill & Cowhurst, 1150 hrs
21 Apr 42	?	5 Bf 109	Swanage, 0712 hrs; 3 +, 15 inj
24 Apr 42	10/JG 2	2 Bf 109	Portland; 2 Bf 109s seen in Lyme Bay, PM, one shot down by *Flak*
	10/JG 26	4 Bf 109	Folkestone gasholder, 0842 hrs

Date	Unit	Aircraft	Details
24 Apr 42	?	2 Bf 109	Bognor Regis, 1645 hrs
	?	?	Hastings, 0845 hrs
25 Apr 42	10/JG 2	5 Bf 109	Solent/shipping, early AM
26 Apr 42	10/JG 26	2 Bf 109	Betteshanger Colliery, 0740 hrs
	?	?	Bognor, 1650 hrs
28 Apr 42	10/JG 2	7 Bf 109	Cowes & warships off in Solent, 0700 hrs
	?	2 Bf 109	Horam, 0815 hrs
	?	?	Newhaven, 1022-1026 hrs
	10/JG 26	2 Bf 109	Lydd & Dungeness
1 May 42	?	5 Bf 109	Bolt Head airfield, 0647 hrs; Spitfires R6775 and AA858 of 306 Squadron damaged Cat AC, Spitfire AB862 of 306 Squadron Cat B. One further Spitfire of 306 Squadron slightly damaged.
2 May 42	?	3 Bf 109	Saldean, 1400 hrs; fishing boats attacked
3 May 42	?	? Bf 109	Hastings, 2100 hrs
4 May 42	10/JG 2	9 Bf 109	Eastbourne, 1350 hrs
5 May 42	?	3 FW 190	Folkestone, 1820 hrs
6 May 42	?	4 Bf 109	Dover Harbour, 0625 hrs
	?	2 Bf 109	Brixham, 1150 hrs; ML No. 160 sunk
	?	4 Bf 109	Beachy Head, 1512 hrs
7 May 42	?	4 Bf 109	Hythe-Eastbourne-Dover, 1511 hrs
8 May 42	10/JG 2	4 Bf 109	Worthing & convoy, 1025 hrs
	10/JG 2	12 Bf 109	Worthing, 1224-1305 hrs
9 May 42	?	4 FW 190	Bexhill/Hastings, 0617 hrs
14 May 42	?	4 Bf 109	Brixham, 1854 hrs; trawler *Our Janie* sunk, 2 damaged
16 May 42	10/JG 2	3 Bf 109	Plymouth Breakwater, 1251 – 1255 hrs; one shot down
17 May 42	10/JG 26	? Bf 109	Folkestone/Hastings, 1010 hrs
	?	?	Hastings, 1310 hrs
18 May 42	10/JG 2	4 Bf 109	Deal, 0620 hrs
	10/JG 26	3 Bf 109	Brighton, 1800 hrs
19 May 42	?	4 Bf 109	Bexhill, 0700 hrs; chased by Flt Lt R W Baker & Fg Off R W Barnett, 485 Squadron, 4 miles south of Hastings
20 May 42	10/JG 26	2 Bf 109	Brighton/Eastbourne, 1205 hrs
	?	2 Bf 109	Needles & convoy SKIPPER; chased by Plt Off Lynch & Sgt Harwood, 501 Squadron, 1045-1210 hrs
27 May 42	10/JG 2	3 Bf 109	Shipping/Solent, 1500 hrs; trawler *Arctic Pioneer* sunk

Date	Unit	Aircraft	Details
29 May 42	?	2 Bf 109	Selsey, evening ?
30 May 42	?	3 Bf 109	Spithead, PM; 3 barges attacked
31 May 42	10/JG 2	? Bf 109	Bognor Regis/Dartmouth/Canterbury; take off for Dartmouth attack 1730 hrs
6 Jun 42	10/JG 26	9 Bf 109	Bournemouth, 1720 hrs; Spitfires from the Middle Wallop Wg (on RAMROD 22) failed to intercept
7 Jun 42	10/JG 2	4 Bf 109	Torquay, 1842 hrs
9 Jun 42	10/JG 26	? Bf 109	East Wittering, 2108-2155 hrs
16 Jun 42	?	2 Bf 109	Shoreham, 0615 hrs
18 Jun 42	?	2 Bf 109	Brixham, 0555 hrs
19 Jun 42	10/JG 26	? Bf 109	(No British record) (German records stated that from 19 Apr to 18 Jun 42, 10/JG 26 flew in the region of 32 Jabo missions with the Bf 109 F-4/R1: 6 shipping targets, 8 railway yards, 5 factories, 2 gas holders, 8 barracks and 2 harbours were attacked)
26 Jun 42	?	2 Bf 109	Brighton, 2148 hrs; hit hospital & gasometer
7 Jul 42	10/JG 2	4 FW 190	Yarmouth/shipping; take-off 0543 hrs. Ship of 10,000 BRT reported sunk by *Oblt* Schröter/*Lt* Wenger and numerous damaged, possibly *Princess Astrid & Joseph*
9 Jul 42	10/JG 2	? FW 190	Shipping/W Portland, 0612 hrs; take-off 0536 hrs– 2 ships sunk, 1 damaged (*Gripfast* sunk?)
	?	2 Bf 109	Friston airfield, 0605 hrs; Hurricane of 253 Squadron damaged (German records state that in the morning, the airfield at East Dean was attacked. An attack on a convoy SW of Portland resulted in one ship and an escort sunk, another damaged)
11 Jul 42	10/JG 2	? FW 190	(German records reported that in the afternoon, Dartmouth was attacked and a destroyer sunk and another damaged by *Oblt* Schröter/*Lt* Nippa. 2 ac attacked Falmouth)
12 Jul 42	10/JG 2	2 FW 190	Shipping/Brixham, 1347 hrs, take-off 1308 hrs (German records state that a destroyer and an escort were damaged in the Channel). MMS No.174 (*Terschelling*) sunk at Brixham
13 Jul 42	10/JG 2	6 FW 190	Shipping, W Dartmouth; take-off 1825 hrs, patrol vessel damaged. Free French Submarine Hunter CH8 sunk 5 kms west of Dartmouth
17 Jul 42	10/JG 2	4 FW 190	Brixham 1245 hrs; tanker *Daxhound* & ML 157 damaged; (German records state that in the afternoon, Worthing was attacked and a 1,000 BRT freighter attacked. In an attack on Brixham, a 3,500 BRT tanker was damaged and a patrol boat sunk)
18 Jul 42	10/JG 2	2 FW 190	Littlehampton, 0622 hrs
21 Jul 42	10/JG 2	2 FW 190	Isle of Wight, 0612-0630 hrs (German records state a radio station on the Isle of Wight was attacked)
22 Jul 42	?	2 Bf 109	Brighton, 1115 hrs

Date	Unit	Aircraft	Details
26 Jul 42	10/JG 2	2 FW 190	Channel/Shipping/Start Point; take-off 1700 hrs (2 FW 190s bombed Torcross, 1750 hrs)
28 Jul 42	?	2 FW 190	Newhaven, 1535 hrs
29 Jul 42	10/JG 2	2 FW 190	Brixham, take-off 1540 hrs, 2 FW 190s attacked ships at 1607 hrs
30 Jul 42	10/JG 26	? FW 190	Channel/Littlehampton, 1210 hrs (German records state that a convoy was attacked south of Littlehampton and a steamship of 3,000–4,000 BRT sunk); ship attacked was the SS *Newglen*.
31 Jul 42	10/JG 2?	2 FW 190	HSL 188 was attacked off Torquay, 1910 hrs; 1 +, 4 wounded; Teignmouth attacked 1920 hrs
1 Aug 42	10/JG 26	2 FW 190	Newhaven, 1010 hrs (one shot down); Southsea attacked at dusk?
3 Aug 42	10/JG 2	8 FW 190	Torquay, take-off 1230 hrs; 8 FW 190s attacked Babbacombe 1300 hrs
5 Aug 42	10/JG 2	2 FW 190	Yeovil, 2109 hrs
7 Aug 42	10/JG 2	? FW 190	Constantine, take-off 1312 hrs; 2 FW 190s attacked Helston & Lizard; 2 FW 190s attacked Bodmin at about 1200 hrs, hitting the town and a military camp
9 Aug 42	?	2 FW 190	Littlehampton
11 Aug 42	10/JG 2	2 FW 190	Salisbury; take-off 1700 hrs. Raid was plotted but was so fast that no aircraft were scrambled to intercept
	?	?	Deal gasholder
13 Aug 42	?	4 FW 190	2 FW 190s attacked Dartmouth, 2 attacked Salcombe, 1217 & 1223 hrs; trawlers *Pierre Descelliers* & *Intrepide* sunk; (German records state that Salcombe was attacked and a patrol boat and a house boat sunk)
	?	7 FW 190	Teignmouth, 1733 hrs.
	?	4 FW 190	Pevensey/Eastbourne, 0550 hrs
14 Aug 42	?	4 FW 190	Eastbourne and ships, 0553 hrs; Flt Lt R R Harris & Plt Off A Eckert of 131 Squadron tried to intercept 5 miles south of Ford
15 Aug 42	10/JG 2	? FW 190	Worthing, take-off 1730 hrs
17 Aug 42	?	2 FW 190	Swanage
	?	4 FW 190	Treleaver, causing damage at Coverak
18 Aug 42	10/JG 2	2 FW 190	Ventnor, take-off 1632 hrs.
	?	2 FW 190	St Blazey, 1820 hrs
19 Aug 42	10/JG 2 and 10/JG 26		Dieppe; both heavily involved
21 Aug 42	?	? FW 190	(German records state that Hythe was attacked)
22 Aug 42	?	2 FW 190	Sandbanks (Bournemouth)

Date	Unit	Aircraft	Details
24 Aug 42	10/JG 2	4 FW 190	Start Point, take-off 1553 hrs; 2 FW 190s attacked Torcross & Culompton, 2 barges sank at the latter (Lysander T1696/AQ-H of 276 Squadron (Plt Off J D Ernst/AC2 S H Fleet) was attacked by *Lt* Wenger and subsequently reported missing; German activity in the area at the time was said to be the cause) (German records state that Dartmouth, Sandwich and Brighton were attacked. In Dartmouth, landing craft were destroyed)
26 Aug 42	10/JG 26	2 FW 190	Eastbourne, 0850 hrs
27 Aug 42	?	8 FW 190	Shorncliffe & Folkestone; 1 +, 4 wounded
28 Aug 42	10/JG 2	? FW 190	Fowey/Pentewan/St Ives, take-off 1541 hrs
29 Aug 42	?	2 FW 190	Brighton, 1450 hrs
	?	3 FW 190	Falmouth, 1239 hrs (German records state that in Falmouth Harbour, a steamship [*Jernfield*] of 5,000 BRT was sunk
1 Sep 42	10/JG 26	4 FW 190	Lydd
2 Sep 42	10/JG 2	2 FW 190	Ventnor, 1139 hrs
	10/JG 2	4 FW 190	Teignmouth, 1556 hrs; take-off 1213 hrs (?) (German records state that the Isle of Wight was attacked and a sailing ship sunk)
3 Sep 42	10/JG 2	? FW 190	Dartmouth; attack aborted because of bad weather
4 Sep 42	10/JG 2	6 FW 190	Torquay & Paignton, 1850 hrs; take-off 1910 hrs; gasworks at Torquay hit
5 Sep 42	?	4 FW 190	Dover
6 Sep 42	?	? FW 190	(German records state that Dover was attacked)
8 Sep 42	?	2 FW 190	Salcombe, 1855 hrs
9 Sep 42	10/JG 2	2 FW 190	Salcombe, 1827 hrs
			(Between 22 Jul and 11 Sep 1942, 10/JG 26 carried out 29 *Jabo* attacks – 13 against ships, 1 against a railway yard, 12 factories and 3 harbours)
15 Sep 42	?	2 FW 190	Rye, 0800 hrs
16 Sep 42	?	2 FW 190	Eastbourne, 1155 hrs (German records state that Rye and Eastbourne were attacked)
17 Sep 42	10/JG 2	? FW 190	Channel/Worthing, take-off 1523 hrs (German records state that Harwich and Worthing were attacked). Bognor Regis attacked
18 Sep 42	?	? FW 190	Boats off Dungeness, Hudson AM821 of 608 Squadron damaged off Gosport
19 Sep 42	10/JG 2	6 FW 190	Dartmouth, 1131 hrs; collier *Fernwood*, coal hulk *Dagny* and pontoon crane sunk
	10/JG 2	2 FW 190	Salcombe, 1528 hrs; take-off 1545 hrs. 2 barges sunk
	?	?	Sandwich
21 Sep 42	?	2 FW 190	Bexhill/Hastings, 0925 hrs

Date	Unit	Aircraft	Details
22 Sep 42	?	4 FW 190	Rye, 1342 hrs
24 Sep 42	10/JG 26	2 FW 190	Seaford, 1330 hrs (German records state that Seaford and Hastings were attacked successfully)
	?	2 FW 190	Dymchurch, 1348 hrs
	10/JG 26	7 FW 190	Hastings, 1630 hrs
26 Sep 42	10/JG 2	? FW 190	Bembridge, take-off 1515 hrs
29 Sep 42	?	2 FW 190	Betteshanger Colliery, 0919 hrs; 2+, 25 wounded
30 Sep 42	?	4 FW 190	Worthing, 1205 hrs
	?	2 FW 190	Rye, 1520 hrs
7 Oct 42	10/JG 2	2 FW 190	Poole Bay/Swanage, 1737 hrs; take-off 1809 hrs. Bombs landed in the sea (German records state that Swanage was attacked and ships sunk)
8 Oct 42	10/JG 2	2 FW 190	River Dart, 1705 hrs; take-off 1718 hrs. No damage (German records state that Hastings and landing craft at Dartmouth were attacked)
9 Oct 42	10/JG 2	2 FW 190	Salcombe, 1122 hrs; take-off 1140 hrs. Barge hit (German records state that 30 – 40 landing craft in Salcombe Harbour were attacked, 6 sunk and 2 damaged. Town also attacked)
10 Oct 42	10/JG 26	? FW 190	Ramsgate/Westgate gasworks/Manston airfield, 0755 hrs
12 Oct 42	10/JG 26	4 FW 190	Brighton, 1230 hrs
	?	? FW 190	Swanage? (German records state that Brighton was attacked)
13 Oct 42	10/JG 2	? FW 190	Shanklin, 1601 hrs; take-off 1636 hrs (German records state that east of the Isle of Wight, 12 tugs and a floating dock of 10,000 – 15,000 tons were attacked by 2 SC 500 bombs and possibly damaged – confirmed by British sources)
14 Oct 42	?	? FW 190	Brixham, 0733 hrs; no bombs dropped
	?	2 FW 190	Rye Harbour, 1355 hrs; Plt Off G G Thomas & Sgt K G Taylor-Cannon, 486 Squadron failed to intercept
15 Oct 42	?	2 FW 190	Dawlish Warren, 1742 hrs
16 Oct 42	?	? FW 190	Deal ?
	?	6 FW 190	River Dart, 1115 hrs; 4 barges sunk (German records state that Gabriel, 6 landing craft were sunk and others damaged)
17 Oct 42	10/JG 2 10/JG 26	? FW 190	Hastings, 1430 hrs
21 Oct 42	?	4 FW 190	Totnes, 1023 hrs, 2 +, 7 injured & damage caused
25 Oct 42	?	4 FW 190	Torquay (Palace Hotel), 1108 hrs, gasometer set on fire.
	?	4 FW 190	Seaford & Littlestone on Sea, 0726 hrs

Date	Unit	Aircraft	Details
31 Oct 42	*JG 2, JG 26, III/ZG 2*	52 (68?) FW 190	Major attack on Canterbury, 1705hrs; take-off 1740 hrs (10/JG 2)
3 Nov 42	8/ZG 2	4 FW 190	Teignmouth, 1249 hrs; 2 shot down by 257 Squadron.
2 Dec 42	?	? FW 190	(German records state that railways and barracks near Deal were attacked; no British records)
5 Dec 42	?	4 FW 190	(German records state that at 1430 hrs 4 FW 190s took off to carry out a *Störangriff* along the railway line from Ramsgate to Dover. Along the route Ramsgate – Sandwich – Deal – Dover nothing seen. 1447 – 1454 hrs, machine-gunned Sandwich railway station, buildings along the road and a factory NE of Dover. Bombed a gasometer which exploded. Set a pick up truck on fire. Defences: along the route Ramsgate to Dover light and heavy *Flak*. East of Ramsgate 2 fighters. On return NE Dover 6-8 Spitfires)
6 Dec 42	6/JG 26	4 FW 190	(German records state that 4 FW 190s took off at 0813 hrs to carry out a *Störangriff* against railway targets in the Folkestone – Ashford – Dungeness area, no railway traffic seen. 0828 – 0842 hrs machine-gunned installations, *Flak* and searchlight positions between Dover and Folkstone and buildings in Ashford a 2 storey building probably storing munitions exploded. 1 *Rotte* attacked the airfield near Brockland [probably decoy airfied of Midley]. 1 Spitfire on the ground shot at. Another *Rotte* attacked buildings in Rye and a heavy goods vehicle with trailer, laden with men. Defences: Light *Flak* from Dover Mole, Brockland airfield and near Rye)
7 Dec 42	I/JG 26	4 FW 190	(German records state that 4 FW 190s took off at 1114 hrs to carry out a *Störangriff* in the Dungeness – Rye area. Machine-gunned buildings in Dungeness, barracks and Rye railway station).
9-12 Dec 42	10/JG 2		detached to southern France
14 Nov-11 Dec 42	10/JG 26		detached to southern France
11 Dec 42	3/JG 26	? FW 190	Spitfires W3445 and BM517 of 91 Squadron damaged Cat B at Lympne, 1205 hrs during a *Störangriff*
14 Dec 42	?	2 FW 190	(German records state that 2 FW 190s took off at 1513 hrs to carry out a *Störangriff/Jabo* attack against Swanage. At 1538 hrs, a military camp NW Lulworth – between Weymouth und St. Albans Head – was attacked from 30 m height with 2 SC 500. 1 SC 500 in buildings complex. 1 SC 500 exploded in a wood due to a techincal problem. On the return flight, buildings between West Lulworth and Swanage machine-gunned. On the return about 30 km N Cherbourg 2 Whirlwinds [Fg Off J P Coyne, Fg Off M T Cotton of 263 Squadron] were attacked but disappeared into cloud)

Date	Unit	Aircraft	Details
15 Dec 42	JG 26	4 FW 190	Deal, Fg Off R L Smith DFM, 137 Squadron claimed 1, 609 Squadron damaged 1 (German records state that 4 FW 190s took off at 1527 hrs to carry out a *Störangriff* against targets in the Sandwich-Ramsgate area. Machine-gunned between Ebbafleet [Ebsfleet] and Sandwich, attacking buildings and barns. At Woodnesborough 1 factory and south of Ramsgate 1 lifting crane. At Ebbafleet 1 herd of sheep of about 40-50 and a herd of cows of about 20. 10 sheep and 5 cows killed).
16 Dec 42	II/JG 26	4 FW 190	(German records state that 4 FW 190s took off at 1204 hrs to carry out a *Störangriff* between Hastings and Bexhill. Machine-gunned buildings in Hastings. Near Winchelsea a thatched farmhouse was set on fire. 1 km W Winchelsea a castle [sic] attacked. One FW 190 damaged by *Flak*.)
17 Dec 42	10/JG 2	4 FW 190	Stoke Fleming, 1213 hrs; damage & 1 casualty (German records state that 4 FW 190s took off at 1133 hrs to carry out a *Störangriff* against Totnes. 1212 hrs attacked Stoke Fleming from 10 m with 4 SC 500, SW Dart Estuary. 1 SC 500 hits a large building. 3 SC 500 in village centre, buildings destroyed. Defences: None).
18 Dec 42	?	4 FW 190	Ashford, 1305 hrs (German records state that 4 FW 190s took off at 1245 hrs to carry out a *Störangriff* in the Hastings – Rye area. Machine-gunned buildings and houses and a bus between Hastings and Rye)
19 Dec 42	10/JG 26	4 FW 190	Deal, 1410 hrs (German records state that 4 FW 190 took off at 1357 hrs to carry out a *Jabo* attack and *Störangriff* against Deal. Target for 4 SC 500 Stommelees, 8 km N Deal. 1 SC 500 hit houses near a factory; fireball observed. 3 SC 500 hit 2 housing blocks and a large house. Big cloud after explosion. 1 FW 190 shot down by *Flak*).
21 Dec 42	?	4 FW 190	(German records state that 4 FW 190s took off at 1605 hrs to carry out a *Störangriff* between Hastings and Eastbourne. Buildings near Eastbourne station machine-gunned)
22 Dec 42	?	2 FW 190	(German records state that 2 FW 190s took off at 1302 hrs to carry out a *Jabo* attack on Hastings. 1324 hrs *Tiefangriff* against Cliffend, 8 km NE Hastings. 2 SC 500 in village centre, buildings destroyed)
29 Dec 42	8/JG 2	2 FW 190	(German records state that 2 FW 190 took off at 1421 hrs to carry out a *Störangriff* against Eastbourne. 1455 hrs 2 SC 500 dropped on buildings in the centre of Eastbourne. Buildings destroyed. On the return flight, 2 Spitfires seen near Eastbourne. 1 Spitfire [EN782 of 91 Squadron, P/O I W Downer] shot down 1458 hrs into the sea 3 kms east of Beachy Head by Oblt Stolle. 1 Spitfire crashed on land 1500 hrs 1½ km east of Beachy Head)

Date	Unit	Aircraft	Details
30 Dec 42	10/JG 2	6 FW 190	Newton Abbot, take-off 0921 hrs; actually attacked Exeter (German records state that 6 FW 190s took off at 0919 hrs to carry out a *Störangriff* on Newton Abbot. 1020 hrs 5 SC 500 from 10 m height. 5 hits on buildings in the town centre. Buildings destroyed)
	10/JG 26	4 FW 190	Bexhill, took off 1458 hrs (German records state that 4 FW 190 took off at 1458 hrs to carry out a *Störangriff* against Bexhill. Attacked with 4 SC 500 a village on the coast near Dungeness [Camber], SW Lydd. Buildings destroyed)
1943			
2 Jan 43	10/JG 2	8 FW 190	Kingsbridge, take-off 1150 hrs; attacked 1236 hrs, intercepted by Plt Off L Zadrobilek & Plt Off K Zouhar, 310 Squadron, 1220 hrs; Plt Off Zadrobilek [Spitfire AR310] wounded (German records state that 8 FW 190s took off at 1150 hrs to carry out a *Störangriff* at Kingsbridge. 1235 hrs attack started with 8 SC 500, 7 hits on buildings in the town. 1 SC 500 dropped in the sea due to technical problems. Kingsbridge then machine-gunned. On the return flight, 2 Spitfires seen off Start Point, 1 Spitfire probably shot down as it was hit by cannon fire)
	10/JG 26	4 FW 190	Bexhill. (German records state that 4 FW 190s took off at 0838 hrs to carry out a *Störangriff* against Bexhill. 0900 hrs Bexhill hit by 4 SC 500. Hits on a large housing block – yellow/grey explosion and heavy smoke. Good hits observed)
3 Jan 43	10/JG 26	4 FW 190	Folkestone. (German records state 4 FW 190s took off at 1427 hrs to carry out a *Störangriff* against Folkestone. 4 SC 500 dropped at 1445 hrs from 4800 m height. 1 SC 500 on the outskirts, 3 SC 500 dropped into habour basin)
	10/JG 2	4 FW 190	Shanklin. (German records state that 4 FW 190s took off at 1604 hrs to carry out a *Störangriff* against Shanklin on the Isle of Wight. 1633 hrs 4 SC 500 dropped on houses in the town and destroyed. Machine-gunned a gas holder and set it on fire. On the return flight, 2 Spitfires seen south of the Isle of Wight, no attacks)
4 Jan 43	10/JG 26	4 FW 190	Sussex, Winchelsea. (German records state that 4 FW 190s took off at 1234 hrs to carry out a *Störangriff* against Winchelsea, 10–15 km NE of Hastings. 1252 hrs Winchelsea hit by 4 SC 500. Hits on housing blocks, grey-yellow and black explosions and clouds. Machine-gunned houses. 1 FW 190 lost over the British mainland – hit the ground and exploded)
8 Jan 43	10/JG 2	8 FW 190	Torquay, 1314 hrs; damage & casualties. Chased by WO J Sala & WO A Skach of 310 Squadron 2 miles south of Brixham. (German records state that 8 FW 190s took off at 1232 hrs to carry out a *Störangriff* against Torquay. 1315 hrs 7 SC 500 dropped on housing blocks and destroyed. Town then machine-gunned. 1 SC 500 dropped in the sea due to technical problems. Defences: Light and heavy *Flak*. On return, 2 Spitfires seen near Torquay)

Date	Unit	Aircraft	Details
9 Jan 43	10/JG 26	3 FW 190	Hastings area; Fairlight, 0910 hrs. (German records state that 3 FW 190 took off at 0848 hrs to carry out a *Störangriff* against Hastings. Hastings was not attacked as at 0905 hrs, a patrol boat 5 km SE of Dungeness warned defences at Hastings. Alternative target was Fairlight, 5 kms NE of Hastings which was attacked at 0909 hrs with 3 SC 500. Hits on houses, destroyed showing grey-yellow explosions. Defences:Light *Flak* at Fairlight)
10 Jan 43	10/JG 2	7 FW 190	Teignmouth, 1439 hrs, Great Western Railway line blocked. (German records state that 7 FW 190s took off at 1348 hrs to carry out a *Störangriff* against Teignmouth. 1425 hrs 6 SC 500 dropped on housing blocks. Machine-gunned Teignmouth. 1 SC 500 dropped in the sea, reason not known. Defences: Very heavy *Flak* of all calibres. 2 Spitfires seen. 1 FW 190 badly damaged 1 FW 190 of 10/JG 2 missing, probably shot down by Flak)
13 Jan 43	10/JG 26	2 FW 190	Rye. (German records state that 2 FW 190s took off at 0820 hrs to carry out a *Störangriff* against Winchelsea; at 0840 hrs 2 SC 500s dropped on housing blocks. Grey-yellow and black smoke from the explosions. Machine-gunned houses and good hits seen. Defences: Machine-gun fire)
15 Jan 43	10/JG 2	4 FW 190	Eastbourne, 1357 hrs. (German records state that 4 FW 190 took off at 1326 hrs to carry out a *Störangriff* against Eastbourne. 1400 hrs 2 SC 500 dropped in town centre, 2 SC 500 near the beach. Houses destroyed and on the flight in and out, town was machine-gunned. Defences: Light *Flak* from destroyers light Flak. 1km S Eastbourne 2 destroyers)
	10/JG 26	8 FW 190	Rye. (German records state 4 FW 190 Jabos and 4 FW 190 as escort carried out a *Störangriff* against Tenterden, SW Ashford. At 1605 hrs 4 SC 500 droppped from 10 m height. Houses destroyed with fierce explosions. On return flight machine-gunned an estate and houses. Defences: Heavy light *Flak* on the return flight near Rye. 1 FW 190 of I/JG 26 shot down by *Flak*)
17 Jan 43	10/JG 2	2 FW 190	Ventnor. (German records state that 2 FW 190s took off at 1645 hrs to carry out a *Störangriff* against Ventnor. 1710 hrs 2 SC 500 dropped on buildings. Machine-gunned houses on flight in and out).
20 Jan 43	10/JG 2	40 FW 190	London, 1235 hrs. (German records state that 28 Jabos attacked London, 1200 hrs 10 Jabos carried out a diversion attack on Tunbridge-Wells 1200 hrs, 2 Jabos carried out a diversionary attack on Ventnor)
23 Jan 43	10/JG 26 10/JG 26	4 FW 190	Hailsham. (German records state that 4 FW 190s took off at 0925 hrs to carry out a *Jaboeinsatz* against Hailsham, 20 km N Eastbourne. Attacked 0950 hrs with 4 SC 500. South of Hailsham an electricitypower station was machine-gunned and set on fire. Defences: Light and heavy *Flak* near Eastbourne. 1 FW 190 of 10/JG 26 missing from the attack)

Date	Unit	Aircraft	Details
25 Jan 43	10/JG 2	6 FW 190	Sandbanks, Bournemouth; damage to military & civilian property. (German records state that 4 FW 190s took off at 1314 hrs to carry out a *Störangriff* against Swanage. Target not attacked due to the wind direction. 1347 hrs 2 SC 500s dropped at South Haven Point, Poole Bay. 1 SC 500 hit a hotel on the beach (Ferry Hotel?). 1 SC 500 on a multi-storey building on the beach. Both buildings destroyed. Because of the wind and heavy *Flak*, alternative target was landing craft at South Deep. Attacked with 2 SC 500, 1 SC 500 failed to explode. 1 SC 500 next to 4 landing craft, boats sunk. Machine-gunned *Flak* positions on return south of South-Haven Point)
26 Jan 43	10/JG 2	8 FW 190	Kingsbridge with alternative target of Loddiswell, 5 km NNW, 1600 hrs. Bombed Aveton Gifford. 2 FW 190s driven away by AA fire at Torquay, 2 machine-gunned a trawler off Dawlish, 6 attacked Aveton Gifford. (German records state that 8 FW 190s took off at 1515 hrs to carry out a *Störangriff* against Kingsbridge. Because of the wind direction, Kingsbridge was not attacked. At 1600 hrs Loddiswell, 5 km NNW Kingsbridge. Houses in the town, including a church, destroyed. Machine-gunned Loddiswell. On flight in, buildings NE Start Point machine-gunned. Defences: Medium to heavy *Flak*. On flight in, 25 km SE Start Point 8 Spitfire seen and followed to mid Channel. 1 FW 190 of 10/JG 2 missing.
	10/JG 26	4 FW 190	Ramsgate (German records state that 4 FW 190s took off at 0817 hrs to carry out a *Jaboeinsatz* against Ash. Due to a compass error with the *Schwarmführers* aircraft, the alternative target of Ramsgate was attacked with 3 SC 500 and 3 hits were seen on buildings. 1 SC 500 was dropped in the sea. Defences: Heavy and light *Flak* at Ramsgate and north of the town)
28 Jan 43	10/JG 26	4 FW 190	Bexhill & Hastings, 1125-1220 hrs. Chased by Flt Lt R W Baker, Flt Lt L S Black & Sgt H Meagher, 485 Squadron, 5 miles south of Selsey & 609 Squadrons. Hit gasworks. (German records state that 4 FW 190 took off at 1100 hrs to carry out a *Jaboeinsatz* and *Störangriff* against Battle, N Bexhill. Attacked 1130 hrs an alternative target of a group of houses between Bexhill and Hastings)
30 Jan 43	10/JG 26	4 FW 190	Margate. (German records state that 4 FW 190s took off at 0819 hrs to carry out a *Störangriff* against Margate. At 0837 hrs 4 SC 500 dropped on a building complex, probably a large hotel. Machine-gunned town)
2 Feb 43	?	3 FW 190	Robertsbridge, 0850 hrs
3 Feb 43	?	8 FW 190	Ashford; 609 Squadron tried to intercept
	?	4 FW 190	Swanage, 1420 hrs (1 +, 1 wounded)
4 Feb 43	?	4 FW 190	Ryde, PM
5 Feb 43	10/JG 26	4 FW 190	Eastbourne/Hailsham/Bognor Regis, 1403 hrs
7 Feb 43	?	4 FW 190	Eastbourne, 1447 hrs

Date	Unit	Aircraft	Details
8 Feb 43	?	3 FW 190	Worthing, Flt Lt H N Sweetman & Sgt L Walker, 486 Squadron damaged 2 (German records state that a *Jabo* attack was carried out against Worthing, 10 houses destroyed and town was machine-gunned)
13 Feb 43	10/JG 2	4 FW 190	Dartmouth, 1125 hrs; take off 1040 hrs. No damage (German records state than in the morning, *Jabos* attacked Dartmouth. 4 fishing boats set on fire)
16 Feb 43	10/JG 2	? FW 190	Kingsbridge,1515 hrs; take off 1431 hrs
17 Feb 43	10/JG 2	2 FW 190	Clacton, take off 1100 hrs
	?	4 FW 190	Shanklin, PM
26 Feb 43	10/JG 2	8 FW 190	Exmouth gasholder, 1214 hrs; take off 1131 hrs. Property damaged & some casualties (German records state that 8 *Jabos* attacked Exmouth, houses hit and a small fishing boat set on fire)
1 Mar 43	10/JG 2	? FW 190	Bognor Regis, 1215 hrs
7 Mar 43	10/JG 2, 10/JG 54	18 FW 190	Eastbourne, 1352 hrs
8 Mar 43	II/SKG 10	2 FW 190	2 FW 190s bombed a trawler north of Eddystone Light House.
9 Mar 43	10/JG 2	? FW 190	Worthing, Hove, 1650 hrs; take off 1625 hrs. Sqn Ldr C L Roberts & Fg Off I D Waddy, 486 & Flt Lt P Howard-Williams, 610 Squadron tried to intercept
11 Mar 43	II/SKG 10	27 FW 190	Hastings, Guestling, 1534 hrs; take off 1510 hrs (10/JG 2) (German records state a surprise attack was carried out by 27 *Jabos* against Hastings in 2 waves at 20 m height)
12 Mar 43	10/JG 2 10/JG 54 10/JG 54, 10/JG 2	19 FW 190	Ilford/Barking/London, 0731 hrs; take off 0704 hrs (10/JG 2)
13 Mar 43	II/SKG 10	5 FW 190	Salcombe 1317 hrs
14 Mar 43	II/SKG 10	4 FW 190	Chivelstone/Salcombe, 1212 hrs
18 Mar 43	10/JG 2	6 FW 190	Walton on The Naze & Frinton-on-Sea, 1411 hrs. take off 1350 hrs
23 Mar 43	?	5 FW 190	Brixham, 1552 hrs (German records state that 5 *Jabos* dropped 5 SC 250 on Kingswear)
	II/SKG 10	6 FW 190	SW England/Dartmouth; bombs dropped in Slapton area 1915 hrs 20 FW 190s attacked Bournemouth 1300 hrs;
24 Mar 43	10/JG 54 10/JG 2	15 FW 190	Ashford, 1003 hrs; take off 0945 hrs
29 Mar 43	10/JG 54	8 FW 190	Brighton/Hove/Eastbourne, 1108 hrs
30 Mar 43	II/SKG 10	8 FW 190	Salcombe & Bolt Head airfield, 0722 hrs
1 Apr 43	10/JG 2	3 FW 190	Ventnor, 1640 hrs; take off 1710 hrs. Sgt Parisse & Sgt Richards, 197 Squadron failed to intercept

Date	Unit	Aircraft	Details
3 Apr 43	10/JG 54 10/JG 2	16 FW 190	Eastbourne, 1146 hrs; take off 1215 hrs (10/JG 2)
7 Apr 43	IV/SKG 10 ?	8 FW 190 3 FW 190	Newport, 0730 hrs; take off 0701 hrs. Some records state attack was carried out by 10/JG 2 Broadstairs, 0710 hrs
9 Apr 43	10/JG 54	4 FW 190	Folkestone, 1753 hrs (German records state that in the afternoon, 4 FW 190s carried out a *Störangriff* against Folkestone. One aircraft was shot down by *Flak*)
7 May 43	II/SKG 10	32 FW 190	Great Yarmouth/Lowestoft, 0710 hrs (German records state that in the morning, 12 FW 190s carried out a *Störangriff* against Lowestoft and another 20 FW 190s attacked Great Yarmouth)
11 May 43	II/SKG 10	18 (20?) FW 190	Great Yarmouth, 0847 hrs; 0841 hrs, 12 aircraft attacked Lowestoft
12 May 43	II/SKG 10	12 FW 190	Shipping off Lowestoft, 0840 hrs
12 May 43	II/SKG 10	25 FW 190	Lowestoft/Kessingland, 2100 hrs (German records state that the town and harbour at Lowestoft were attacked by 24 FW 190s. Good results were obtained and off Lowestoft, patrol boats were attacked)
15 May 43	*Stab* I & II/SKG 10	26 FW 190	Felixstowe-Southwold, 2200 hrs
23 May 43	II/SKG 10	20 FW 190	Hastings, 1300 hrs
23 May 43	IV/SKG 10	26 FW 190	Bournemouth, 1300 hrs; take off 1230 hrs
25 May 43	II/SKG 10	19 FW 190	Folkestone, 2200 hrs (German records state that 19 FW 190 were to carry out a *Tiefangriff* against Folkestone but due to the considerable fighter defences encountered, the attack was carried out by 4 FW 190s and one aircraft was lost)
30 May 43	IV/SKG 10	24 FW 190	Brighton, 1220 hrs; take off 1155 hrs
30 May 43	II/SKG 10	21 FW 190	Colchester/Frinton-Walton/Essex, 1925 hrs
30 May 43	IV/SKG 10	22 (26?) FW 190	Torquay, 1441 hrs; take off 1400 hrs
1 Jun 43	I & II/17 SKG 10	(20?) FW 190	Margate, 1310 hrs
2 Jun 43	IV/SKG 10	9 (10?) FW 190	Niton, St. Catherines Point lighthouse, 1126 hrs; take off 1100 hrs
2 Jun 43	II/SKG 10	16 (17?) FW 190	Felixstowe/Ipswich gasworks, 0525 hrs
4 Jun 43	IV/SKG 10	18 (17?) FW 190	Eastbourne, 1126 hrs; take off 1058 hrs (German records state 15 FW 190s)
6 Jun 43	II/SKG 10	16 FW 190	Eastbourne, 1338 hrs

APPENDIX 9

Graph of Confirmed 'Tip And Run' Attacks March 1942 – June 1943

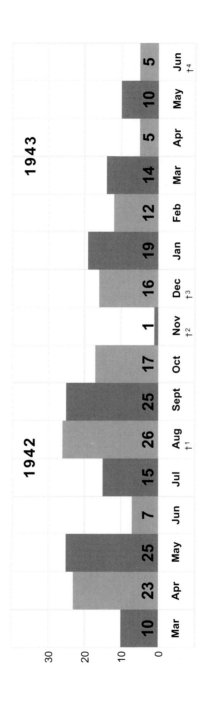

Confirmed 'tip and run' attacks by month and as detailed in Appendix 8.

†[1] Does not include Dieppe Raid 19 Aug 42
†[2] *Jabostaffeln* deployed to southern France
†[3] Includes *Störangriff*
†[4] 1-6 Jun 43 only

APPENDIX 10

Luftflotte 3 Einzelmeldung For 20 January 1943

The following is a translated précis taken from the *Luftflotte 3 Einzelmeldung* for 20 Jan 43 and only refers to the *Jabo* and associated escort missions for this day. The footnotes have been added by the Author.

20 January 43, 1115 hrs:

SECRET

Einzelmeldung **No.1 – 20 Jan 43:**
Reconnaissance missions – aircraft against England (including the Atlantic) on 19/20 Jan 43:
2 FW 190s (0848 hrs) visual reconnaissance Dungeness – Eastbourne.

Results:

0910 hrs, 7 merchant vessels 2,000-3,000 BRT 5-6 kms south of Hastings, course West, medium speed.
Off Eastbourne 2 small ships, course West, medium speed.
- Defence: during return flight attacked by 2 Spitfires†[1].
- Losses: 1 FW 190 of III/*JG* 26 shot down†[2].
- Weather: 8-10/10 clouds at 1,000 metres height off Brighton, showers of rain, visibility 30-50 kms.

21 January, 0305 hrs:

SECRET

Results of the day – 20 January 1943:

Against England:

8 aircraft – security patrols
8 aircraft – free-lance missions
2 aircraft – weather reconnaissance
1 aircraft – photo-reconnaissance Hull and Newcastle
148 fighter aircraft, including 40 aircraft on 3 *Jabo* sorties, 2 of these missions were diversionary attacks:
33 fighters on three *Jabo* escort missions, 39 on 3 missions escorting *Jabos* on the return flight, 32 on 8 air-sea rescue missions, 2 on a reconnaissance sortie – 2 scrambled for a defensive mission (167 aircraft altogether).

Successes:

Against enemy aircraft:

Combat victories by fighters: 3
1236 hrs – 1 Spitfire north of Canterbury†[3]
1242 hrs – 1 Spitfire near Ramsgate†[4]
1312 hrs – 1 Spitfire near Ardres†[5]
Probably shot down:
1312 hrs – 1 Spitfire near Boulogne†[6]

Against ground targets:

See *Einzelmeldung* No.1 of 21 January 1943:
- London: collapsed multistorey houses, high losses among civilian population probable.
- Wadhurst: collapsed houses, high losses among civilian population probable.
- Ventnor: collapsed buildings.
Own losses: 1 FW 190 of 10/*JG* 26 missing†[7]

2 Me 109s of *ESt(Jabo)/Süd* missing†[8]
1 FW 190 of I/*JG* 2 shot down†[9]
1 FW 190 of I/*JG* 26 missing†[10]
4 Me 109s of II/*JG* 26 missing†[11]
1 FW 190 of III/*JG* 26 shot down†[12]
1 FW 190 of III/*JG* 26 shot down†[13]
altogether 6 Me 109s and 5 FW 190s.

21 January, 0025 hrs:

SECRET

Einzelmeldung No.1 – 21 January 1943:

Combat report on *Jabo* attack against London on 20 January 1943.

I) Strength: 112 aircraft altogether –

28 aircraft (*Jabo*) – attack on London
10 aircraft (*Jabo*) – diversionary attack against Tunbridge Wells
2 aircraft (*Jabo*) – diversionary attack against Ventnor
16 aircraft (*Jabo*) – close escort (FW 190s)
39 aircraft (29 FW 190s and 10 Me 109s) – diversionary advance and escort for return flight
17 aircraft (FW 190s) – protection of the landing.

II) Take-off:

1150 hrs – 2 FW 190s (*Jabo*), diversionary attack on Ventnor, Isle of Wight area
1200 hrs – 10 Me 109s (*Jabo*), diversionary attack on Tunbridge Wells
1201 hrs – 8 FW 190s as close escort for diversionary attack
1200 hrs – 28 FW 190s, *Jabo* attack against London
1202 hrs – 8 FW 190s as close escort for main attack
1210 hrs – 29 FW 190s and 10 Me 109s, diversionary advance direction Thames estuary and also as escort for return flight
1235 hrs – 17 FW 190s to protect the landing

III) Operation:

A.) Jabo **attack on London:**

1.) Strength: 28 FW 190s
    25 aircraft attacked London between 1230-1235 hrs at 20-50 metres height. 20 SC 500 and 5 SC 250 bombs dropped.
    2 aircraft attacked Eastbourne as alternative target because of technical problems; 1220-1222 hrs, low-level flight.
    1 aircraft aborted mission because of technical problems (1 SC 500 was dropped into the sea).

2.) Observed hits:
    22 bombs in a district within following boundaries: Tunnel Avenue (East), the curve of the river Thames (North), and southern banks of the river Thames – Maze Hill Street – West-Combe Park (West).
    3 bombs north of the big curve of the river Thames near the northern part of Manchester Road.

3.) Effect of the attack:
    Very good grouping of hits in blocks of flats and crowds of people, violent detonations. Collapse of multistorey houses observed. Busy streets, obviously there was no air raid warning before the attack. High losses among civilian population probable. Big fire in a small factory

near the southern banks of the big curve of the river Thames.

Effect on alternative target:

Direct hits in blocks of flats in the eastern part of the town. Collapse of buildings observed.

4.) Assessment of effects:

Complete surprise and the weather situation were favourable for the attack. According to what was observed by the crews it is probable that there had not been any air raid warning. The attack was carried out almost without any defence. The effect of the attack against houses and live targets has to be described as good.

Attacks with guns against barrage balloons over the southern parts of the town. Attacks with guns against live targets and villages until crossing the coastline east of Newhaven.

5.) Results:

10 barrage balloons shot down over the southern part of London. 12 lorries and 2 gas holders set on fire in a railway station. 1 (railway) engine exploded after several hits. Crowds of people, residential buildings and vehicles effectively attacked.

6.) Defence:

Line of approach: No defence.

Over target: One heavy *Flak* calibre battery with scattered fire. A few barrage balloons, rising. 2 squadrons of Spitfires at about 1,200 metres height did not attack.

Return flight: Light and heavy *Flak* fire in the area of Newhaven. 2 squadrons of Spitfires, flying low-level – only short combat.

7.) Own losses:

1 FW 190 (*Jabo*) 10/*JG* 26 missing (parachute jump seen over the sea near the English South Coast)†[14]

B.) Diversionary attacks:

1.) Diversionary attack against Tunbridge Wells:

Operation:

Strength: 10 Me 109s (*Jabo*)

9 Me 109s attacked alternative target Wadhurst at 1241 hrs because of strong fighter defences high above main target.

Height of attack: 20 metres

Amount of bombs dropped: 9 SC 250

1 Me 109 aborted mission because of technical problems.

Effect of the attack:

Good grouping of hits in town centre. Very busy streets observed. Houses collapsed. High losses among civilian population probable.

Defence:

Some light *Flak* fire over target. Precise light and heavy *Flak* fire east of Hastings during return flight.

Fighters: 1249 hrs – 11 Spitfires at 500 metres height south of Hastings, short combat.

Own losses: 2 Me 109s of *Jagdgruppe Süd* missing†[15].

2.) Diversionary attack against Ventnor, Isle of Wight area:

Operation:

Strength: 2 FW 190s (*Jabo*) with 2 SC 500, low-level flight, 1226 hrs.

Effect of the attack:

Buildings near the beach and in the town centre were hit. Collapsing buildings were seen.

Defence:

Precise *Flak* fire with all calibres.

Own losses: No losses.

C.) Close escort:

1.) Jabo **attack on London: 8 FW 190s**
Flying height: from low-level up to 6,000 metres.
Combats: none
Results of strafing: 4 farms were set on fire in the area of Newhaven.

2.) Diversionary attack on Tunbridge Wells: 8 FW 190s
Flying height: from low level up to 1,500 metres.
Combats: 1310-1312 hrs – 3 Spitfires 20 kms northwest of Boulogne.
1312 hrs – 1 Spitfire probably shot down 20 kms northwest of Boulogne.
Own losses: 1 FW 190 of I/JG 26 missing[16].

D.) Diversionary advance direction Thames Estuary and escort mission for return flight:

Flying height: from low level up to 6,000 metres.

Combats:

1.) 1235-1238 hrs – 4 FW 190s with 2 Spitfires at 3,000-4,000 metres south of Thames estuary.
 1236 hrs – 1 Spitfire shot down north of Canterbury at 3,000-4,000 metres height[17].

2.) 1235-1240 hrs – 13 FW 190s and 10 Me 109s with 15 Spitfires at 3,000-5,000 metres height over Thames Estuary.
 Losses: 4 Me 109s of II/JG 26 missing, it had been seen that two Me 109s collided mid-air[18]. During return flight 1 FW 190 of II/JG 26 crashed into sea off Calais because of combat damage[19].
 1250-1301 hrs – combat with 4 Spitfires over the sea off Etaples at 3,000-4,000 metres height.

3.) 1235 hrs – 12 FW 190s with some Spitfires near Margate at 5,000-6,000 metres.
 1242 hrs – 1 Spitfire shot down near Ramsgate at 5,000-6,000 metres height[20].
 1310-1315 hrs – combat with 10-15 Spitfires between Cap Gris Nez and St. Omer at low level up to 5,000 metres.
 1312-1314 hrs – 1 Spitfire shot down at 50 metres height, Ardres area[21].

E.) Protection of the landing:

Was carried out by 17 FW 190s without enemy contact.

IV) Weather:

Airfields during take-off and landing: 9/10 layer of clouds at 1,500 metres and 6/10 higher than 6,000 metres. 10-20 kms visibility.
Approach and over target: 7-9/10 clouds at 1,000-1,500 metres. 20 kms visibility. Over London haze (from industry).

V) Complete combat victories:

3 Spitfires shot down, 1 Spitfire probable.

VI) Losses:

Jabos: 2 Me 109s and 1 FW 190
Fighters: 4 Me 109s and 2 FW 190s

21 January 43, 0140 hrs:

S E C R E T

Einzelmeldung **No.2 – 21 January 1943:**
Combat report No.1 *Jafue* **3 – 21 Jan 43:**

2 FW 190s (take-off 1408 hrs) – air sea rescue mission for a FW 190 which had crashed 15 kms north of Calais (*Jabo*-mission London). Without success.

1446-1448 hrs – combat with 18 Mustangs at low level 20 kms northwest of Calais. No combat victories.

Losses: 1 FW 190 shot down in flames and crashed into the sea[22].

[1]These were two Typhoons of 609 Squadron

[2]FW 190 A-4, *Wk Nr* 7037 coded Black 8. *Lt* Hans Kümmerling killed. Shot down by Fg Off R Lallemand, 609 Squadron

[3]Claimed by *Maj* Josef Priller, *Stab*/JG 26

[4]Claimed by *Hptm* Klaus Mietusch, 7/*JG* 26

[5]Claimed by *Hptm* Klaus Mietusch, 7/*JG* 26

[6]Claimed by *Oblt* Fülbert Zink, 2/*JG* 26

[7]FW 190 A-4, 2409, Black 2. *Lt* Hermann Hoch POW

[8]Bf 109 F – 4, 13101, Yellow 9 of 3/*Jagdgruppe Ost*. *Oblt* Karl Frentzel-Beyme – *St Kap* – missing. Bf 109 F – 4, 8623, Red 23 of *Jabostaffel*/*Jagdgruppe Süd*. *Lt* Eberhard Dau missing

[9]FW 190 A-3, 5674, 3/*JG* 2. *Fw* Josef Burkel killed. Also FW 190 A-4, *Wk Nr* 5684 of *Stab*/JG 2 returned with *Lt* Heinz Ebersbach wounded

[10]FW 190 A-4, 2375, Black 7 of 2/*JG* 26. *Ofw* Paul Kiersten missing

[11]All Bf 109 G – 4s from 6/*JG* 26: 16141, Brown 11, *Lt* Kurt – Erich Wenzel missing; 16102, Brown 7, *Uffz* Heinz Budde POW; 16113, Brown 12, *Uffz* Heinz Marquardt POW; 16094, Brown 6 *Uffz* Hellmuth Peters killed

[12]FW 190 A-4, 7102, Black 4. *Uffz* Robert Hager wounded

[13]See footnote 1

[14]See footnote 7. *Lt* Hoch force – landed at Capel in Surrey

[15]See footnote 8. One ac was from *Jagdgruppe Süd*, the other *Jagdgruppe Ost*

[16]See footnote 9

[17]See footnote 3. The identity of this ac has not been ascertained

[18]See footnote 11. Ac that collided were flown by *Lt* Wenzel and *Uffz* Budde

[19]See footnote 12

[20]See footnote 4. Spitfire BL333 of 91 Squadron. Plt Off B Fey baled out slightly wounded

[21]See footnote 5. Spitfire BS252 of 332 Squadron. Lt P G Mollestad fatally wounded

[22]FW 190 A-4, 2460, Black 5 of 5/*JG* 26. *Fw* Alfred Barthel killed. Probably shot down by Flt Lt A Atkinson, 609 Squadron

BIBLIOGRAPHY

Published Sources

Admiralty (1947) *British Merchant Vessels Lost or Damaged by Enemy Action During Second World War* (HMSO, London).

Balke, Ulf (1997) *Der Luftkrieg in Europa 1941-1945* (Bechtermünz Verlag, Augsburg).

Bigge, Jupp (unknown) *Jagdgeschwader Richthofen Nr 2* (Privately published).

Caldwell, Don (1996) *The JG 26 War Diary, Volume One 1939-1942* (Grub Street, London).

Caldwell, Don (1998) *The JG 26 War Diary, Volume Two 1943-1945* (Grub Street London).

Dahlman, Kurt (unknown) *Die Nachtschlach -Gruppe 20* (BA-MA RL 10-510, held by Bundesarchiv, Freiburg).

Dierich, Wolfgang (1993) *Die Verbände der Luftwaffe 1935-1945* (Verlag Heinz Nickel, Zweibrücken).

Fock, Harald (1995) *Flottenchronik* (Koehlers Verlagsgesellschaft mbH, Hamburg).

Franks, Norman (1992) *The Greatest Air Battle: Dieppe, 19th August 1942* (Grub Street, London)

Frappé, Jean-Bernard (1977) *Jabo Sur La Manche* (Le Fanatique de L'Aviation, Paris).

Galland, Adolf (1953) *The Battle of Britain* (Air Ministry, London).

Galland, Adolf (1975) *The First and the Last* (Fontana/Collins, London).

Goss, Christopher (2000) *The Luftwaffe's Battle of Britain: The Fighter's Battle* (Crécy, Manchester).

Krebs, Karl Klaus (1942) *Der Kanalschreck greift an* (W Conrad & Co, Leipzig).

Neitzel, Soenke (1995) *Der Einsatz der deutschen Luftwaffe über dem Atlantik und der Nordsee 1939-1945* (Bernard & Graefe Verlag, Bonn).

Obermaier, Ernst (1989) *Die Ritterkreuzträger der Luftwaffe 1939-1945, Band I* (Verlag Dieter Hoffmann, Mainz).

Obermaier, Ernst (1988) *Die Ritterkreuzträger der Luftwaffe 1939-1945, Band II* (Verlag Dieter Hoffmann, Mainz).

Pomeroy, Sqn Ldr C A (1995) *Military Dorset Today* (Privately published).

Prien, Jochen with Gerhard Stemmer, Peter Rodeike and Winfried Bock (2002) *Die Jagdfliegerverbände der Deutschen Luftwaffe 1934-1945, Teil 4 – Einsatz am Kanal und über England 26.6.1942-21.6.1941* (Struve-Druck, Eutin).

Rahn, Werner und Schreiber, Gerhard (1992-1994) *Kriegstagebuch der Seekriegsleitung, Teil A, Band 35-46* (Verlag E.S. Mittler & Sohn, Herford).

Ramsey, Winston G (1990) *The Blitz – Then and Now*, Vol. 3 (After The Battle, London).

Routledge, Brigadier N W (1994) *History of the Royal Regiment of Artillery: Anti-Aircraft Artillery 1914-55* (Brasseys, London).

Rohwer, J / Hümmelchen, G (1968) *Chronik des Seekrieges 1939-1945* (Gerhard Stalling Verlag, Oldenburg).

Scherzer, Veit (1992) *Die Träger des Deutschen Kreuzes in Gold der Luftwaffe 1941-1945* (Scherzer's Militair Verlag, Bayreuth).

Steel, Nigel & Hart, Peter (1997) *Tumult in the Clouds* (Hodder & Stoughton, London).

Vasco, John J (1990) *Bombsights over England – The History of Erprobungsgruppe 210 Luftwaffe Fighter – Bomber Unit in the Battle of Britain* (JAC Publications, Norwich).

Wood, Tony & Gunston, Bill (1977) *Hitler's Luftwaffe* (Salamander, London).

Ziegler, Frank (1993) *Under the White Rose: The Story of 609 Squadron* (Crécy, Bristol).

Documentary Sources

Abschussunterlagen, Luftwaffen – Personalamt (held by Bundesarchiv/Militärarchiv, Freiburg).

AI 1 (K) Report No 781/1940 *Bombing with Me 109* (held by Air Historical Branch, London).

AI (K) Report February 1943 *Further Report on Three Aircraft of JG 26 Brought down on January 20th 1943* (held by Air Historical Branch, London).

Analysis of South Coast Tip and Run Incidents (held by Air Historical Branch, London).

AWA Report Numbers BC/G/11, BC/18, BC/19, BC/20 (held by Air Historical Branch, London).

Belegungsübersicht der fliegenden Verbände März-Juni 1943 (by Kommando des Flughafenbereiches 8/VIII, Caen).

Diary of Day Raiding – April and May 1943 (held by Air Historical Branch, London).

Einzelmeldungen der Luftflotte 3 (held by Bundesarchiv/Militärarchiv, Freiburg).

HQ No.11 Group Operations Record Book (Air 25/205) (held by Public Records Office, London).

Meldungen über Flugzeugunfälle und Verluste bei den fliegenden Verbänden Gen.Qu. 6.Abt. (held by Bundesarchiv/Militärarchiv, Freiburg).

Meldungen über Flugzeugverluste bei den fliegenden Verbänden (held by Bundesarchiv/Militärarchiv, Freiburg).

Namentliche Verlustmeldungen der fliegenden Verbände der Luftwaffe (held by Deutsche Dienststelle, WASt, Berlin).

Parliamentary Debates Commons 1942-43 Vol 386 (held by Public Records Office, London).

Personalakten ehemaliger Flugzeugführer (held by Bundesarchiv-Zentralnachweisstelle, Aachen-Kornelimünster).

Report WT.16628 83/6/43 (held by Air Historical Branch, London).

'Richthofen' Jagdgruppe – Ein Jahr im Krieg (wartime magazine, published 1941).

Royal Air Force Bolt Head, Operations Record Book (Air 28) (held by Public Records Office, Kew).

Royal Observer Corps Narrative 1942 (held by Air Historical Branch, London).

Royal Observer Corps Narrative 1943 (held by Air Historical Branch, London).

Setzer, Fritz (Private letter dated 1989).

Shelter Damage Special Report Yeovil M.B 5/8/42 (HO192/875) (held by Public Records Office, Kew).

Index